THE

VOLUNTEERS

THE VOLUNTEERS

*A memoir of
conservation,
companionship
& community*

CAROL
DONALDSON

summersdale

THE VOLUNTEERS

An Hachette UK Company
www.hachette.co.uk

Summersdale Publishers
Part of Octopus Publishing Group Limited
Carmelite House
50 Victoria Embankment
LONDON
EC4Y 0DZ
UK

www.summersdale.com

This FSC® label means that materials used for the product have been responsibly sourced

MIX
Paper | Supporting responsible forestry
FSC® C104740

Printed and bound by Clays Ltd, Suffolk, NR35 1ED

ISBN: 978-1-83799-327-7

Substantial discounts on bulk quantities of Summersdale books are available to corporations, professional associations and other organisations. For details contact general enquiries: telephone: +44 (0) 1243 771107 or email: enquiries@summersdale.com.

CONTENTS

Prologue	8
Chapter One	14
Chapter Two	36
Chapter Three	67
Chapter Four	89
Chapter Five	106
Chapter Six	126
Chapter Seven	150
Chapter Eight	166
Chapter Nine	188
Chapter Ten	211
Chapter Eleven	231
Chapter Twelve	249
Chapter Thirteen	264
Chapter Fourteen	282
Acknowledgements	296
About the Author	298

PROLOGUE

The smell of smoke drifted across the clearing. It ghost-gathered, hanging like a spectre amid the birches, glowing brightly in the pared-down winter palette of the woods. There was Roy, flapping away at the fire with a biscuit-tin lid, trying to get air to the flames. He tackled most things in life with the same boyish enthusiasm, despite now being in his sixties. Embers flew and alighted on his fleece, adding yet more perforations to the garment that already looked like it had been eaten away by moths. Meg stood on the opposite side, cutting the huge pile of brash into neat chunks, laying each branch carefully on the fire. She was our oldest member but showed no let-up in her fitness either.

"Butts and tips, tips and butts," Roy reminded her as the branches were laid first one way, then the other. Meg didn't need telling – she was a naturally neat woman and knew how to lay a fire as well as anyone – but Roy meant no harm. Butts and tips was an in-joke; there were lots of them among the volunteers. Jim emerged carrying a huge bundle of bramble on a pitchfork and dumped the lot of it in the centre of the fire, sending a rush of flames into the air and scattering the neatly assembled pile. Jim's mop of white hair glowed from the heat but his luxuriant eyebrows always seemed to escape the flames unscathed.

"Just pile it on," he said. "Once the fire's got to this stage it will burn through anything."

Roy didn't protest. We all knew Jim was right – he usually was. Jim had a natural authority but, unlike some of the other volunteers, he didn't try to take charge. He didn't need to, he only had to chip in a word or two of advice from the sidelines to make me reconsider my approach. I knew by now that Jim's advice was worth listening to.

Josie and Kit, our youngest members, appeared from a thicket of scrub, dragging a huge pile of branches. Josie leaned back against the weight of the tangle, tugging away – she loved nothing better than pitting her strength against an ensnared bundle of bramble. Kit was the same; I knew by now when he was swinging an axe or a scythe he was in his happy place. The pair of them were laughing and stumbling over the rough ground. It was a world away from the morose, closed-off youths they had first appeared to be when they had joined. When they were in their early twenties, Josie had hidden away from life and Kit had dismissed the world as not worth bothering with. Now, it seemed, they had forgotten themselves and looked like they were having fun.

"Don't just pull those branches, cut them up," Val instructed the pair. "Josie, put a long-sleeved shirt on or you'll get a thorn in your arm and end up with blood poisoning." Val was right, blackthorn had ferocious spikes that could cause infection. She looked down at Roy who was now blowing vigorously into the base of the fire. "Roy, stop breathing in all that smoke, your lungs are damaged enough." Val had been a nurse for many years and still expected her orders to be followed. She struggled to rein in the impulse to take charge. I sympathised, knowing I could be the same. We were both natural bosses and, maybe because of this, we respected and liked each other. Val's great virtue was that she could laugh at her foibles and apologise when she knew she had gone too far. I watched her now as she shot a glance at Bevan, who was leaning on the fire fork, chatting.

Bevan often appeared to do more talking than working. He was a natural people person, which seemed to me at odds with his former life as an accountant. He was also a master of uncovering a person's life story and would usually find out all the background information on a new group member in 10 minutes flat. Bevan's own life story was less on display; his buddy Jim probably knew all the facts, but Jim was no gossip and was not about to tell. Meg said they had a bromance. The men in the group had supported each other through life's knocks in the undemonstrative way that men do.

Esther and Wayland were bundling up piles of long straight poles, tying each with twine so they could be hauled away and stored. I hoped they wouldn't get arrested at the weekend when they were going on another Greenpeace protest against fracking. They weren't reckless but, if it came to it, were quite willing to put their liberty at risk for a cause they believed in.

The light was leaving us, sinking rose gold beneath the bare trees. As the sun lowered, it bronzed the bracken and beech leaves, firing them into life, the rich colour of chestnut ponies. Spider webs hung from the bracken fronds, each one backlit, tinselling the woodlands in the run-up to Christmas. Winter momentarily softened and was kind before the coming of the night.

Our work was part of a cycle of management that had taken place for hundreds of years in these woods. We coppiced the hazel trees, cutting the stems down to the ground to make use of the tall poles that would regrow in a few years' time. Next year, this part of the wood, flooded with light, would be alive with bluebells – but would I be there to see it?

The scene could have been part of another century, resembling a Brueghel painting of peasants at work in the woods. If those peasants could have stepped into this clearing they would have felt quite at home. There was the same chatter as we worked beside each other, the same tools, wooden handled and fired metal. Our clothes, patched, bagged and smoke smeared, were not so very different. We were part of the woods, as they had been, rooted in this landscape in a way that can only happen when you work on the land and meet it on its terms.

A crow called overhead and somewhere up above, a buzzard mewed. I felt that happiness wash over me that I could never quite pin down; the happiness that comes from working outdoors with your hands alongside your friends, doing something that feels worthwhile.

I loved being part of the volunteer gang. I loved being their leader. After six years of working alongside this group of characters, my love for them was so big that it swelled up inside me. We had been there for each other in a way I never would have expected when I took the job in a panic as my life hit the buffers and the money ran out. With my family and my friends far away, the volunteers had come into my life and filled that void. The group had become something much more than a job. It was a fundamental part of my happiness. All of it, the physicality, the connection to nature, the laughter, the in-jokes, even the slight annoyances that were bound to arise when you spent time with a bunch of strong-minded individuals. I couldn't picture life without these people, and I knew that the group meant something of equal importance to each one of its members. With some I could only guess at what that void had been in their own lives; with others they had opened up and told me. We all need something, don't we? Whether you are 21 or 79 we all need the same things. Friends, support, acceptance, a sense of belonging, a feeling of purpose. Outside, in the real world, everyone was so busy and rushed and absorbed with their own lives that these things could be hard to find, but inside, with the volunteers, we had time for each other and the patience to get to know the person beneath the exterior.

Now though, things had changed. A chance had risen up before me that I had to take. Nothing comes without loss, I told myself, but how was I to leave behind this community that I had helped to create? How would I say goodbye to these people who had become necessary to me in a way I hadn't expected?

"Tea's up," I shouted. The others downed tools and wandered across to where the mugs were lined up; orders I knew by heart, already served. Not yet, I told myself. I have this for a little longer, the decision doesn't have to be made yet.

CHAPTER ONE

Six Years Earlier

When the phone call came to offer me the job I was sitting on the pillbox watching the brent geese come and go on the estuary.

On the far bank the riverside towns glowered at me under the heavy sky, but here there were just the broken ribs of barges and the suck and spring of mud as the geese paddled out to the tide. Rain was blowing in from the sea, blotting out the three cranes that guarded the river entrance. Soon I would be blotted out too and I wasn't planning to move an inch to stop that.

I had been there for 4 hours, thighs stiff with cold, bladder bursting from too much coffee, which I had drunk from a flask smelling of baked beans. But I was grateful for this little bit of freelance work I had been given and was being paid £15 an hour to sit and count geese, and it was money sorely needed.

Dog walkers occasionally appeared, trudging head down and determined into the wind. We didn't greet each other. I was clearly odd, a woman in tattered layers sitting on a pillbox. I resented the dog walkers, disturbing the peace. I wanted only the sound of the moorhens purring in the ditches and the rattle of wind in the bramble. I was, once again, fringe dwelling. At 36 I had been cast out of the sanctuary of a job and the relationship that I had been cocooned in for the last 14 years.

A curlew lamented somewhere out on the tideline. My phone rang. It was the man I had met last week. I was surprised to hear from him; to my mind the interview hadn't gone well. It had been tempting to stay safely under the duvet that morning but instead I had hauled myself out of my single bed, consumed half a bottle of Bach Rescue Remedy and forced myself not to think sad thoughts as I drove along the motorway. I'd arrived in the pouring rain at some farm buildings in the middle of nowhere to be greeted by two steely eyed women, a gangly man who appeared to be the boss and a giant shaggy hound who had rested his head on my lap throughout the ordeal.

By that time the Rescue Remedy had kicked in, making me high on flower power to the point of being swaggering and expansive. I became full of stories about my previous work and the projects I had run. The man looked delighted. It was the technical questions where I felt I'd floundered as I tried to dredge up facts on managing chalk grassland and hedge planting from the countryside-management course I had done six years previously. I came away thinking I had probably blown it, and that maybe it was time I bit the bullet, put the conservation career on hold and found a job, any job, in order to pay the bills.

To my surprise, however, the man was now sounding upbeat.

"I'd like to offer you the post," he said. "You'll be running the volunteer group, undertaking weekly habitat management tasks, fencing, coppicing, river work. You know the kind of thing?"

"Yes," I said. I did, in theory. I had a postgraduate degree that said I was qualified; the certificate looked great; I had read all the books and, after all, it wasn't that long ago that I had been a volunteer. "My practical skills might need a bit of refreshing," I said honestly.

The man brushed this aside. "You've worked for the RSPB," he said, as if that was all he needed to know. The RSPB is the biggest wildlife-conservation charity in Britain. They are not universally loved and they don't always get it right but, within the world of nature conservation, they are well respected. I guess people presume they pick only the best to work for them.

For the last four years I had been the community officer for the RSPB reserves. I organised events, wrote walk guides and, yes, on paper, ran a volunteer group, but one which mainly did fairly soft tasks such as litter picking and the occasional bit of footpath maintenance.

Now this man was explaining that I was to "write management plans, do water vole surveys, ring barn owls…"

It sounded marvellous. It sounded like the kind of job I had always dreamed of; finally, an opportunity to put into practice all I had learned and never had the chance to use because, at the RSPB, there was always someone better qualified than me to do it.

"So do you accept?" he said.

I still had one question. "What salary are you offering?"

He quoted a figure, a low one.

The estuary blinked back a metallic eye at me. It wasn't enough. The rain reached me, clattering down, bouncing back up from the pillbox, bristling back off the mud. The geese vanished, the cranes vanished. I watched as the storm swept over the jumble of abandoned boats at the edge of the marina, tossed into one another by wind and tide. I thought of the unpaid bills and the cold flat I'd recently moved into. I was in no position to argue but that figure wasn't going to be enough.

I held my nerve. "I was hoping for more."

His voice lost some of its previous enthusiasm. "That's all I'm offering," he said.

I took a deep breath, summoning up my tattered confidence.

"I was running a team of five staff at the RSPB," I told the man. It wasn't a lie. When the redundancy came in the autumn, I was managing four field teachers and the reserve's admin officer. "I think my experience justifies the top end of the pay scale."

"I've never paid a member of staff that much," he said sharply.

I thought of the redundancy cheque running out and the black mould sprouting on the living room walls.

"I'm worth it," I told him.

I had no idea if I was but a deal was done. In a moment of bravado with a gas meter ticking down to zero, I became the leader of the Kingsdown Partnership's conservation volunteer group.

I pushed down hard on the clutch and clunked the protesting gearbox of the old Land Rover Defender, owned by the Kingsdown Partnership, down a notch as I turned off the fast road. I began to weave my way down through the woods, avoiding the tree branches that had dropped in winter storms. It was March, three weeks into my new role and not enough time to master the intricacies of driving this battered old beast. Kirk, my new boss, followed in the minibus with the volunteers.

The Kingsdown Partnership was one of several Countryside Management Partnerships dotted throughout the county. I confess that, until I'd seen the job advertised, I had never heard of its existence. A bit of background reading prior to the interview had revealed that the Partnership was nominally part of the county council, who provided the office accommodation at Greengate Farm, where the Partnership was based, and gave a small yearly grant to keep the organisation running. However, the Partnership was expected to be mainly self-sufficient and to find the majority of its funding from running projects. The reality of this meant that its staff had to turn their hand to anything that might bring in an income.

Over the last few weeks, while Kirk ferried me round project sites, I had learned that the Partnership undertook habitat management on council-owned land, wrote guides to walking and cycle routes, did wildlife surveys and restored rivers. It ran guided walks and education programmes and wrote management plans for landowners. It seemed to me that the Countryside Management Partnerships were full of unsung, underfunded and often unappreciated heroes who worked hard for nature and kept much of the countryside accessible for people to enjoy.

The Kingsdown Partnership did all of this fine work from a dilapidated porta cabin with two full-time employees (me and Kirk), two part-time women (Gemima, who did a similar job to mine and ran a volunteer group in a different part of the county, and Mel, whose work, at that time, focused on more urban areas), and three large dogs, who received equal billing on the staff pages of the Partnership's website. In addition, each area had its own weekly group of volunteers who met up every Thursday to carry out various conservation tasks.

Today was my first chance to meet the gang of retirees that made up the volunteer group I was to manage. The day's task was hedge planting, and in the back of the Land Rover, spades and pickaxes clanked away. I hoped I had packed everything we would need. That morning Kirk had handed me a list and told me to load the vehicle, but most of the items on the list were a mystery to me. I knew what a mattock was but what exactly was a rabbit spade? I didn't feel I could ask. Kirk didn't seem to like too many questions. Maybe that was one of the reasons my predecessor, James, hadn't lasted long in the job.

Today was an opportunity to prove to Kirk that he had employed the right person. So far, I felt he hadn't been impressed. At the end of week one I had stood beside him in a dried-out meadow down by the river as he told me that I was to design a wetland restoration plan, which would flood the land to benefit wildlife, but not so much that it would endanger the nearby railway track or road.

"I don't really feel confident designing a wetland," I had confessed. "But I could ask someone at the reserve I worked at for advice."

"Why would you need help?" he had said. "You worked for the RSPB."

"I didn't really have anything to do with managing the marshes," I told him.

"Weren't you the warden?" he said, aghast.

"No, I never said I was the warden. I was the community officer. I ran events."

Kirk looked as if he'd been hoodwinked and strode away to the car.

But I never said I was the warden, I wanted to call after him. *It clearly said on my application form that I was the community officer. Didn't you read it?*

I felt he had yet to recover from his disappointment, but today maybe I could prove my worth. For the last few weeks Kirk had been running the volunteer group while I was sent on courses for first aid and heavy lifting. This week I was to shadow Kirk and learn the ropes and from next week I was to be the one in charge.

I pulled into the village where we were to be working and the roof of the tithe barn rose up from behind the trees.

The tithe barn was a thing apart; it held the power of age, the ability to hush the world for a moment and quieten the traffic rushing through the village on the way between the city and the coast. The long roof was thatched with straw which had become sun bleached until it resembled a silverback gorilla's fur. The barn was a cresting wave which looked like it was forever caught at the point of crashing over into the churchyard beyond. Its blackened timbers, weathered with the pustules of age, had become sucked in by the weight of the roof, the thatch foaming out above. Once, the barn had been owned by monks. As recently as 1960 it had stored the crops from the fields. Now, the builders and the monks and the farmers lay in the churchyard, dust to dust, circling in the light cast between the beams.

Kirk parked the minibus up beside the barn and the volunteers tumbled out: a gang of six men and one woman. He opened up the back of the Land Rover, revealing a jumble of wheelbarrows and tools. He started pulling out saws and loppers, big long-handled shears used for chopping back shrubs. The volunteers unloaded the little foot-high, bare-rooted trees, called whips, which were bundled into hessian sacks to prevent their delicate roots drying out in the March winds. Everyone seemed to know their role and I felt suddenly shy, wanting to be helpful but not sure what I should be doing.

I spotted Roy among the unknown faces and felt a rush of relief. I had met Roy on my first day at work when I had found him on top of the Partnership porta cabin with a broom, sweeping away a pool of water which had gathered on the sunken roof line.

"I'm just trying to keep the office watertight for you," Roy had called out jauntily from his elevated position. He'd given the broom an extra-enthusiastic swoosh and had sent a fountain of water cascading down the windows, narrowly avoiding giving me a soaking.

Despite this, Roy had quickly become a bit of an ally in the office, where he volunteered one day a week on top of the task days.

He was a friendly and enthusiastic presence in the workplace, which was great as, so far, I had found the atmosphere at work a little lacking in bonhomie.

Today Roy was wearing an assortment of layers, a tattered coat mended with colour co-ordinated gaffa tape and a faded sweatshirt peppered with burn holes. The rest of the group were in similarly patched clothes: dirty jeans, fleeces so singed with embers they looked like lace work, battered hats and rucksacks. These items, I suspected, were worn with pride; the burn holes appeared like war medals – the more holes, the longer you had been on the campaign trail, battling bramble into submission around winter bonfires. In comparison, my own recently acquired work layers were unblemished and marked me out as someone with limited experience on the front line.

Roy threaded his way through the group towards me. Even in a few weeks I'd already realised that, without Roy, the Partnership, or at least their office, would have literally crumbled away. The porta cabin at Greengate Farm, which housed the Partnership, must have once been a uniform green, but it had become faded and blotched with patches of bitumen paint that had been splashed around the walls to stop the rot. A sign proclaiming "Kingsdown Partnership" hung at an angle from one remaining screw. Roy turned up cheerily on his bike every Monday and single-handedly waged war against the sagging building, which appeared close to collapse. He did his best to keep it watertight, but even so, the carpet inside was covered with dark stains where water had seeped in and buckets were propped up on top of filing cabinets and photocopiers to catch the water that dripped from the ceiling in every rain shower. When he wasn't fighting with the office accommodation, Roy battled away in the tin barn at the back of the site, ransacking the shelves for mangled wire and odd screws with which to mend the racks of tools. It hadn't always been like this, I knew – at some point the Partnership had clearly had money enough to buy the Land Rover, minibus and an array of smart chainsaws and other equipment that crowded the barn. After a morning of fighting the decay, Roy would spend his afternoon tucked away in a darkened corner of Kirk's office, undertaking piles of admin. To begin with I had chatted to Roy when he was in the office. He owned an ancient caravan on the Yorkshire Moors where he went to stay for weeks at a time in the summer. As I had also spent three years living in a 1970s caravan on the marshes while working for the RSPB, we had a lot in common and our talk cut through the silence of the porta cabin. It took a while to realise that talking during work hours was something Kirk disapproved of.

So far my days in the office had passed with hardly a word spoken as the clock ticked, the dogs farted and the boss wandered through sporadically to check that I was working. Gemima and Mel seemed to be a tight gang of two and shared an office, from where I could occasionally hear them talking to each other, but mainly they seemed to keep their heads down, typing away furiously at their computers. Kirk occupied a separate room where ivy crawled across the windows, blotting out the light, and flies lay dusty and blue-eyed in spider webs.

I found the long days of silence hard knowing they would now lead to equally long nights on my own. I had come from an RSPB reserve full of banter, music and digger drivers perched on the edge of tables, chewing the fat. A place where I had held my own, joking with the wardens. Now I felt myself begin to shrink a little, my personality stifled by the atmosphere.

On Mondays, when Roy was in, I could at least wander over to the barn for a moment of respite. Here, beneath the broken-down roof, surrounded by "Danger Asbestos" signs, Roy emerged as a man full of enthusiasms. He had been a customs officer, he told me, until he took early retirement at 56.

"For years I loved the job," he said. "I enjoyed whizzing off on the launch to inspect the ships. I liked the characters and the camaraderie. Then it changed. It seemed to become all about paperwork."

"Did it get boring?" I asked.

"No, it was the opposite," he said. "You were forever on the alert, looking for something. It affected the way you interacted with people. I started to think how long can I do this for? But I didn't know how to make the change, and then I read that book."

Roy had mentioned *Clear Waters Rising* before. I had already realised that Roy was a man in love with culture. Each Monday, in the barn, he raved about the book he was reading or the film he had seen at the weekend, as if literature and cinema were new art forms he had just discovered. He devoured ideas with a relish that others reserved for gourmet meals. *Clear Waters Rising* was an account by Nicholas Crane of a walk across the Pyrenees. According to Roy, reading this book had been life-changing.

"I sat in my office at the port," he said, "and read about the villages the writer passed through and the amazing scenery he was seeing, and then I looked out of the window at the brick wall opposite my office and something just lit up. I thought, I'm only fifty-six. This isn't what my life was meant to be about."

So Roy decided to opt for early retirement and set off on the Camino de Santiago.

"It seemed like one day I hung up my uniform and pulled down the shutters on that life and the next day I went and walked across the Pyrenees."

When he returned, he joined the volunteer group. "You'll find they're a funny bunch," he said, "but I wouldn't be without them."

Now, Roy pushed past the members of this "funny bunch", smiling warmly at me. "Lovely to have you with us," Roy said as the other volunteers gathered around the minibus, selecting tools from the pile of loppers and bow saws on the ground.

"That's Val," Roy whispered to me, as a determined-looking woman searched through the loppers.

She selected two pairs and took them off to snip at a nearby bush in order to test their sharpness. She looked disapprovingly at one pair.

"Here, you can have these," she said to a tall man with wild blue eyes and a thatch of sandy hair as she clutched the other pair to her.

"That's Alex," Roy said. "He's a bit..." he paused, "funny in the head. Had a car accident when he was young, in Zimbabwe, although he will never call it that; to him it's always Rhodesia."

Alex was digging the blade of Val's rejected loppers into the ground, which I couldn't imagine was increasing their sharpness.

"That's Jim," Roy said, as a man with a mop of silver hair stepped forward and began searching the glove box in vain for a matching pair.

"The Oracle," interjected a jolly-looking Welsh man who had been listening in from behind. "We call him that because he knows everything."

"No, Reuben is the one with all the knowledge," Roy said, looking slightly put out that this man had butted into his introductions.

"I mean Jim keeps the list," the Welsh man said.

"What list?" I asked, feeling more than a little confused as I tried to remember everyone's names.

"A list of all our tasks, what we do, who comes out."

"I'm Bevan," the man said, extending a hand. "How are you finding the job so far?"

In truth I was finding it exhausting. It was only week three and already I had 10 hours of overtime. The Partnership's grant from the local council had recently been cut back so Kirk was scrabbling around trying to make up the shortfall in funding by saying yes to every new project which came his way. He had asked me to arrive early each morning for long days of site visits and Gemima and Mel seemed routinely to work until gone 6 p.m. When I had asked about time off in lieu the boss looked astounded, as if the concept had never before been raised.

"In conservation everyone does loads of overtime and never gets it back," he said. "We're all dedicated to the job."

I was also dedicated to making a difference for wildlife, but I had learned from experience that long hours led to burnout and workplaces rarely returned the loyalty. I was already wondering how I could keep up with Kirk's expectations coupled with the 2-hour commute to and from Greengate Farm. Thankfully, I was rescued from relaying this to Bevan, who had the sort of face you confided in, by Kirk calling the gang to order.

Our job that day, he explained, was to plant up the gaps in the hedge which encircled the ancient barn. Marley, Kirk's dog, was sniffing at the trees. He was a long-limbed beast with a shaggy beard and appeared none too bright, but his devotion to the boss was clear. Every day he lay in his basket in the office, never taking his eyes off Kirk, and leaped to his feet to pin his body to Kirk's leg every time the boss moved. He was Baldrick to the boss's Blackadder and now he appeared to have a "cunning plan" concerning the trees. We all waited for him to cock his massive hind leg while the boss began a talk about the correct way to use the tools.

I got the impression that certain members of the gang felt this was unnecessary. Jim started digging a spade into the bank to test the soil and Val had already disappeared with the sharp loppers, intent, it seemed, on doing what she felt was needed regardless of Kirk's instructions.

"Hedge planting is easy," Roy whispered to me. "You just stick your spade in the ground, wiggle it around and push the tree into the slot."

"Jim's going to think this is a stupid task," Bevan whispered. "We'll be done in an hour."

I could see the boss glaring at me from his elevated position on the back of the minibus, as if I was the one encouraging the chatter.

"So, we are going to begin by digging a trench," he announced.

"A trench?" Jim said, looking up from where he was unearthing a massive flint.

"Yes," the boss said.

"Why aren't we slot planting as always?" Val interjected from somewhere deep inside the hedge.

"Because I think the trees have a better chance of survival if we dig a trench," he said.

There was a muttering among the group.

Jim wandered over. "It's ridiculous," he said to Bevan. "It's completely unnecessary for such tiny trees and this ground is full of flints."

Bevan sympathised. "You know what he's like. He feels his decision is final."

Jim rolled his eyes.

"Reuben wouldn't come out at all," Bevan continued. "When I told him who was running the task, he said he wasn't coming out if that vile canine was going to be here."

"Are you sure he was referring to Marley?" Jim said, and the two men laughed.

The grumbling continued as the group spread out along the bank and set to digging holes. It was a bumblebee warm day, one of those days when the spring sun surprises the earth with its warmth and the fat-bodied hummers go a-searching through the purpling ground ivy for a place to make their nest. We laboured like a chain gang in the growing heat under the great wedding flush of a magnolia tree in flower as wrens sang bright and clear in the sunshine. Layers were soon piled up along the hedge bottom as we sweated away at the baked ground.

Kirk had told me that, during the spring, the volunteers did work ranging from weeding newly planted hedges to footpath maintenance to removing birch saplings on heathland. If the tapestry of habitats and rights of way which make up the British countryside are to be maintained, then volunteer labour is needed to do the work that farm labourers did for hundreds of years before mechanisation.

Footpath maintenance, for instance, mimicked the job of the medieval foresters who had kept the drove ways through the woods clear and used the cuttings for fuel. Birch removal would have been carried out by gamekeepers, keeping the heather clear for the grouse to feed on, although our work was done not for game birds, but to benefit nightjars – nocturnal moth hunters who favoured open habitat for hunting forays. Patching up the hedges, mending the fences and keeping the scrub off the pasture was part of a yearly cycle of countryside work that had gone unchanged until after the Second World War when the skills of the traditional farm workers, passed down from father to son, had been replaced with machines that ripped and slashed where the hedge layers and woodsmen had coaxed and tended. Those woodsmen would not only have understood the work the volunteers carried out but they would have recognised many of the tools they still used to do it.

I had taken a mattock from the pile at the back of the minibus; a versatile hand tool used to dig out tree roots and remove stones from hard ground. The first mattocks were made by Mesolithic people from deer antlers; when you use a tool like this you are connected with humanity all the way back to the beginning of cultivation. You can feel this in the hefting of the weight of the mattock head, which has a double blade, combining an axe with a pointed pick; the releasing of muscles as you swing the tool through the air. Your body is doing what human bodies have done for centuries and, as the mattock connects with the earth, you are directly experiencing the start of agriculture.

"Hold your hands further apart," Roy whispered from his position a few feet away, after I had been using the tool for a while. "Let the weight of the blade carry it down at the top of the arc." He put his loppers down and came over. "Here, let me show you."

He went to take the tool off me but I held on. I didn't want to look incompetent; after all, from next week, I was supposed to be the one leading the group. *I know what I'm doing,* I wanted to say. But did I? It had been years since I'd done any hard physical labour, not since the start of my career when I had volunteered on conservation groups to get work experience. Decent tools had always been in short supply in these groups and, even if you did manage to get hold of something like a mattock, it was only a matter of time before some man would pop up and want to take it from you because they felt they could make more of an impact with it; at least it seemed that way to me.

"I'm OK, Roy," I said. "It's best I do it myself." I rolled my eyes towards the boss meaningfully.

Roy took the hint, winked and wandered off to the other men, who were gathered at one end of the trench as far away from the boss as possible.

I noticed no one stepped in to show Val how it should be done. She had already shed her winter layers and was down to a vest top, her wiry muscles working away with practised skill. Bevan, I noticed, was not breaking much of a sweat.

"It's not a social club, Bevan," Val said as she hacked away at the soil.

Bevan made a few reluctant stabs at the dirt but, in truth, a social club was exactly what it seemed to be.

A constant hum of chatter and laughter rose from the group. I was sure Kirk wouldn't approve, but most of the volunteers were older than him and not likely to be intimidated. As the thatch on the tithe barn warmed in the sun and the greenfinches rasped overhead, the volunteers worked alongside each other companionably, as generations of men and women must have done at the barn in the past.

I was beginning to see that the reason for joining a group like this was as much about being part of a community as a desire to plant hedges. It was fulfilling some essential need to be a social species and work alongside each other with the sun on our backs.

I was jogged out of these thoughts by the approach of Alex, the man from Zimbabwe. He had abandoned the loppers bestowed on him by Val and found a much more exciting mattock.

"She thinks she's the boss," he said, indicating Val. At least I think that's what he said as it came out in a slur. Roy had already told me that Alex had suffered brain damage after a car accident when he was young, and it had obviously affected his speech, but clearly in other ways his mind was still sharp – his comment about Val was spot on.

"How are you finding the work, Alex?" I asked. Kirk had already told me that, without guidance, Alex was "hard to motivate".

Alex rolled his bright eyes. "Working with him is no fun," he said, pointing openly at Kirk in disgust. "He forgets he doesn't pay us and he doesn't bring biscuits. But I'll work for you."

As if to prove this, Alex began attacking the soil with gusto, swinging the mattock with abandon, causing flakes of flint to fly from the rocky ground.

I stepped back as Alex banged the sharp metal blade into the earth. "You're working really well there, Alex," I said, hoping Kirk was noticing how keen Alex now seemed to be.

"That's because you're nicer," he said in a rush. "I'll bring you a gift."

I laughed. "No need for that, Alex," I said. "Just keep up that mattocking."

At lunchtime we sat with our backs against the crumbling red brick wall of the nearby manor house as the others produced an impressive array of packed lunches and banana holders that kept their fruit unbruised. Val brought out homemade flapjacks for everyone. "To mark your first day," she said briskly, and seemed almost embarrassed to be caught displaying such kindness.

"Alex's taken quite a shine to you," said Bevan, who sat shoulder to shoulder with Jim. I had already noticed from their banter that the two men appeared to complement each other: Jim seemed quiet, only saying what needed to be said, Bevan was all jovial chatter. I had heard the two of them planning on taking a countryside ramble together the following day. It seemed their friendship stretched beyond the Thursday volunteer group. "You want to watch Alex," Bevan said. "Has he offered you a gift yet?"

I admitted he had.

"It won't be something he's bought," he said. "It will be something..." he paused. "Something he has acquired, from the care home where he lives."

"Why does he do it?" asked Roy, who always wanted to be in the thick of the conversation.

"I think it's just his little bit of rebellion," Bevan said.

"I don't blame him," said Jim. "If I had lost control over my life I might do what I could to rebel, too."

"Even so," said Bevan, "Alex has a habit of becoming enamoured with women in the group. You'll have to tell him you're with someone."

"I'm not, I'm single," I told him. It still didn't feel right saying it. After so many years as part of a couple, my new status felt unreal.

Before the redundancy, my life had looked – on the surface – like a success. I had had a good job and was engaged to a man I had known since university. When the redundancy had been announced at the end of autumn, I took it in my stride. It was an opportunity,

I told myself. I was sick of being employed, one short-term contract after another. I was going to take charge of my own destiny and start my own business running wildlife tours. It was sure to be a success because... I willed it to be so. I had a company name, a company logo and a two-page business plan with some figures that admittedly didn't seem to quite stack up, but I was convinced it would all work out well.

This life plan had ended on Christmas Eve when I discovered my partner's affair. "It's been over for ages," he said.

I guess it had but he'd forgotten to tell me. It was true my partner and I had lost our way a little as a couple after calling off our wedding the previous year, but we were still together, in a fashion. I had thought that in the new year we were going to get some relationship counselling and get back on track.

In the blank space of shock that followed the break-up, I wrapped myself in blankets in front of the electric fan heater in the damp flat I had moved in to and tried to hang on to the one thing I had left: the business plan. In January I watched the news of the banking collapse with growing alarm. I wasn't the only one being made redundant. Government cutbacks were forcing people onto benefits and into food banks. People were losing their homes, everyone was tightening their belts and no one, it seemed, would have money for such luxuries as wildlife tours.

Somewhere in January, as people with friends and lovers played snowballs outside my window, I finally forced myself to look at the figures. There was no hiding from it; even the most optimistic of sales projections told me what I already knew. It wasn't going to work. As a single woman with rent and bills to pay, the business wasn't going to make enough, and besides, I was in no fit state to set up a company on my own – for that you need confidence, and mine had just gone walking. I sat up all night, through those hours when the water bubble of fear swells to fill the whole room, when the world sleeps and your life hangs in front of you. By morning I had made a decision. I needed stability and for that I needed a solid income and for that I needed a job. My relationship status was a trickier issue and not so easily "fixed".

Bevan must have noticed the look on my face. "Well, I'm sure you won't be single for long," he said.

I found myself hoping he was right. Part of me wanted to be out of the wilderness. Filling in forms saying I was 36 and single felt like failure.

Bevan kindly changed the subject. "So how are you finding the task?" he asked.

"It's hard work," I admitted. "I think I'm going to feel it tomorrow." Jim snorted. "I think we all will."

"Particularly Alex," Roy said. "I don't think I've ever seen him work so hard."

"I don't think I've ever seen him work at all," Jim said dryly.

After lunch I struggled to pick up the mattock and begin work again. *How did the others do it?* I wondered, as I watched them planting and back-filling the trench. Most of them were about 30 years older than me and yet they didn't seem as tired. I had a feeling it might be something to do with pacing yourself. I had started too hard; my arms were now bands of fire from the constant reverberation along the wooden shaft as the blade of the mattock bounced off the rock-hard ground. I'd been trying to prove myself, in front of Kirk, in front of the other volunteers, but maybe I was, once again, proving that I was just a bit green.

I felt myself slowing down, as the shadow of the beech trees worked across the lawns and the pigeons cooing marked the passage of time as surely as a cuckoo clock. It was 4 p.m. by the time the boss called it a day. The others were still in good humour, but I longed to press a magic button and transport myself home to a bath and bed. Ahead lay the drive back to Greengate Farm, offloading the vehicle and washing the tea kit before I could start the commute home. How was I going to do it every week?

Roy must have seen my exhaustion. "You'll get used to it."

"Will I?" I whispered.

"You will, you wait. I've never once questioned why I pull myself out in all weathers to do this. You wait, you'll get it."

I hoped he was right.

CHAPTER
TWO

For the next few weeks, I busied myself in the office writing management plans for wildflower meadows, phoning farmers and ordering in materials for the volunteer tasks. The work was absorbing and at last I felt I was doing a "proper" countryside job: hands on, practical and directly achieving things for nature. It was a steep learning curve but I relished the chance to learn more about a subject I loved. At times, though, the amount of work felt overwhelming.

"Everything on your to-do list needs to be completed by the end of the month," Kirk told me.

The problem was the list expanded daily as Kirk accepted more projects for me to manage without any consultation.

It was in sharp contrast to my role at the RSPB: there I had been presented with little more than a job title and some overall aims and left to get on with planning projects. I had prided myself on taking an idea and running with it; it was what I was best at, and my RSPB boss had been delighted that I had needed so little management. At the Kingsdown Partnership, things were different. Kirk made the decisions and you did the work. This management style seemed so archaic to me, like some 1950s factory where the roles of boss and workers were clearly segregated. Having so little say over my day-to-day work didn't sit easily with me, but at least on Thursdays, when the volunteer tasks took place, I was – nominally at least – in control.

My Thursday mornings quickly fell into a routine. The 6.30 a.m. alarm, the quick glance out of the window to see another rain-heavy morning. The hour-long drive, along the motorway, through the country lanes, cursing the tractor in front. Turn left and down, down through the woods, like a dive into dappled water as the sunlight filtered through the leaves. The woods giving way to hedgerows and the downs rising up, a knobbly spine, ridge backing away towards the sea. Then over the crossroads and descending again into the ancient village, before, wham, halt, as the level crossing closes.

The level crossing seemed always to be closed – it seemed to me that it shut after only 20 seconds and stayed shut for 20 minutes at least. By now the stress is building; *I'm going to be late, I'm going to be late,* chattering in my head. The rain still hammering down, the crossing opens, on I drive, over the stone bridge, beneath which the river churns into life as it tumbles over the weir of the old corn mill. The swishy-haired mums chat beside empty strollers on their return from the prep-school nursery as I rattle by in my old Nissan Micra. Time to negotiate the nightmare drivers in the village, a lethal combination of elderly people and massive farm vehicles with loaded trailers. Past the squat little church with its churchyard full of wind-blown daffodils and headstones where the lichen picks out the names of farming families long rooted in this land. Escaping the confines of the village, up the lane, swinging to a halt beneath the cherry trees. Quick time check: 8.30 a.m., good, now 50 minutes exactly before I have to leave again to pick up the volunteers in town.

On this particular Thursday, I quick-marched past the faded entrance sign, which listed the names of a number of other wildlife companies as being resident on site. It was true that there was once a time when the rutted path, spongy with moss, and the jumble of buildings strung with sagging wires were busy with staff from these organisations, but they had long since left to more watertight premises elsewhere. Now the only businesses at Greengate Farm were the Kingsdown Partnership and a man who fixed tractors.

The farm was once a poultry unit, where generations of chickens lived out miserable and short lives housed in long, dark, wooden sheds. These buildings, dotted around the site, were now pitch black and empty with doors that creaked in the wind.

I gave the porta cabin door a well-aimed kick on the spot where the lacquer of mould and snail trails had worn away from many years of staff booting the door to release its swollen wood from the splintering frame, and wrestled with the pesky burglar alarm. I grabbed the kitchen key and stepped across the path to another building, which housed the kitchen and mess room.

Outside, guttering sagged and cracked downpipes leaked in slimy rivulets of algae. Ivy clambered through the rotten wood of the window frames and the corrugated iron roof was fluorescent with moss. I unlocked the kitchen and kicked open this door as well. An old sofa, black with mouse droppings, sat beneath a faded wall of photos showing old volunteer projects. A water heater hung broken on one wall, lined with cracked blue tiles.

"There's no lighting, or hot water," Kirk had informed me on my first day, "but the fridge works."

I turned on the dripping tap, slow, slow leaking of water into the furred-up kettle. As one kettle boiled I packed all the tea and coffee supplies for the day. The first kettle was to scald the cups over which the mice had jigged, the second kettle was to fill the Thermos flasks.

Beyond the kitchen lay a series of rooms where only the truly brave ventured. In one room the ceiling had collapsed, sending a shower of broken wasp nests and dead wasps across the floor. The whole building smelled of Camembert cheese, a sure sign that mice had died somewhere within the walls.

Kirk had proudly taken me on a tour of these buildings on my first day and asked me what I thought.

"Well, it's certainly atmospheric," I told him, struggling to think of something positive to say. "It would make a great film set."

He had frowned. "Well it needs some fixing up," he conceded, "but Roy can do that. My plan is for us to move in when the porta cabin comes to the end of its life."

It wasn't like I was expecting pristine offices. I had worked in conservation long enough to be used to tumbledown conditions. The staff usually moaned but pulled together to keep things watertight and safe. However, here it felt as if no one, other than me, noticed that anything was wrong. Gemima and Mel had covered the black fingers of mould in their office with pictures of butterflies and Kirk seemed to see only the world portrayed in the faded volunteer photos on the kitchen wall. These showed a bygone era when the porta cabin was new, the equipment shiny and Kirk had hair. In his mind it seemed nothing had changed.

The Kingsdown Partnership had been formed back in the heady and hopeful days of the early 1990s, which saw a resurgence in environmental awareness that unfortunately seems to wax and wane. The 1992 Earth Summit gave the world Agenda 21, a global action programme to deal with the environmental crisis and promote sustainable development. The document was wildly ambitious; business and government less so. Most of the actions have never been completed, innovative ideas swept aside for short-term gains. Still, on this wave of optimism, councils across Britain sprang into action and began setting up recycling schemes and creating local action plans, which involved lots of tree planting, allotment gardening in inner cities and volunteer groups.

It was in this world that the Kingsdown Partnership was formed. In the age of hope and sufficient budgets. Between 1996 and 2001, government spending on conservation had risen by 40 per cent and continued to rise right up until 2008 when the banks collapsed and council budgets were slashed. There had been money at the Partnership in the past, that much was clear, but it was also obvious those days had flown.

It looked like times were likely to get harder, and maybe the rose-tinted spectacles were just the staff's way of staying positive. After all, what could Kirk really do? The council seemed in no rush to rehouse the Partnership and Kirk was clearly struggling to keep the ship afloat and the staff paid amid cutbacks.

I shook myself out of my reverie about the Partnership's finances as the kettle finally boiled. Time was ticking by and I still had to load the vehicle. I poured the hot water into the Thermos flasks and carried them out towards the big silver barn where the tools were stored. Alex arrived, dropped off at the farm gates by cab. Alex, I had discovered, lived in his own flat at the care home. I imagined it to be some converted stately home, but this was because faded grandeur would suit Alex. He had no family nearby, as far as I was aware. His parents lived in Ireland, Alex had informed me proudly. Alex was sent to visit once a year.

I opened the workshop – yet another Rubik's Cube of locks which needed to be pushed in and out and fiddled with in a way that no one had explained to me – while Alex chattered at my ear.

Tool list for that day in hand, I raced around the dark, leaky workshop gathering what I needed. Loppers, ten, must remember Val's, she likes the green pair; bow saws, ten; fire fork; wheelbarrows, all carried out to the trailer attached to the Land Rover. Alex helped, lifting the wheelbarrow in, carrying anything he decided was too heavy for a lady, but he needed to be kept focused otherwise he would wander off and I would find him slipping things into his pockets. I hadn't yet received the "gift" he'd offered but I had found the teaspoons vanishing at the end of each task.

"We will have to ask for his room to be searched to recover them," suggested Gemima but I stifled a smile. I was of Jim's opinion; it seemed a small act of defiance and one that maybe we could turn a blind eye to, as long as the tools didn't go walkabout.

Trailer loaded, I locked up the heavy metal doors of the workshop, picked up the tea kit, checked the time: 9.20, good.

"Alex, time to leave," I called. Time to escape before Kirk arrived with instructions of things to do on the way or pick up on my return.

I swung the vehicle out of the gates and along the lanes. Bedraggled pheasants were hiding in hedgerows, a kestrel was wrestling the wind on the field edge, its body a miracle of minor adjustments, all alive into the wind. Alex told me his life story, a colonialist's story of servants and land and a pet wild dog. He produced a photo to show me, of a spotted dog with huge bat-like ears sitting on a bearskin rug.

"It's beautiful," I said.

He grinned with nostalgic pride as if the dog and the house and the land were still his, and we swooped down from the hills to the river valley, swollen across its banks with the early spring rains. It was April and the world had become all lamb in the last few weeks. They tumbled away from me across the fields, long tails dangling behind.

I hit the main road and urbanity crept across the countryside with the traffic. A sprawl of business empires, caravan sales rooms, garden centres. I thought of the volunteers waiting in the car park. The rain had given way to a fine drizzle, maybe it would be dry after all. I began to plan the day's task, how I would explain the work, what we needed to achieve.

"Left or right, Alex?" I asked as I got stumped at a junction. The route from the farm into town was still new and confusing.

"No idea," Alex said.

"But you've been driven this way for years," I told him.

"No idea," he said, crossing his arms stubbornly.

I rolled my eyes. I'd noticed this about Alex. I suspect, like the teaspoons, the stubbornness was an attempt to keep control of his life, but it didn't make him the most compliant volunteer.

After the first task at the tithe barn his work ethic had dropped off considerably. Normally, within half an hour of starting the job I would find him sitting down watching the others work.

"Alex, I need everyone's help to get this job done," I'd say to him. "You've got to pull your weight the same as any other volunteer."

"Don't want to," he'd reply.

"But that is what the volunteers do," I'd tell him. "They volunteer, to work."

"I didn't volunteer," he said, which was probably true; he was probably told to come along by a member of the care staff. Alex was sent on lots of activities that were seen to be therapeutic. Maybe due to his speech impediment he had also developed a way of getting his point across in a few words.

I knew by now that once he'd decided not to answer me, there would be no budging him.

I sat at the junction for a few seconds, feeling the drivers fume behind, and then decided. We wove through the congested city, through the ancient gates, across the river bridge, around the corner and into the car park and there they were, waiting by the wall, with patched layers and packed lunches: the volunteers.

On that particular morning I'd woken early. Not, for once, by the murderous dreams about the ex which were frustratingly still a regular feature of my sleep, but by the realisation that today I would have to drive the Land Rover and reverse the trailer through the car park in full view of the volunteers. For the last few weeks I had been using the minibus, a big beast but easy enough to drive as long as you remembered to swing it wide round the tight corners of the old city. I knew though that there was no way the minibus would cope with the rough ground of that day's worksite.

I am probably going to insult a whole legion of devotees when I tell you that I am no lover of the Land Rover Defender. Iconic vehicles of the British army they may be but, in my opinion, they are a pig to drive. The Partnership's old Defender seemed little more than a tin bucket on wheels. It had no heating and an ominous hole in the front windscreen which looked as though someone had taken a pot shot at it in the not-so-distant past.

To make matters worse, I had the trailer in tow. Kirk had realised that I might need some extra instruction on trailer driving and had told Gemima to give me a lesson. The problem was, Gemima appeared to have been reversing trailers round corners at pony club meetings since she was knee high to a grasshopper and swung the thing around with such dexterity it made it look easy.

"You'll pick it up," she said casually as I jack-knifed the trailer against the barn door for the third time. I wasn't so sure that I would.

The problem with reversing a trailer, as you will know if you've ever tried it, is that it is counter-intuitive; turn the wheel right and the trailer zooms off to the left. It has something to do with the ball joint which you hitch to. You have to push the front of the trailer in the opposite direction to where you want the back to go. On top of that, the lumbering steering of the Land Rover, which normally needs an acre in which to accomplish a turning circle, suddenly becomes supersensitive and likely to send the trailer veering off course if you get overly excited. Looking in the rear-view mirror while microscopically correcting the wheel and trying not to burn out the clutch was difficult enough when I had practised at the farm, but now I had to do it in a city car park as tourists walked past, gazing in wonder at the ancient architecture, oblivious to vehicles. What's more, I had an audience.

It was the audience that was worrying me, or more specifically two elements of it. First there was Jim. I wanted to look competent in front of Jim. I felt that somehow his approval was necessary. He had seen many group leaders come and go in his time as a volunteer, which was evident from the list he kept of each task, and I was a long way from earning my stripes. My predecessor James had lasted less than a year and didn't seem to have left much of an impression, but the leader before him sounded like some superefficient and practical wildlife expert that Jim admired.

"We worked long days," he had told me, "but everything was done to a high standard." I felt that it was inevitable I would prove a disappointment.

So far, Jim had been tolerant as I'd hashed my way through a series of Krypton Factor style tests, masquerading as weekly volunteer tasks, which the boss had devised. There had been the week that we were sent to cut scrub on an abandoned railway embankment so steep that the only way we could attempt to work on it was to lash ourselves to trees with ropes. Then there was the week I was sent to waymark a footpath route, which involved dropping small groups of volunteers off at one spot and picking them up hours later from another, where I learned that people of a certain age have a passionate dislike of leaving their mobile phones on. It had been late in the day before I had finally tracked them all down.

The second person in the group I didn't want to look a fool in front of was Laurie. From what I had seen of him so far, I felt that he would sneer at my ham-fisted efforts to reverse the trailer. Laurie had joined a few weeks before, a sullen man with his fair hair scraped back in a ragged ponytail. He didn't want to be there, that I felt was clear, but he had a Community Service Order and, at the end of each task, he presented me with a form to sign as proof that he had turned up, handing it across like it was a dirty rag and clearly nothing that anyone would normally associate with him.

The other volunteers were trying to make him feel included in the team. From my position in the driver's seat I had heard Bevan asking him about his life.

"I have nothing to do with any of my family," Laurie snapped in his upper-class voice. "No, I'm not working," he said in response to Bevan's enquiry. "I've been a waster my whole life. I am on the dole. I spend most of my days watching television and smoking pot." He glared at the volunteers, challenging any of them to pass judgement.

"And have you got a girlfriend?" Bevan asked mildly.

"Women are bad news," Laurie said loudly. "Women drove me to drink, I want nothing to do with them."

I waited for Val to explode, but she turned away and stared out of the window. This man wanted an argument and she wasn't about to give him the satisfaction. Laurie caught my eye in the rear-view mirror and seemed satisfied that I had heard but I looked away, in silent agreement with Val.

His polished voice spoke of public school and country estates. *What had he done*, I wondered, *to be on community service?* I had been given no background information and Laurie clearly didn't invite inquiry. Whatever it was, mummy and daddy appeared to have cut him loose some time ago if his work boots were anything to go by. I had already noted the broken seams and what appeared to be carrier bags poking through, presumably as waterproofing. Back at the workshop there were spare boots I could have offered him, but I hesitated. He didn't strike me as a man who wanted me to offer him spare boots.

I could see him now, watching me as I slowly edged the Land Rover backwards down the car park, slamming on the brakes each time a student strolled into view, gazing at their phone screen. Finally, with relief, I pulled to a halt.

Jim wandered across, opened the passenger door of the Land Rover and climbed in. Alex shifted over reluctantly, he seemed to feel that the front seat was his territory alone, and viewed all other men as rivals for my affections.

"You did OK," Jim said as the others clambered into the back and, if the day had ended there, I would have been happy.

We set off from the city, Jim directing me through the streets while Alex sat, cross-armed and sulking beside him. Outside the town we plunged down through narrow lanes between high hedges laced with blackthorn. After a long winter everything was suddenly honey-scented and twittering with light.

"Pull in here," Jim said as we reached a dark green gate with peeling paint and a height barrier. "Give me the keys and I'll open the car park."

I handed him the key labelled with the site name which I had snatched from the cabinet that morning.

"And the other one," Jim said.

I felt a surge of panic. "That's all I've got," I admitted. "No one told me I needed two keys."

Jim sighed and I felt the point being chalked up against me. "I guess we're walking from here," he called to the others in the back.

A groan went up, which felt unfair.

"No one told me I needed two keys," I said again feebly. Back at the porta cabin there were hundreds of site keys in the cabinet all with worn-away labels and mysterious abbreviations. How was I to know there were two locks on this gate if no one had told me? My words were lost as the others tumbled out of the back and peeled back the cover on the trailer to get at the tools.

Kirk had given me two tasks to complete that day. The first was pretty straightforward: remove the little blackthorn bushes that were beginning to grow up and smother the flowers of the grassland that sloped down a hill towards the sea. The second was more of a challenge: install a kissing gate at the point marked on a hand-drawn map.

"We're going to have to carry that huge gate," a small, brisk-looking man said, gazing at the wooden gate strapped to the Land Rover roof.

"That's Reuben," whispered Roy. "Cambridge scholar, very clever."

I had heard Reuben's name mentioned by group members in the previous weeks but this was the first time we had met. Reuben was one of two new faces for me that week. The other was a tall, chunky man who walked slowly and seemed eager to please everyone.

"Bastian," Roy said. "He's been with the group forever and he always tries to be helpful."

I was surprised to see Laurie in the thick of the action, clambering onto the roof of the trailer and undoing the ratchet straps that were holding the gate on.

"He's keen all of a sudden," Jim said as he wandered past.

Soon the tools were loaded into wheelbarrows and we set out beneath the fizz of static from overhead power lines. Laurie, I noticed, was carrying the heaviest part of the gate on his back, but for the first time since he had joined he looked happy. Maybe after all that TV watching and pot smoking it felt good to be doing something physical. He was younger than the other group members probably by about 25 years and his body didn't speak of someone who was habitually inactive. It had a languid confidence that hinted at a past life of physical effort. He had hefted the weight of the gate onto his shoulders with a practised confidence like someone whose muscles remembered what physical work was. Maybe his brain was finally catching up and remembering he liked this kind of activity too.

The site was a remnant of meadow and scrubland sandwiched between main roads. It had been opened with some fanfare by the local council a few years before, but its isolated location and tucked-away car park meant it soon became a magnet for fly tipping, dogging and other unsavoury activities that haunt the urban fringes. After a few months, the council had been forced to lock the car park and the site became lost once again. The remains of old fridges and tyres still poked out of the blackthorn bushes. Cowslips nodded in the shadows and bees swarmed in a happy bonanza amid the ground ivy colonising the piles of household rubble that had been left behind.

Chiffchaffs were calling in the scrub as we hauled the tools uphill along the muddy path, churned into a quagmire by the hooves of the Konik ponies who were let loose to graze.

Eventually we emerged at the top of the hill and looked down upon the nearby coastal town and, beyond, the sea, today the colour of a speedwell's eye. Two swallows flew over, arguing as they sailed across to the coast. As they flew they snacked on the clouds of St Mark's flies which rose in the early warmth, their black legs held in supplication beneath their hairy bodies. Below us the flatlands of the marshes swept away, dancing with grass, mirroring the waves blowing in from the sea, an endless interplay of wind and current.

The hill fell away before us, a tapestry of meadow and scrub. Where the scrub had been cut back, it revealed a carpet of bird's-foot trefoil and clover, but dotted throughout the flowers were tiny shrubs of blackthorn and bramble ready to reclaim this sunny hillside if given half a chance.

Blackthorn and bramble are both valuable native species for wildlife. The mass of blossom was great news for the bees and butterflies busy collecting nectar, and the dense tangle of branches was great for sheltering the nests of birds such as the whitethroats which could be heard calling across the site, along with three brief notes from a nightingale hidden deep inside the scrub.

Blackthorn and bramble are also nature's barbed wire. They are trees that bite back. Bramble ensnares the legs of volunteers, sending them flying face first, and blackthorns are covered in alkaloids which, once buried in the skin, can rapidly lead to blood poisoning. Despite this, revenge is not the reason that conservation volunteers spend so much time hacking these plants down and putting them onto bonfires.

The flower-rich grassland on which the volunteers and I were standing was not a natural habitat in the full sense of the word.

Nowhere in Britain is fully a natural habitat. Our countryside is varied and diverse because of our long history of land management.

Woodland is thought to have once been the dominant habitat of most of England. To quote Julius Caesar's impression of the country upon landing in Sussex, the whole island was pretty much "one horrible forest". That doesn't mean it was wall-to-wall trees. There would always have been natural processes occurring that created clearings in the woodland: storms toppling trees, floods leaving land scoured clean and wildfires burning off the vegetation and allowing opportunities for new growth to flourish. These clearings would have been exploited by large herds of grazing animals, whose behaviour in turn would have been governed by predators.

When people began to clear the forest from around 5000 BC, they provided opportunities for the pioneer species, present in the pockets of open ground, to break out and colonise new areas. Our most precious and rare meadows have been managed in a traditional round of cutting and grazing, sometimes for thousands of years. As such they contain communities of plants and insects which are dependent on this clearance.

If this grassland of wildflowers and butterflies were left alone, it would eventually become dominated by coarser grass and then scrub and eventually trees. Flower-rich grassland – known in conservation as an early successional habitat – is very scarce in Britain. Around 97 per cent of meadows have been lost since the Second World War, most of it ploughed up and reseeded with grass species more nutritious for livestock or turned into arable farmland. The grassland at this site had survived because the hill was too steep to plough.

Some of our most precious wildlife in Britain is reliant on sites which are early successional habitats. Much of the habitat management carried out on nature reserves is aimed at freezing natural processes and keeping the land suspended at an early stage – a policy sometimes criticised by exponents of rewilding.

Rewilding is an idea that has gained momentum in Britain in recent years. According to the organisation Rewilding Europe, "it is about letting nature take care of itself, enabling natural processes to shape land and sea." Through rewilding, they feel, "wildlife's natural rhythms create wilder, more biodiverse habitats."

Outspoken supporters of the rewilding movement such as George Monbiot have also challenged long-accepted views of habitat management. Monbiot has questioned conservation organisations over why their management favours one community of wildlife, such as chalk grassland butterflies, over another, such as birds associated with woodland.

Asking questions about established practices is always healthy, and rewilding parts of Britain is a great idea, especially on land that has limited wildlife value in its current state. However, allowing natural processes to take place on sites like the hill we were now standing on would be the quickest way to lose the 3 per cent of meadows we have left in Britain and the species associated with them. Without regular scrub management and grazing, plants like the salad burnet with its crimson flowers and the golden joy of bird's-foot trefoil, the burnished beauty of small copper butterflies and the captured prism of sky which makes up a common blue butterfly's wing would vanish from the site and these species would have nowhere else to go.

The volunteers' task that day was to cut down the foot-high blackthorn bushes dotting the site, in the hope that the semi-feral ponies, which we could see wafting their tails over each other's backs in the shade, would graze down any regrowth and allow the wild flowers to thrive.

I explained some of this in a rush to the volunteers, who, to my amazement, looked interested and listened.

"Can we have a fire with the little bushes?" Laurie piped up. He was smiling again. He had a front tooth missing, I noticed. "I love making fires," he said.

I hesitated; maybe his Community Service Order was to do with an arson attack? I'd never asked.

"A small fire," I said.

Laurie beamed.

"You'll be needing this," Roy said and produced some newspaper and a lighter from inside his jacket, which, I'd realised, operated like a Swiss Army knife of useful gadgets. Roy's choice of clothing was often unconventional; during the winter months he stuffed a layer of cardboard inside his clothes. "It's good insulation," he assured me. Today he was in summer mode, wearing a vest top, a pair of knee-length shorts and wellies. "For protection against nettles," he had volunteered when I'd looked at them quizzically.

He handed the newspaper to Laurie.

"Many thanks," Laurie said, and set to scrunching the paper into balls, whistling a tune as he did so.

It seemed this task was bringing out the best in him.

"I'm going to need a few of you to come with me and help install the kissing gate," I said. "Have any of you had experience of doing this before?" A bunch of hands shot up, which was a relief as my own experience was limited to say the least.

It had been hard at the RSPB reserve to find opportunities to get involved in the day-to-day management of the site. The all-male team of wardens possessed years of experience and had worked their way up the ranks by passing through such legendary places as Fetlar and the Farnes, where all proper wardens cut their teeth and self-reliance was necessary.

I had bypassed this well-trodden route into conservation by having two things which, in those days, few wardens possessed: an ability to talk to people and a degree in creative writing, which allowed me to write passable copy for press releases and run guided walks.

I had worked my way up different ranks, from publicity officer at a reserve in Dorset to community officer. In the 1990s when I started my career in conservation, these were the jobs that women could get. Wardens were another breed. I am not making a big thing about this but I had heard that the RSPB in those days had an annual beard count at their legendary and hard-drinking wardens' conference, which kind of says it all.

Slowly, at the RSPB reserve, I had edged my way into the men's world. I had begged my boss to send me on brushcutter and tractor-driving courses and had run scrub-cutting and pond-clearance tasks with the little volunteer group I ran, but most of the practical work of the reserve had been the domain of the wardens.

Today's mission was a step up from the previous weeks at Kingsdown. In our previous tasks, the worksites had been a challenge, but the work of scrub cutting and litter removal had been within my comfort zone. Something as technically challenging as installing a kissing gate on a steep slope so that it swung correctly and closed with a satisfying knock on each post was, I knew, another level.

Still, before I could worry about erecting the gate, I first had to find out where it needed to be installed. I set off with the group of volunteers who had experience of installing kissing gates and left the rest of the volunteers cutting scrub on the hill. It took all six of us to manhandle the gate over a fence, through the long grass of the next field and downhill, following the hand-drawn map with a large "X" which Kirk had given me. Above, a red kite patrolled, watching us, before twisting its fork tail and banking away towards a distant wood.

"So now where?" said Reuben as we all collapsed in the shade of an oak at the bottom of the hill.

"It should be here," I said, gazing despairingly at the endless line of thick hedgerow in front of us.

"Didn't you visit the site in advance and check?" asked Reuben.

I had suggested this myself. "Wouldn't it be useful to do a recce before the task day?" I'd asked Kirk a few days earlier.

"It's not necessary," he had said. "It's perfectly obvious where you need to go."

Looking at the site now I could see it wasn't.

"No, I've not been here before," I confessed.

Jim snorted.

"We can't be dragging this thing around in the heat all day," Reuben said.

"Stay here," I said, blustering. "Have a cup of tea. I'll look for the spot."

I could hear the grumbling begin as I set off rapidly across the next meadow. Where the hell was the gate supposed to go? I could imagine the look on the boss's face if I brought it back and told him I couldn't find where to put it.

I was halfway across the field when I heard a shout from behind and turned to see Roy jogging towards me.

"We've found it," he panted. "It was tucked away further down the hedge, but Jim wants to know where the peeler bar is."

In the week before, I had scoured the office bookshelf and searched the internet for advice on installing a kissing gate. It wasn't like I was a complete novice. I had installed a gate before. Well, no, I lie. I had been present when a kissing gate was installed by the RSPB volunteers but, now I thought about it, I seemed to remember that some competent men had set to with mysterious tools and told me to go off and paint the rails with wood preserver. Still, I had seen it done and, what was more, I had read the TCV handbook which told me how to do it.

These handbooks, first published in the 1980s by an organisation called The Conservation Volunteers, are pretty much the bible for all volunteer tasks. They provided clear instructions on all the types of gate you might need to install and how to organise your volunteers to do it. I had packed all of the tools mentioned – true, there had been a few that I'd never heard of but I was pretty sure the TCV book hadn't mentioned a peeler bar.

I followed Roy back to the group. The bits of gate had been laid out along with the tools and Val was in the process of digging a hole for the fence posts.

Jim looked up. "I can't find the spike," he said. "So we've started digging the post holes with a rabbit spade but now I can't find the shuv holer."

I had no idea what he was talking about. "I don't think I used one last time I did this," I hedged.

Jim raised an eyebrow. "Well how do you suggest we get the dirt out of the bottom of the hole?"

I looked at the deep, narrow hole Val had created and could see we had a problem.

The group waited for my reply.

"Oh, let's just get on with it," said Reuben impatiently, and he lay full length on the floor, reached with his arm into the deep hole and began scooping out the dirt with his hands.

I stood impotently to one side. "I'll make a cup of tea," I mumbled.

Bevan wandered across as I squished teabags into cups and watched the volunteers struggle to remove the dirt from the holes. "They're like a big pair of sugar tongs," he said. "They're kept just inside the doorway. Just in case we need them again." He smiled.

I smiled back weakly. "Thanks," I said.

He patted my arm. "Jim doesn't like his teabags squished."

Under Jim's expert guidance, by midday the gate posts had been installed, creating a three sided box and a sturdy-looking post on which the gate would swing. I had been handed a paint brush and was sitting in the shade slapping on wood preserver.

"Right, we're doing well," Jim said, coming across to me. "Just the gate to install now, so we're going to need the adjustable wrench?"

My heart sank. "I brought a socket set," I said quietly.

"A socket set?" Jim said. "No wrench?" He rolled his eyes to the heavens. "Come back, James, all is forgiven," he called, summoning up the departed spirit of my predecessor.

"And we never thought we would say that," said Reuben.

Jim turned to Bevan, who lived in the seaside town at the foot of the hill. "Do you have one at home?" he asked.

Bevan nodded.

Jim sighed deeply. "Come on then," he said and I watched as they disappeared off across the meadow and vanished in the heat haze.

"Is an adjustable wrench really that necessary?" I said to Roy.

He nodded and put a hand on my shoulder. "Don't worry," he said. "James was put in the same situation too, sent out with only half the information he needed."

It was Roy's kindness that pushed the button, and I knew that if I didn't walk away right that moment I was going to cry.

"I'm going to check on the others," I said quickly. "You lot have lunch."

I walked briskly away up the hill. *Suck it up, suck it up,* I told myself, but the tears were already rolling down my cheeks. They came so easily these days. Since the break-up everything seemed much closer to the surface. My feelings were like an overfull tea cup always threatening to slosh out into the open. I was trying so hard to get to grips with my new life, to not dwell, to keep battling on, but I felt in over my head with this job: the long hours, Kirk's expectations, the days of silence in the office and all those blank spaces in my diary showing empty nights and weekends looming large.

Within the safety of a relationship I had become complacent. My ex had been my best friend and making new friends hadn't felt that important. I had friends of course, good friends I had known for years, but nowadays they were all scattered across the country, busy with work and their own relationships and, in the last few weeks, it had come as something of a shock to realise how few people I knew locally.

The truth was that, after years of working on reserves, everyone I knew locally was a man and most of them were happily married men at that. In the past few months these men had been kind. They had rallied round, declared the ex a bastard who they had never liked, even though I knew this wasn't true. They had offered me solidarity in the form of gruff words, unexpected phone calls and unexplained gifts but they were, for all the right reasons, not available to go out with on a Saturday night.

I had been trying so hard to hide how I was really feeling from my family, my colleagues and the volunteers. I wanted to look like I was coping and now I felt exposed. It must be obvious to the volunteers, I felt, that I didn't have the knowledge or the practical skills to do this job. They could all see it. I reached for my phone and began dialling home. Not my flat – it was a sanctuary where I could hide away, but it didn't feel like home. Not the ex – I had my pride. The place that I knew would always shelter me when things went wrong. I wanted to cry down the phone, "Dad, I can't do it."

The phone rang, once, twice. I knew what my dad would say: "Come home. I'll help you out."

Bless him. It is what my dad would always say. Whenever I faced any big challenge that I was scared of setting out on, he would always be there protecting me but, if I gave in to that impulse to run home and hide under the duvet, then what? I couldn't live with my parents. Giving in to that impulse was a slippery slope. Thinking of my dad helped; he didn't come from a generation that threw in the towel and wailed, "I can't do it." I pressed the red button and disconnected the call. Onwards and upwards was my dad's mantra.

I stomped up the rest of the hill and just before the top I met Laurie. He was coming across the field towards me and had his shirt off, revealing a smattering of hair across his chest. I smiled, suddenly shy, not sure what to do when confronted with a semi-naked man. Yes, look. I know I was in my mid-thirties and it's the twenty-first century, but forget that and instead imagine it is 1700 and I'm 16, because I might as well have been for all my woman-of-the-world knowledge. Since the age of 22 I had been faithful in what I had thought was a solid relationship. It had been a long while since I'd spent time with an unknown bare-chested man.

"I was coming to see if you needed any help," he said pleasantly. His change of attitude that day had been a surprise. For the last few weeks he had seemed determined to paint himself as a woman-hating pothead with a criminal record. It was like he wanted to show us that he wasn't a likeable person. However, whatever point he had been determined to prove, to us, to himself, had failed. None of us had risen to his challenge and instead he had been met with polite friendliness and a lack of judgement. Now it seemed he had given up and decided that maybe he would give us a chance after all.

He had pulled his hair out from the ponytail and it now fell beyond his shoulders. He looked at me.

"Are you OK?" he asked. "You look, well, you look like you've been crying."

I wiped my face with the back of a dirty hand.

"It's not going well," I admitted. Somehow it was easy to say it to him. I hadn't really considered what age he was before. He had seemed old and grumpy in his black layers with scraggly fair hair and a permanent scowl. Now he looked as if the sunshine had cracked him open from his winter shell and I guessed he was close to my own age.

"What's up?" he said with genuine concern.

"I'm getting it all wrong," I said. "I don't know the names of half the tools or what I'm doing really."

He was the one person in the group I didn't feel I needed to look sorted in front of. Somewhere along the way, this man's life had taken a wrong turn too and, unlike the others, I doubted he had ten years' experience of putting in kissing gates. He wasn't about to roll his eyes to heaven and ask me where the peeler bar was or pray for the return of my predecessor.

Laurie smiled; he really had a very nice smile. "They'll forgive you," he said. "I'm sure they are charmed by you too." Then he blushed; the cocky, snotty man who thought all women were bad news, blushed.

"Thanks," I said, feeling flustered and suddenly aware that we were alone. Up until then I had only dealt with the volunteers in a group. I had been wearing my public face. Maybe this man had been doing the same, and suddenly, in this little dip in the hills, there was just the two of us and we could both risk letting the act drop a little.

He likes me, I thought with a shock. I think he might even fancy me a bit. Believe me, it was a revelation. An unbelievable thought that a man my own age might be attracted to me. The ex at times had seemed to only have eyes for other women. Now, to my surprise, I realised I was free to like Laurie back. A door opened before me after a long dark winter. *You're single,* I thought, and for the first time the thought made me smile. If I chose, I mean, if only I possessed the courage, I was free to spend time with this man and, glory be, take it as far as I wanted. The thought was way too much to cope with.

"I need to have a wee," I stammered, and shot off up the hill to hide behind a bush, leaving Laurie looking after me with bemusement.

Back on the hilltop, among the safety of the other volunteers, all suddenly seemed sunnier. We had lunch under the sheltering shade of a hawthorn, newly minted with leaves. Laurie spent the afternoon trimming a tree into the shape of an umbrella. Topiary wasn't really the point of the task but he looked so happy that I didn't have the heart to stop him. It turned out that Bastian was a dab hand at cake making and he produced a slightly squashed lemon sponge from his knapsack. And, when Jim and Bevan returned with the adjustable wrench, they sorted the kissing gate out in no time. When we left the hill that evening everyone seemed quite happy. Somehow I had muddled my way through yet another task day.

Back at the farm, the staff had left for the day. Alex hopped out of the passenger seat and strolled off determinedly for his waiting cab as soon as I parked. I sighed. It looked like I was on my own getting the trailer back in the barn.

I pulled open the big metal doors, propped them open and hopped back into the Land Rover cab. The barn yawned darkly behind me.

"Come on, Donaldson," I said aloud. "Just this one thing to do."

It wasn't true, there were still about a hundred things to do but, if I thought of that, I would be undone.

I clunked the Land Rover into reverse and tried to hold the clutch and spin the wheel in the precise way Gemima had demonstrated. The trailer veered off wildly towards the wall of the barn. I pulled forward and tried again; the clutch was so stiff it felt like pushing your foot through a vat of quick-drying cement. My knee ached in protest as the muscles struggled against the resistance. This time I succeeded in jack-knifing the trailer against the Land Rover lights and, as I pulled forward, I realised the whole thing was now at an impossible angle to manoeuvre.

I was so, so tired. I laid my head on the steering wheel. I couldn't go on like this, looking a fool in front of the volunteers, muddling through each task. *I want out,* I thought. *I want to be done with this job I am no good at, with a boss whose expectations are impossible to meet. But then,* I thought, *wasn't that what people always expected of me?* In my twenties I had gained a reputation for flicking my metaphorical skirts at managers I couldn't handle, coming out with a magnificent leaving speech and vanishing from their employ.

Whenever I had any big decision to make, my thoughts turned to my old boss Graham. I had first met Graham after one of those spectacular departures from a job. Following a series of short-term contracts with wildlife-conservation charities, I had landed what I felt would be my dream job, back in my home town, managing a project based around the river valley I had grown up playing beside. It was an opportunity to bring wildlife back to this blighted landscape and encourage the locals to care for it, I told myself.

From day one I realised that things were wrong. There was no money, no clear plan and in-fighting among my employers. I struggled on for three months, feeling increasingly depressed and angry that I had been employed in such circumstances. In the end, I resigned and wrote a letter to my boss, venting my frustration. In reply he told me I would never work for any conservation organisation in the county again. Instead of rising up the career ladder, I found myself on the dole, living with my parents and needing to hide out in a place where no one knew me in order to lick my wounds and figure out what came next.

It was then I'd seen the job at College Lake. "Summer warden wanted for unique reserve set within a former chalk quarry. Volunteer position but board and lodging provided."

As Graham drove me around the reserve in his battered Land Rover during my interview, volunteers seemed to be everywhere, patching up and repairing hides, painting the little huts which served as information centres on bees, bats or fossils. Baking cakes in the tea room, weeding the wildlife gardens, rounding up the reserve's chickens and guinea pigs.

"Guinea pigs?" I questioned Graham. "What conservation purpose do they serve?"

"Can't have a nature reserve without guinea pigs," Graham said in his country burr, and winked at me.

Graham laid out the story of College Lake's creation as we drove around the site. He had created all of this himself over a period of 20 years with the help of the army of volunteers. College Lake had been a quarry owned by a cement company and Graham had been a lorry driver for the company with a keen interest in natural history, which he sometimes indulged while driving his lorry around. On one of his trips he noticed the orchids growing along the edge of the quarry, glow-worms lighting up the banks and the untouched arable fields above holding a seed bank of rare cornfield flowers, which were rapidly disappearing from intensive arable fields. Graham was a man of vision. He could see that under the normal run of things the quarry, at the end of its useful life, would be reverted back to arable land and the orchids and wildflowers and glow-worms would be sprayed into defeat by the noxious chemicals of industrial agriculture.

Graham saw obstacles as things to be broken through. His initial approaches to the quarry owners to turn the quarry into a nature reserve fell on deaf ears, so he went through the back door. He knew the quarry owner's wife was a keen painter, so he invited her painting club along to paint the orchids while at the same time explaining to them the rarity and fragility of the habitat. The quarry owner's wife convinced her husband that the site should be turned into a nature reserve and Graham volunteered to give up lorry driving and instead manage the site's restoration. I was hooked both by Graham's force of personality and the individuality of College Lake.

Up until then all I had seen was the world of corporate conservation: matching uniforms, spreadsheets, budgets, targets and objectives. This reserve had personality, along with a second-hand bookshop and a collection of ancient farm machinery, which Graham still used on a daily basis to cut the wild flower meadows.

There was a feeling of happiness about the place too. It buzzed in the air above Graham's volunteers like a little cloud, sealing everyone into this nest. I was intrigued. When Graham asked what I thought, I told him I wanted the job.

"Don't speak too soon," he said. "You haven't seen the accommodation yet."

We pulled up outside a 1960s caravan, painted forest green, with a hand-carved wooden sign on the door saying "The Lodge". It was set behind a picket fence in its own little garden of scrub elder and hawthorn trees.

"It has gas heaters and electricity but no running water," Graham said. "You won't want to stay here."

The caravan had a view of the lake and a desk to write upon. "When can I start?" I asked.

Graham looked surprised. "But you won't last," he said. "I've had a string of young men take on the job before you and they all found it too hard and caved in. You won't last."

I dug my heels in. *I bloody well will,* I thought, and from that point on I was determined to make the job a success.

I had to remember that girl now. That College Lake girl. There was no way that Graham would want me to give up my career in conservation. Working at College Lake had helped me believe in myself again, and I had to summon up that self-belief now.

You have two choices here, Donaldson, I told myself. *Quit or take control. What would Graham do?* I knew what he would do, he would take control. *Bugger Kirk,* I thought. *You cannot go out on another task without taking the time to properly prepare.*

The boss might want to be the one issuing the orders, but when it came to the volunteer group I was in charge. I was the one who was responsible for what went on during the tasks, not him. I was the one who had to stand up in front of the volunteers every week and look like an idiot if I hadn't done enough preparation. From now on, I was going to run the group the way I thought it should be run, and if that meant visiting sites in advance and asking endless questions then Kirk was just going to have to learn to live with it.

CHAPTER
THREE

For the next few weeks we stayed on the sunny hillside. It was a happy time, as the hill spun into the gold of spring and a blanket of flowers was thrown across the land. The job of cutting back the little blackthorn bushes was easy compared with installing the kissing gate and I used the time to talk to the volunteers about the tasks they had done in the past and enjoyed. Back at Greengate Farm I was putting together a work programme for the next few months and it wasn't proving easy.

Practical conservation volunteer groups such as the one I was running have been around in some form or another since about the 1950s when the Council for Nature was formed "to make people of all ages conscious of their responsibility for the natural environment". Originally these groups were seen as a way of giving young people, in particular, some of the benefits previously provided by the recently abolished national service. Later, in the 1970s, the group morphed into the British Trust for Conservation Volunteers, or TCV as it is called today.

The number and scale of these groups continued to swell as more people became aware of the toll human actions were having on the natural environment. Throughout the 90s, groups focused on objectives such as community involvement in local green spaces. During the millennium celebrations, they planted trees for millennial woods but now, at the beginning of the twenty-first century, things were changing – and not for the better.

Government funding for conservation and biodiversity had continued to grow right up until 2008 and, at that point, the Kingsdown Partnership volunteer group could afford to focus on doing work simply because it provided ecological benefits or improved access to the countryside for people. Now, we all had to face up to the fact that times were rapidly changing. Funding had already been slashed and further cutbacks were sure to come. If the Partnership were to survive, Kirk had to become a bit more hard-headed. The volunteer group had to be cost-effective and the only way to supplement the fuel for the group's minibus and the staff wages was to introduce a charge for the group's services.

Suddenly community groups and private landowners, who had happily had the volunteers laying their hedges and cutting the meadows on their land for years, had to pay for the privilege. I had the unenviable task of phoning people and explaining that, from now on, they would have to pay around £200 a day if they wanted the volunteers to come out. Some felt affronted, some simply couldn't afford it.

"Is this your doing?" one man barked at me down the phone. "We never had to pay before you got the job."

I'm just the messenger, I wanted to say, but the man had already put the phone down. Between the exit of James, the previous project officer, and my arrival, finding work for the volunteer group to do had suddenly become much harder. I had to find ways to fill the weekly programme with work that was not only worthwhile and suitable for volunteers, but paid.

Consequently, I was happy to canvas the group for ideas, which I did over lunch during one of the tasks. Bastian, in particular, was full of suggestions; he had been with the group longer than anyone and had a wealth of knowledge about previous tasks.

"We can't cut scrub in the summer months, Carol," he informed me, "because the birds will be nesting in it."

"That's right, Bastian," I said.

He leaned on the rake he had been using to gather the little blackthorn twigs before putting them on the bonfire. To be honest,

Bastian spent almost every task raking. He had mild cerebral palsy and was not very agile. I had noticed he quickly became out of breath on the walk up the steep hill. Gentle raking didn't call for much fitness and, thankfully, Bastian seemed happy to do it every week.

"In the summer we usually spend a lot of time doing footpath surveys," he said. "Kirk has published many, many walk guides and we have to make sure the paths are easy for people to use."

"Too right he has," said Jim, who happened to be passing. "Most of them are mouldering in that cavern at the farm."

Bastian ignored him. "We make sure that the walks are passable and mend the stiles."

"Does everyone enjoy doing that?" I asked.

Bastian shot a look at Alex who was scouting around the tea kit for the biscuits. "They don't all like doing it. Alex will tell you his feet hurt and he doesn't want to walk."

I smiled, knowing that this was probably true, but I had also noticed that Bastian often said things that might get Alex into trouble.

Before working at the Kingsdown Partnership I had never known anyone with a brain injury and had thoughtlessly presumed that Alex and Bastian's minds would somehow work the same. I couldn't have been more wrong. Alex had experienced 20 years of unimpaired brain function and, in many ways, was as sharp as a tack with a swagger that came from a privileged upbringing. Bastian's brain injury, according to Gemima, had happened at birth when he had been starved of oxygen which, I believe, had caused his cerebral palsy. Bastian's mind also worked spectacularly well in many areas, especially when it came to recalling names and dates, but he had been born and raised at a time when disabilities of all sorts were less accepted. I felt Bastian had been brought up to be "good" and not a nuisance. Consequently, he was apologetic and eager but with a little boy's love of telling tales on the "naughty" group member.

"Do you like doing footpath surveys?" I asked.

Bastian looked glum. "I don't mind," he said, "but people don't like doing it with me because I am too slow."

I could imagine that was true as well. I struggled to keep up with Jim and Reuben when they were walking across country. "What else does the group do in the summer?" I asked.

"Sometimes we take care of hedges and trees we've planted, making sure the grass doesn't cover them or the trees don't die of thirst. Sometimes we work on heathland, keeping it open for nightjars and sometimes we work near the river. I don't like that," Bastian admitted. "I'm sorry, Carol. I can't swim and water makes me nervous."

"You've got very good knowledge though," I told him. "You've been a great help."

Bastian beamed with pride. "And don't forget the jolly," he said. "We always have a jolly, a nice day out to thank us all. You mustn't forget that, it's very important."

"I won't forget," I told him.

With Bastian's advice I finished off the task programme and wafted it briefly in front of Kirk for his approval.

"Try to get more work that will pay next time you create the programme," he said, "but it will do for a first attempt."

The volunteers were more enthusiastic when I handed it out the following week.

They took the sheets of paper eagerly and devoured the list to see what their summer had in store.

"Mallet's Wood!" said Val. "We haven't been there in years."

"What's this?" said Reuben. "Austrian scything?"

"Yes," I said. "Kirk's managed to find some funding so we can be properly trained to cut the meadows."

Reuben looked delighted. "I will look forward to finding out more about it."

"Do we get new scythes?" asked Roy tentatively.

"No, there's no money for that, Roy," I said. "I've been meaning to ask you if we can try to mend those old ones in the workshop."

Our eyes met as the vision of the rusted blades and woodworm-eaten handles swum before us.

"I'll do my best," Roy said, and I knew he would.

"It looks like an interesting programme of work," Jim said. "You've obviously put a bit of effort into it."

I smiled. My relationship with Jim had improved over the last couple of weeks. A few days after the kissing gate saga I had emailed him. "Dear Jim," I wrote. "Turns out I don't know much about installing kissing gates, but I know a man who does. I wonder if you would be so kind as to give me a list of tools I will need for tasks like this, should we do it again."

Jim's comprehensive list of tools for fencing arrived in my inbox the next day and became my go-to reference document. If Jim wanted monkey strainers, then I would damn well find out what they were and make sure they were packed. If Jim wanted an adjustable wrench, I fought my way to the back of the barn and found one amid a pile of old wire Roy had been saving. "Just in case," he'd said. I thought of the scythes again. He was probably right.

Slowly I was edging my way into being group leader. I had long ago realised that I was not by nature a communal-decision sort of person. Once, at a climate change camp, I had watched a very egalitarian meeting take place in which a talking stick was handed round and everyone had equal say over how the "action" should take place. As one person after another chundered on with frankly ludicrous ideas, I felt a growing desire to grab the stick, rap the nearest protester over the knuckles with it and say, "Now shut up, you lot, this is what we are doing." I clearly was not cut out for the world of communes and was temperamentally quite suited to being group leader.

To be fair, I did try in those first weeks to involve others in the decisions but some of the volunteers didn't seem keen to take on that responsibility. "Has anyone got any suggestions on how we should do this job?" I'd ask.

"You're the leader," Jim would say. "We've spent a lifetime making decisions, we don't come out here to do your job for you."

Fine by me, I thought. At the end of the day, Jim was right. I was the only one being paid. It would be me phoning their relatives and waiting with them in A&E if someone had an accident. I had to take responsibility for getting the job done safely.

After four weeks we had cleared the tiny bushes on the hill and left the ponies in peace. We headed back into the city to a large wasteland on the edge of town. It covered an area as big as a supermarket car park and was possibly destined to become one in the not-so-distant future if the developers had their way. But for the last 20 years this place had been left to its own devices and had become an edgeland paradise for all the free-roaming creatures who occupy the urban fringes.

Surrounding the wasteland were streets of old-fashioned council houses. Here the kids still played on the street or trailed in and out of open front doors, watched over by adults who sat in weedy front gardens discussing the comings and goings of their neighbours. It was the part of the city the tourists never saw. Their vision ended at the growing ranks of executive flats which were sweeping such communities away.

I led the group across the wasteland. Beneath our boots the thin soils of the site smelled sickly with chemicals leached from old industrial processes, but the wild flowers were not finicky. Red and white campion, selfheal and buttercups covered the old scars, blooming with the profusion reserved for pioneer plants who knew that the season to make merry would be short. All around, the scrub rang with the calls of blackcaps, a bird seemingly indecisive over its song – it sounded like a robin with a sore throat. Whitethroats were less fussy, having travelled across North Africa to get here – they scratched away in the bushes to south Saharan beats.

Beyond the scrub, tucked away amid a thicket of nettles, lay the river, accessible only to the hardiest kids who were prepared to traverse the jungle. Many clearly were: a ladder attached to the riverbank gave access to a deep pool and rope swings hung precariously from the cracked willows above. Tucked away in this unprepossessing part of town, the river was at its most beautiful, dancing with the flowers of water crowfoot which drifted in vast rafts across the surface of the water. Birds and butterflies sped along this highway where few adults ventured.

Nature and children ran unchecked here. It was the kind of place I had grown up alongside. An edgeland, places all too vulnerable to developers who see only quick profit in these brownfield sites close to town. My childhood playground had been an old Second World War airfield on the edge of a working-class neighbourhood. Like so many other places to the east of London, it had been dug for gravel in the 1970s and became a danger zone of flooded workings, sinking sand and, occasionally, unexploded bombs that caused all the surrounding streets to be evacuated. It was a fabulous place for the local kids who explored the gun emplacements, underground tunnels and air-raid shelters. We fished and swam in the local river and would occasionally eyeball a rat but, as far as I'm aware, no one ever got sick from these adventures; in fact, we were probably healthier because of them.

It was in the wasteland on my doorstep that I first fell in love with nature. The nature diaries my mum had encouraged me to keep were full of observations made over "the back", as we called it. My first cuckoo, my first water vole, a grass snake hunting for frogs in a pond, all spotted on trips to the airfield. I escaped there at every opportunity, often, it has to be said, when I should have been in school. However, like many nature-loving children, I'd drifted away in my early teens. It was necessary really; I was a terribly shy child with bushy red hair, bad acne and a double row of braces. Frankly, in a tough Essex comprehensive I was already doomed. If I had revealed that I spent my evenings reading nature books and my weekends examining insects in pitfall traps in the garden, I never would have survived.

It was only when I was at university that I rediscovered my love of the countryside. Keen to escape the claustrophobia of halls and explore a new part of the country, I bought a bike and spent my weekends cycling in the Peak District. Later I became fascinated by the lives of the blue tits occupying the nest box outside my bedroom window, mainly as a distraction from writing my dissertation.

When I left university, however, I still didn't know what I wanted to do for a job.

"What were you into when you were young?" my boyfriend asked.

"Wildlife," I answered immediately. "I read nothing but nature books."

"Why don't you go and volunteer somewhere?" he had said. "See if you still enjoy it."

It was excellent advice. I did and I never looked back.

The volunteers and I were in this wasteland to tackle something else which had escaped the confines of the city and was running unchecked.

"Today we are hunting for Himalayan balsam," I told the group as I handed round printed sheets showing the mature plant with deep-bellied, pink bells resembling gnomes' hats. It was a beautiful plant that had first been introduced to Britain as a garden flower in 1839 but had escaped, and now brought a joy of colour to the swathes of nettle-lined riverbanks and a flush of pollen to bees.

"We have to grab it now," I told the group, "before it creates seed pods." I pointed to the picture of the seed pods, little pointy closed parasols that exploded with a twist. They could project the seeds up to 4 metres.

The sheets had been printed during the lunch hour when the boss was walking Marley. I had realised the knack to getting things done at the Kingsdown Partnership was to do them when the boss wasn't there. Lunchtimes were handy for awkward phone calls and, on days when Kirk was out of the office, I began taking the opportunity to visit sites and work out the plan for each task. It meant I was forever looking furtive but it saved the hassle of having to justify my actions to the others and meant the tasks were beginning to run more smoothly. Things still went wrong of course. I still failed to bring the right tools, I still forgot the milk for the tea, I still drove us to the wrong part of the site and everyone had to walk for miles, but I was trying – the volunteers could see I was and I felt I was slowly winning my place.

I searched around at my feet and plucked one of the plants of Himalayan balsam to show the group. "You can eat it," I said. "Take a bunch of young plants home and cook them up for tea. But not if you've got gout," I added as an afterthought, "or arthritis. They are a bit too rich in minerals and likely to aggravate it."

Reuben perked up. "Really," he said. "Which minerals?"

I should have anticipated this. Reuben was a lifelong scholar and loved new facts. He liked to explore every idea fully and often asked me technical questions about wildlife that left me floundering. It wasn't that Reuben was trying to catch me out, he just gave me the compliment of assuming my level of knowledge was on par with his own.

When I first met Reuben I had imagined he came from a middle-class background. His voice was cultured, he loved to listen to evensong on Radio 3 and, after all, he had gone to Cambridge. Coming from a very different background, to me these things added up to someone who was just a bit posh. Over the last few weeks, however, I had found out that this wasn't the case at all.

"How did you come by your knowledge of natural history?" Reuben had asked me one week.

I had told him that, because I'd been bullied at school, I had spent much of my youth locked in my parents' bathroom, refusing to go out.

"I spent my time reading nature books," I said. "I probably got a better education that way than I would have done in a school where the teachers hid under the desk while the children pelted them with wet newspaper."

Reuben looked horrified. "But you went to university and did a further degree. You must have got some formal education."

"I loved learning," I told him. "I changed to a more disciplined school when I was fourteen and did well in my exams."

Reuben told me that he had also fought hard for his education. Far from being posh, it turned out he was a lad from a council house, not the natural background for a Cambridge student in the 1960s. He had also failed the eleven-plus, an exam which, in those days, tested people on a certain type of intelligence, one which involved being good at riddles.

"Even now I couldn't solve a cryptic crossword," said Reuben. "I wouldn't have a clue. It's not how my mind works."

But at his secondary modern school Reuben had worked hard and finally transferred to the grammar school for his A levels.

"Still, the eleven-plus coloured my life," he said. "Many of the boys I had known from my youth still wouldn't speak to me at the grammar school because I had failed the exam and been marked as non-academic."

Even after getting excellent A levels Reuben still had to struggle against the expectations of his social class. "My dad thought I should work," he said. "So at nineteen I got a job at British Rail, but I was coming home every night and falling asleep in front of the fire like an old man. I thought, I've worked my socks off for an education and I am going to university whether my dad likes it or not."

Reuben went to Hull to study geography and then got a research award to pay for his maintenance at Wolfson College, Cambridge.

Even after completing university, Reuben continued his studies. He often picked up on some piece of information I gave the group, went home to study the subject further and came back with useful information on the following task, so it was typical that he would want to know exactly which minerals in Himalayan balsam were bad for gout. I didn't want to disappoint Reuben by revealing that my natural history knowledge was not good enough to answer his question, but I knew it was best to be honest.

"I'm afraid I don't know which minerals are in Himalayan balsam," I confessed. "I'll look it up and come back to you next week with an answer."

"I'll also look it up," said Reuben, "in my library."

Reuben's great luxury was a membership to the London Library, where he went on a regular basis to further his knowledge. He also, I knew, had an extensive natural history library at home. I could picture him, later that evening, sitting by an open fire in a leather chair, with a glass of whisky and a large plant atlas showing the national distribution and properties of all the flora in the British Isles. In my fantasy of Reuben's home life, this book would be written entirely in Latin.

I liked the image. There was something about Reuben that seemed to belong to another era. He certainly was no lover of twenty-first-century technology as he had no mobile phone and no computer. All correspondence with Reuben had to be in writing or through Bevan, who would phone him and hope that Reuben picked up. He was toying with the idea of getting an answerphone but it was a concession to modernity that didn't come easily. I sympathised. I didn't appreciate the intrusion of technology into our lives either and was secretly delighted to support someone who refused to bow to the expectations of modern life.

"Why are we pulling the Himalayan balsam up then?" asked Laurie. "If it's so nutritious?"

Over the last few tasks I had seen the change in Laurie. Now he sang his way through the task days on the hillside, slashing at the mini scrub as the days slowly warmed and clouds of blue butterflies rose from the grassland. He had a good voice and we all liked to hear him sing. There seemed something old fashioned about that too. The kind of thing people did to entertain themselves while they worked before iPods were invented and everyone shut themselves off in a world of their own music.

Since the moment he had found me tear-stained, Laurie had appointed himself my assistant, helping me out by handing out tools and making the tea for the others.

"I'm glad you're here," I had told him as he took orders and ladled coffee into cups.

"I'm glad you're here, too," he said, and I thrilled at the thought that his gladness implied something quite different than mine.

There was something intoxicating about these baby steps we took in getting to know each other. All the tiny touches of arms and hands that seemed to happen while exchanging tools, looking up from my work only to find him watching me and smiling, the text messages he sometimes sent me during the week telling me about a small incident that had happened to him that day. We live in an age when it is far more acceptable to jump into bed within hours of meeting someone than to take your time but, working alongside each other, things could evolve naturally.

Over the last few tasks, Laurie had begun to open up and provide a little information on what had brought him here.

"I'm on probation because of a fight," he'd revealed one day as he handed over the form which I needed to sign to prove he had attended. "I just lost it," he mumbled. "Got charged with GBH, but I had thought it was going to be worse."

I waited for more explanation but that seemed as much as he was currently prepared to give and I reined in my desire to find out more. I had already realised that, if you dug too deep with Laurie, he was likely to shut you down with some comment designed to shock and push people away. It was best to stick to the facts.

"So, how long is your Community Service Order for?" I asked.

"Another few months," he said. "I'm enjoying it though. I know I'm not meant to say that but it's all practical and outdoors, which is good for me."

Over the last few weeks I had seen that Laurie had become much more interested in the work. Like Reuben, he had a questioning mind and liked asking questions, so it was typical of him to ask why today's task involved pulling up a plant that was nutritious.

"Because Himalayan balsam is non-native and invasive," I said. "The seeds float downstream like little coracles and colonise new areas, given the chance. By the end of the summer this plant could grow to eight feet tall and shade out all the other native plants beneath it."

"So we don't like it because it's foreign?" he said.

"Well," I said, thinking, "it's more to do with it being invasive than foreign; some non-natives don't cause much damage at all."

I looked at the rest of the group. Removing a plant as attractive and bee-buzzing as Himalayan balsam was bound to make people question whether this was a good use of their time and, if the volunteers were going to spend a whole day in baking heat removing it, then they deserved to know all sides of the argument.

"Some people think we should just leave Himalayan balsam alone," I told them, "because it makes parts of the river quite pretty and without it the riverbank would just be lined with nettles. But, like I said, it out-competes native plants and it also has very shallow roots. This is good news for us as it means it is easy to pull up, but it also means that, when it dies back in the autumn, there is no root system to hold the banks together and they get washed away in winter floods."

To be honest I sometimes doubted the wisdom of balsam bashing myself. In town centres it didn't feel quite right to remove the only bright spot of colour and useful nectar. But downstream the meadows were alive with such delicate delights as ragged robin and tubular water dropwort plants, and I wouldn't want these beauties lost beneath the balsam's dark canopy.

"Right oh," Laurie said, and enthusiastically began searching for the plant.

Jim sidled up to me and watched him. Laurie was wearing a battered T-shirt with the arms cut off. "He's a nice lad," he said to me now, indicating Laurie, "but he is going to regret doing that work without gloves on by the evening."

As always, Jim was right. Himalayan balsam pulling was not a task to do with bare hands. The plants spent their first few weeks sheltering beneath dense beds of nettle and, without protection, everyone's hands and wrists would become swollen into angry red welts.

I wandered over to Laurie. "You're doing a great job," I said. "But you might want to do it wearing these." I handed him a long pair of red rubber gloves, the kind of thing that vets use to extract calves from the back end of cows.

"Groovy," Laurie said.

He beamed at me, revealing that missing front tooth. He had lost it in the fight, I knew that much by now. He had volunteered up some more information a few weeks before. "It was someone I knew, vaguely," he had said. "He said something I objected to."

What? I wanted to ask. *What could anyone say that made you inflict such damage on them that you would be charged with grievous bodily harm?*

Laurie though continued to be vague about the details and didn't seem interested in explaining or helping other people understand. If anything, he appeared to want people to judge him harshly – after all, it was how he appeared to judge himself, and any whiff of sympathy was quickly shut down.

"This isn't the first time I've been in trouble with the law," he had told me as I had signed the Community Service Order form. "I broke into a girlfriend's house after smoking too much pot. The police were called then, too."

The revelation had the desired effect. I imagined the girlfriend scared at the appearance of a different Laurie, the one who was angry and obviously had a propensity to violence. I handed the form back to him silently.

Laurie appeared to revel in telling me his many misdeeds and, knowing no better, I took it at face value. Now, I suspect his internal monologue went more like this: "I like you but you won't like me and it's best that you don't so I am going to show you what terribly bad news I am and why it's best that you reject me. Please stay away. Please don't like me. I don't like myself all that much."

Mental health issues are discussed much more openly these days but at that point, I had never knowingly met anyone who had an issue. When I was growing up it was not a topic for discussion. Now I think there must have been people in my immediate vicinity who were struggling with depression or bipolar disorder, but these problems were just absorbed into something more palatable, a case of the blues or eccentricity.

Laurie had said that being outdoors with the group was good for him and I was also beginning to realise that I felt happier at the end of each volunteer task. In the silence of the office or my flat I dwelt on the past but, on my days with the volunteers, I was too busy and social to think of such things. Being out on the hillside laughing with Roy, or beside the river listening to the banter between Jim and Bevan, or working alongside Reuben having long intelligent conversations, I realised that I felt more myself again. My head cleared of the internalised fug and I felt surer that things would be OK. That I was OK.

There is growing evidence that social prescribing in the form of exercise, volunteering in the community, gardening, singing and, yes, conservation volunteer groups, can have a positive impact on people's mental health and reduce the amount of time spent at the doctor's. In many ways it seems madness that so many of us need to be told by a doctor that getting off the sofa, being outdoors, exercising, being part of a community and giving something back to society, will make us feel a whole lot more positive about life. Still, we can all fall into a dark spiral and it can be a damn sight harder to buck your ideas up if you have limited education, poor housing, no fulfilling work and everyone around you is in the same boat.

I didn't know it then but Laurie was someone who was falling through the cracks of the NHS mental health system. He had clinical depression but wasn't getting the help he needed. The pot smoking and drinking were just ways of coping with thoughts he couldn't manage.

Laurie lay his criminal record and mental health problems on a platter before me, but in spite of what he said about himself, it was hard not to warm to him. Everyone seemed to because, when he was in a good mood, he was hard-working, well-mannered and a pleasure to be around. I had pushed those early days of gloom and sharp-tongued answers to the back of my mind and now what I saw on a weekly basis was an enthusiastic, handsome man, with a ready smile, who offered me support. It was the buzz of excitement and boost to my confidence that I needed at that moment.

Our days together felt so much more real than the stilted conversations I was trying to conduct on the internet dating site my friend Lynn had signed me up to. Lynn was one of my best friends but she lived in Shropshire, sadly too far away to be company on those lonely evenings. She had, however, come to visit not long after the break-up with the ex and in her practical, farmer's-daughter way, had taken me in hand.

"You need to get back on the horse," she assured me. "Dip a toe in the water. It will be fun."

However, the people I had so far encountered on the dating website seemed to occupy a world entirely alien to me. Judging from their profile photos, the other women all seemed to possess impossibly shiny hair and manicured nails. They listed their hobbies as watching box sets and shopping. In contrast, the profile Lynn had written for me said I enjoyed nettle-beer making and wild camping, and my photo showed a woman with wild red hair, wearing a duffel coat she had picked up 15 years before in a charity shop for a fiver. Lynn said this made me look niche. I wasn't so sure that men wanted niche, but what did I know? My male friends were mainly bird watchers; they weren't the best people to canvas for advice.

Clearly, though, there are men out there who are attracted to women resembling Stig of the Dump, as my inbox was swamped by messages from men who wanted to "chat". I felt invaded – the flat was my sanctuary, the only place I could switch off and not have to appear like I was fine, but with the laptop reporting to my potential suitors that I was online, I felt watched.

Out of politeness I had begun answering the men's messages one by one. More messages shot back; it was too much, I wasn't ready. I had switched off the computer and spent the rest of the evening feeling guilty. With Laurie it was different, there were no expectations, it was possible to enjoy the tiny things: a look, a touch for all that it contained without any pressure to move things along.

I think if Laurie had made a move in those early days, actually asked me out on a date, I would have danced away in terror. I had just come out of a 14-year relationship, and I wasn't so certain I wanted to get into another one. I had felt locked down in that relationship, unable to want the things a woman in her thirties is meant to want: marriage, home ownership, babies. The men of my age who flashed up on the internet dating site had done all these things and had done them young. Whatever their actual age, it felt like they were far older than me. I still wanted fun and adventures, camping by rivers, travels to exciting places and a man who would accompany me on such things.

Laurie on the surface seemed so much like that man. He wasn't about to question why I wasn't married and didn't have children, as many of the men on the internet did. He wasn't about to judge my financial compatibility or frown because I had chosen a job that was fun and meaningful over one that provided a fat pay check. Why would he? He had problems, that much was clear, but who was I to judge? My baggage was piled up around me like Paddington Bear.

Back on the river the heat was building. By the afternoon our backs ached from the endless pulling of the Himalayan balsam and in spite of the rubber gloves, everyone's arms above the elbow were swollen with nettle stings. We sweated and were stung and by nightfall our arms would be hot flames and bubble like smallpox victims. The coolest place to be was in the river, and many of the volunteers were happy to slip into the shallows between the black darting fish to hunt for outlying plants growing in hard-to-reach places.

Mayflies were rising on the river, godly arms held wide as they ascended to the heavens. The mayflies rose in hope only to be knocked from the air as sparrows tried to catch them and missed. The buffeted mayflies fell back into the water, where they made valiant attempts to lift off again on their maiden flight. Slowly their wings became sodden with the oily embrace of the river. Their one day of strength and flight used up, they tried and then tried again to lift from the water and then, humbled, drifted with the current towards the sea.

Reuben was in the river in his thigh waders and a pair of shorts. He saw me watching the mayflies.

"It's so sad," I said.

Reuben was philosophical. "Their Latin name is *Ephemeroptera*," he informed me. "Derived from the Greek word *ephemeros*. They are a creature meant only to exist for a short time."

"Like many things in life," I said; I had thought my relationship with my ex would last a lifetime but I had been wrong. I had not seen the ending coming. I had not predicted that at the age of 36 I would be starting on a new chapter. It seemed everything in life has an ending. "The Buddhists believe we suffer when we do not accept life's impermanence," said Reuben. "We try to cling on when we need to let go."

I hadn't clung on to the ex. I had let him go and knew there was no way back, but I had suffered over the way our long relationship had ended. Maybe it was time I stopped looking back and began to look at what life had to offer now.

"The trick is to enjoy the moment," Reuben said.

I looked out across the river. Damselflies were emerging between the flag iris. Fish quivered among the weedy tresses of crowfoot and occasionally a trout rose and snatched a midge from those that spun in dizzying clouds above the surface. Dark holes under trees spoke of otters, edging back into the county using arteries such as this. It was all ephemeral, like the mayflies, and could be gone, would be gone, so easily. It was inevitable, we were told, it was progress, regeneration. The people and the wildlife would be swept away by developers who signed such places off as brownfield land and therefore, in the eyes of many, worthless. All of the plants and creatures that lived here were making the most of this moment, mating and fruiting as the sun passed in its zenith. I needed to learn to do the same.

So, as the swallows skimmed the water and clouds of willow down blew like confetti from the trees, I played beside the river; holding Laurie's hand as I leaned out over the bank to reach a lone plant of Himalayan balsam that had escaped the others' attention. It was a moment of dancing light and laughter, and maybe for now that was all I was ready for.

CHAPTER
FOUR

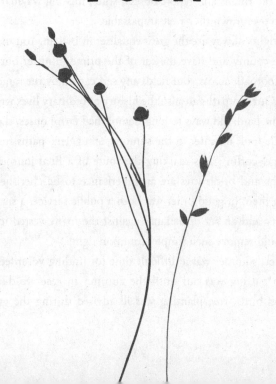

Spring became summer and the songs of the birds grew wistful: a tale of winners and losers in the fight for procreation, who had mated and created, who had been left behind. There were those who had almost triumphed only for a babe to be snatched away in the jaws of a cat or the claws of a sparrowhawk. The young of these birds, the survivors, wanted nothing of such tales. For them life was new. Starlings flew in jubilant teenage gangs around the rooftops of the old city, joined by the swifts, sky-anchoring in a joy of tumbledown flight. Out in the fields, flowers fell across the downs and the grass was a hot mass of butterflies.

The volunteer gang and I took to the footpaths. Footpath maintenance was summer work and a handy way to fill a gap in the programme, as Bastian had said. I sent the group off in teams to inspect the routes and report broken stiles, missing waymarkers or paths so overgrown they were impassable.

Our rights of way are the great equaliser in Britain. You may own half the county and have the ear of the prime minister but if you have a footpath across your fields any serf can enjoy the same views as you. Our footpaths are also the history of ordinary lives writ large across the land: old ways to long-demolished farmhouses, the route the cattle took to water in the summer, smugglers' paths from bay to village, coffin paths marking the route of a final journey. Our footpaths and bridleways are an inheritance to be cherished, and keeping them in good order was both a public service, a statement of liberty and an act of defiance against the many vested interests that would remove such simple, common rights.

Besides, summer was a difficult time for finding volunteer tasks – scrub cutting was out until the autumn in case we disturbed breeding birds, tree planting was ill advised during the growing season as the shock of transplanting young trees could kill them, and it was too early for hay making. Thankfully, the volunteers seemed to enjoy footpath maintenance as it was useful and sociable – the main requirements of a good volunteer task, I was beginning to realise.

The skill to making it enjoyable was in putting together teams of people who would enjoy each other's company and walk at a similar pace. There was no point matching Jim with Bastian, for instance, if the experience was to be pleasurable for either of them. Jim's long strides could eat up the miles and Bastian would have spent the day apologising for his shuffling gait. Jim, Bevan and Reuben were the ideal team; the three men loved a good walk and regularly met up outside of the Thursday tasks to take strolls together along the coast. I could imagine that the conversation on these days out was as quick and lively as the pace. I could see no benefit in forcing people into teams they wouldn't choose for themselves; after all, I wanted the volunteers to enjoy their days as they were giving their time and labour for free.

My time with Graham at College Lake had taught me how fulfilling it could be to volunteer. I had never worked harder than I did during my time there. Each day I would wake in my narrow bed in The Lodge by the lake and hear the birds singing. I would fire up the smelly paraffin heaters to ward off the damp air and make myself a cup of tea on a two-ring hob. Outside, I would sit on the picnic bench in my garden and watch the sun rise over the lakes. *In a moment I will go and feed the chickens,* I would think, *and then maybe, later today, I will paint that old shepherd's hut.*

When he arrived I would present my list of prospective jobs to Graham.

"Needs doing," he would say as he drunk tea in the little hut known as The Bothy, which the volunteers had built and used for a mess room. That was all the encouragement I needed to head off to spend the day painting, hedging or weeding. The work was all practical and easy on the head. There was no such thing as office work. The reserve, in those days, didn't possess a phone line, let alone a computer. That was why I understood Laurie when he told me how the practical nature of his Community Service Order was helping him process what had happened in his life. I knew what it was like to fall off the ladder of life and need to hide out in the country doing something that didn't involve any big decisions. After months of my own swirling thoughts, College Lake had been what I needed. I was never happier or felt more authentic than at College Lake. I volunteered late into the evening and on my days off because I wanted to be involved, because there was nothing half so much fun going on as being with Graham and the other volunteers.

I was entranced by Graham, I don't mind admitting. I wanted to be him. He had a kind of glow around him that made you want to follow where he led. He was a tall man with a sweep of silver hair and dressed in the outfit of all countrymen: corded trousers, wide-checked shirt and a jacket with multiple pockets. He probably always had a hand lens and a penknife in these pockets. He was the epitome of every illustration I had seen in my childhood nature books of what a nature reserve warden should be. Watching Graham, I learned how to treat each volunteer as a valued member of a community, whatever their quirks might be. Graham matched the volunteer to the job in order to get the best out of both, and he could only do that if he found out who each person was and what they enjoyed. Graham showed me that the tea and talk were an important part of the day. That if people had a good time and felt they had contributed, they would want to come again.

The Volunteer Functions Inventory identifies six reasons that people volunteer: to act on values important to them; as an opportunity to increase their knowledge of the world and develop or practise skills that might otherwise go unused; to enhance their self-esteem; to cope with inner anxieties and reduce feelings of guilt or inferiority; to gain experience to help their careers; and to be part of a social group.

People in charge of conservation groups sometimes fail to consider why people volunteer. In the past I had seen task leaders set work that was just a dull slog and expect volunteers to do it cheerfully all day long, for nothing. Alex was spot on when he said volunteering for the boss was no fun because he forgot he didn't pay. The payment must come from somewhere.

However, it wasn't only volunteer group leaders who sometimes didn't get it. My dad was equally perplexed by all these people choosing to work for nothing.

"Why don't they get paid jobs?" he'd say over Sunday lunch, when I returned to my parents' and told them exploits from the latest task.

"Most of them are retired," I would explain.

"So why would they want to keep on working for nothing?" he'd counter.

It was a question I put to the volunteers over tea break the following week.

"My wife suggested I join," said Bruno, a long-term member of the group and our most senior volunteer. "It was about six months before I retired from my job as a chemist. She found a leaflet in the farm shop about the group and said it would suit me. She knew I would be at a loose end and I liked the idea of putting something back into the countryside."

"I found a leaflet in the bakers," chipped in Bevan. "I'd been retired about three months and had caught up on all the DIY I'd been meaning to do when I was working and thought, now what?"

"I put those leaflets in the bakers and the farm shop," Bastian said eagerly, seemingly delighted that his hard work had reaped such rewards. "We didn't have many volunteers at the time and I told Kirk I would help."

Bruno and Bevan exchanged smiles. If it hadn't been for Bastian's diligent promotion, then the last few years of their lives may well have been entirely different.

"So what appealed to you about joining the group?" I'd asked them.

"I had always fancied doing a job like this," Bevan admitted. "Accountancy paid, but every now and then I would see a warden job advertised and fantasise about a very different kind of working life, but it would have meant losing half my salary so it wasn't realistic. When I retired I suddenly could please myself."

Roy's story was similar. "When I retired, I could have done something easy," he said as he sanded down the new handles he was making for the scythes, in preparation for the Austrian scything workshop that was to take place later that year. "I could have opted for playing golf and going on cruises but I wanted to still be contributing. I think without the volunteering I would have no sense of my place in the world."

My dad had tried. Like Roy, he'd taken early retirement from his job at the Royal Mail. He never seemed to enjoy the job and I guess he initially welcomed the free time. Like Bevan, he had gone on a DIY spree, but now he was often bored.

A report by the Joseph Rowntree Foundation in 2005 advocated for phased retirement schemes, in which people approaching retirement took time off during the working week to try out different forms of volunteering with a range of organisations. "Typically, they might start with half a day a week in the year running up to retirement and increase the time commitment as retirement gets closer."

Why hadn't a big company like the Royal Mail been enlightened enough to offer this to my dad? If it had, he may have realised that there was more to be gained from useful employment than wages.

Bevan had worked in London and had told me over the tea break the previous week that when he had left work he felt he had lost all his colleagues at once. "I still kept in touch with some of them, of course," he said, "but it wasn't the same. I missed the social interaction. Now I feel that the volunteers are my colleagues."

I felt that volunteering after retirement would have helped my dad make new friends too and, as a kind man, he would have loved using his fabulous practical skills to help others. I could well imagine him standing beside Roy in the barn making tool handles. My dad's world would have benefited from volunteering but now, in his late seventies, ill health had closed that door to him. Maybe it had always been closed.

UK surveys consistently show that you are more likely to volunteer if you are the lucky recipient of a higher education, occupational status and income. My dad left school in Stratford, east London, aged 14. A clever man with a talent for mathematics, his hopes of an engineering apprenticeship had been cut short by the early death of both his parents. The Royal Mail, in those days, offered good stable employment for a working-class lad, but it came with long hours and low pay.

Unlike my dad, the volunteers were almost exclusively from professional occupations: former accountants, chemists and civil servants. Around 35 per cent of people in managerial and professional jobs volunteer, as opposed to 16 per cent of people in routine jobs, and only 13 per cent of the unemployed. Studies into volunteering often describe it as an altruistic activity, so does this discrepancy in the occupations of the people who volunteer mean that accountants are more altruistic than postal workers? Probably not, it's just that there are barriers both real and implied which stop people with lower levels of education and money from volunteering.

The Institute for Volunteering Research felt that barriers included a lack of time, a lack of self-confidence, attitudes of other volunteers and staff including direct discrimination and prejudice, practical barriers such as concerns over losing benefits, a lack of knowledge on how to get involved and the cost of transport and childcare.

I think one of the other barriers to volunteering comes from the experience many working-class people have had in the workplace. If you have been paid a low wage for your labour and had little autonomy or fulfilment from your employment, then maybe you are less inclined to give anything to "the man" for free. Traditionally, the people in charge of charities, in conservation at least, have almost always been from a middle-class background, which is the same as, "the man". Until wildlife charities employ a broader section of the population in public-facing roles, then I feel they will fail to attract a cross-section of people to volunteer.

Still, my own recruitment drive, which followed Bastian's plan of leafleting likely venues, had yet to attract any obviously working-class volunteers. Many things about the Kingsdown Partnership, at that time, were slightly archaic, and the website was one of them.

It had presumably been created many years ago and no one had had the time to update it. Consequently, the Partnership's social media presence was pretty much non-existent. Amazingly, volunteers were still finding us through our limited online presence as well as through leaflets and word of mouth, and in some ways we were becoming a more diverse bunch. I now had three new women in the group, one of whom came from a background other than white British, something of a coup in the world of conservation I assure you as, at the time, 99 per cent of volunteers, according to the National Trust 2011 volunteer survey, were white.

Kay was a solicitor who had been put on a four-day week when the recession hit, and was taking advantage of her reduced hours to get involved in something she had long wished to do. She was in her thirties, intelligent and driven. "It's so different from the day job," she said, but we could all see how much she was loving donning dirty jeans every Thursday and getting stuck in.

Meg was in her late sixties, a genteel, cultured woman. She loved John Betjeman poetry and early English choral music, but in her younger days she had thwarted her family's expectations to live in a caravan, work on a farm and zip around the country lanes on a Vespa scooter. Although officially retired, she was still working one night a week at a boarding school, helping children with their reading, and was the gardener at the local convent. Her full life had involved meeting and befriending endless interesting characters that could have filled the pages of a Dickens novel. I loved lopping and chopping alongside her and hearing these tales unwind.

This was the thing with the volunteers: if I had passed many of these people on the street, I would have possibly made assumptions about them based on their appearance, but working alongside each other you realised that the image people presented to the world was rarely the most interesting thing about them. In the casual conversations that started up while working beside someone you discovered the rich depths of who a person really was. In many ways the facts of a person's life, their former job or their marital status weren't important or sometimes even mentioned; it was the stories people told that created deeper, more meaningful connections.

Esther and Wayland were a case in point. Esther was a former social worker and Wayland had worked in a children's home. They had a solid marriage and three grown-up children. They had recently moved to a large, rambling house on the outskirts of town. Stand behind them in the queue at the supermarket and they would have looked like a conventional couple in their early sixties doing the weekly shop, but dig a little deeper and you would realise that Esther and Wayland were committed conservation activists.

Esther could be found at weekends in the supermarket but, instead of doing the weekly shop, she would be stickering cans of tuna to protest against unsustainable fishing, or heading to a climate crisis rally dressed as a polar bear. Wayland might be in London looking after the welfare of protestors locked to a bank's headquarters, making sure they were treated with respect by the police when arrested and had a lift home when they got bailed. They cared deeply about the climate crisis and had endless energy and integrity to live by their beliefs and hold others accountable.

None of this had been evident when they first joined. To begin with we had been a little unsure how they were going to fit into the gang, not because of their political activism but because they had vocal marital spats which sometimes caused the rest of us to fall silent in embarrassment. Soon, however, we realised that the sparring masked a huge amount of love for each other and a great partnership.

"I'm not working with him," Esther would say, waving her hand at Wayland, and they would go off and make their own friends in the group, Wayland swinging tools with huge gusto, ensuring everyone kept a wide berth, and Esther a sunbeam that lit up every edge of a woodland she worked in. At the end of the day Wayland would come over and kiss Esther on the head. Outside of the volunteer group, they were a tight team with shared values. They took on an allotment, kept bees in the tumbling garden of their house and stocked the cavernous cellar with chutney, honey and wine.

They were soon core members of the gang and we knew we were lucky to have them. They were great role models for me and all the younger members of the group of what an active old age should look like. If only the benefits of volunteering could be understood by more people, my dad included.

By the third week of footpath surveys, I had a good idea of who to pair with who to do the work. I sidled up to Esther and Meg.

"Would you mind taking Bastian with you?" I asked. "He loves working with you and I know you won't make him feel rushed." They were both kind women and agreed to help, although I knew that Meg would have preferred to stretch her legs with a good, fast yomp.

"I'll walk with Bruno, Kay and Reuben," Val declared.

It was a good team. Val had strong views on many things and was likely to shoot down in flames anything she disagreed with. Bruno was a quiet, considered man. Kay had a sensible, balanced opinion and Reuben was likely to steer the conversation in philosophical directions.

Jim and Bevan were already edging into a gang with Roy, but I was eager to get everyone's attention before they shot off.

"The routes are all different lengths," I explained, "so choose one that is suitable for everyone's abilities." I shot a meaningful look at Meg and Esther. "Make sure each group has a hammer and you take a good supply of waymarker discs, blue for a bridleway, yellow for a footpath, and only bang the discs into posts or field gates, not trees or garden fences, and KEEP YOUR MOBILE PHONES ON," I bellowed over the gaggle of discussion. "Jim," I shouted, "I don't want to phone and hear your answerphone tell me that you only switch your mobile on once a day."

Jim smiled.

Laurie sidled up to me. "I'll come with you," he said.

"That's fine," I said casually, trying not to look too pleased.

"Me too," Alex said, almost pushing Laurie to one side. It seemed Laurie and I weren't going anywhere without my chaperone.

The three of us set off on a footpath upstream from the city. A place where properties with sweeping lawns lined the river, pleasure boats bobbed along the banks and people who could afford to dawdled away summer's afternoons in riverside pubs. The river became idle too, lazily making its way between banks all flush with summer growth. A storm was threatening, the heat rose in muggy waves from the grassland and thunder flies crawled through the hairs on our arms. Tall willows and alders wafted in the breeze as blowsily as a Gainsborough painting, and horseflies dogged our progress, attracted by the heady scent of sweat and sun cream.

Laurie walked along in front with his shirt off, revealing a smattering of light hair across his chest and a large scar on his arm. He tucked his T-shirt casually into the waistband of his jeans.

"I feel miles away from the city out here," he said. He juggled with the hammer. "Give me a hammer and some nails and I'm a happy man."

"I'm glad," I said.

"I could build you a tree house out here," he said. "I loved building tree houses when I was young. I was a happy boy scout."

"I bet," I said.

"Me too," Alex said quickly. "I was a good boy scout too."

"I bet," I said again.

"I was in the air cadets," Alex continued. "In Rhodesia."

"Really?" Laurie said. "I tried out for the air force too, all I ever wanted was to be a fighter pilot, but they turned me down."

"Why?" I asked.

"They offered me helicopter training instead, but I said no."

"So *you* turned *them* down?"

"It's my biggest regret," Laurie said, the sunshine leaving him. "I messed my whole life up right there. I'll never forgive myself."

I pursed my lips. I was beginning to realise that Laurie was happiest when he forgot that he had labelled himself a failure who was angry at the world. I was learning that you had to jog him out of this mood or it would take over.

"I'm not prone to regrets," I said. "Other people will give you a hard time, so why beat yourself up over things you can't now change?"

Laurie was silent. A point of balance, which way would it fall?

"So why do it?" I said, jogging him with my elbow and laughing.

"OK, OK," he said surrendering with a smile. "I get it."

The sun returned. We walked on between tall stands of hogweed where orange-bellied soldier beetles indulged in three-way orgies between the flowers, and sedge warblers chittered with an endless buzz of sound. Finally, we came to a fork in the path where a waymarker disc was needed.

"Which disc do I need?" Laurie asked.

"Yellow, for a footpath," Alex said proudly, to show he'd been listening.

I pulled one of the plastic discs out of my pocket.

"Give me a nail, Alex," Laurie said.

Alex held on. "I'll do it."

Laurie shrugged and handed the hammer over.

Alex positioned the nail and banged away with enthusiasm. The nail bent in two, as did the next one. He stood back and looked at me as if to say, "Will that do?"

"I can't really leave it like that, Alex," I said. "I think the council will complain if they don't look smart."

Alex's face fell.

"Sorry Alex," I said as I wrenched the disc off with the claw of the hammer.

Laurie set a new disc in place, but did little better.

"I think you're both hitting a knot in the wood," I suggested.

Laurie handed me the hammer. "Go on then," he said. I placed the disc slightly to the left and banged the nails in briskly. They went in smoothly and stayed flat; I had, after all, spent years marking out guided walk routes as part of my role for the RSPB. Without thinking, I tucked the hammer into my belt strap and walked on. Alex and Laurie followed behind.

I wasn't the most practical woman in the world. I didn't really have the patience or accuracy for DIY, but I had spent years helping my dad out with projects round the house, the chippy to his master carpenter, and years more on reserves struggling to fix, open and mend things because I didn't want to be the weak link among the men, the one who was always asking for help. In this way I had learned the secret of why men seemed better at practical things than women. Many women lacked confidence in their physical ability whereas men would worry away at a problem until they either fixed it or it broke. I found that if I also refused to give up, I could usually solve the problem alone.

After a while, it came naturally to me to have a go. My ex had never been a practical man and for years I had got on with my mending and fixing without even thinking about it. As we reached the next waymarking point, however, I noticed that neither Laurie nor Alex stepped forward to help and, for the first time, I wondered if maybe I should appear less practical than I was. After all, did men really want girlfriends who could hammer things in better than them?

"You do this one," I said to Alex, not wanting to show favouritism, and handed him the hammer.

At lunchtime we stopped to eat our sandwiches on an old concrete embankment jutting out into the river. Alex kept his distance from the edge as Laurie and I lay on our stomachs and gazed down into the pool, watching the minnows circulate.

"We could come down here and fish," Laurie said. "Make a little fire, catch a fish and cook it."

"That sounds lovely," I said. *It sounds like a date,* I thought wildly. *Is he suggesting a date?*

"I'll come too," Alex said and stepped forward quickly, not wanting to miss out. In his haste his boot kicked the hammer that had been left lying on the path. It shot through the air and fell with a splash into the pool below.

We all looked at the hammer, its outline wavy at the bottom of the river.

"I don't like water," Alex said quickly and stepped back.

Laurie, normally so keen to help, looked equally uncertain. "It looks a bit cold," he said hesitantly.

"I'll get it," I sighed. "I can't leave it in the river."

Rolling my jeans up to the thigh and taking off my work boots and socks, I slid down the steep bank on my bottom, falling with a plop into the river. Laurie was right, it was icy and much deeper than it had appeared from the bank. The water reached to my waist band.

"Just brilliant," I said aloud, feeling annoyed and thinking of the long drive home in sodden clothes, but it was too late to turn back now. Slowly I inched forward until I could feel the hammer with my toes.

Laurie and Alex watched me from the bank.

I bent over and stretched my arm down into the river but couldn't reach the bottom.

"Now what?" Laurie said.

I sighed again, took a deep breath and ducked down beneath the water, blindly grabbed the hammer from the bottom and re-emerged, with water streaming from me.

I looked up at the two men above. "I think," I said, "I am the only one here that could actually cut it in the armed forces."

Laurie's face fell.

It was a low remark and didn't make for a happy group as I slopped my way along the rest of the path, but why had Laurie, who was normally so chivalrous, not offered to help? Had my prowess with the hammer convinced him that I was the kind of woman who didn't appreciate a man literally wading in on her behalf? Was I that kind of woman?

Why should I expect him to rescue me anyway? I thought, later that evening as I sat in the minibus driver's seat on a plastic bag so as not to sog up the seat. The others had long ago finished the task, but Esther, Meg and Bastian were still out, slowly making their way along the footpath they had chosen. I would be late getting back home, but that was part of the deal; after all, I was the group leader. It was my job to make sure everyone got back safely at the end of the day and it was my job to wade into rivers and rescue hammers. *You want to be seen as capable by the volunteers, don't you?* I told myself. *You can't have that but then expect to be treated like "the little woman" when it suits you.*

I was conflicted. I had long ago learned how to be accepted in the male-dominated world of conservation. Have a go, drink pints and be good at banter. But did that somehow disqualify me as girlfriend material? I wanted a man to like the real me, but was the larky "one of the lads" persona really me or was it a shield? Had I spent too long wearing ripped jeans and baggy T-shirts to hide the fact that a woman had snuck in among the rank and file? After all, it was no longer the early 1990s, and even the world of conservation had changed. Perhaps I no longer had to pretend to be one of the boys to fit in.

CHAPTER
FIVE

"Thank God for that," Esther said as I pulled off the narrow, fern-lined road and into a clearing beneath the trees. She wrenched open the door of the minibus and the volunteers emerged from the cramped, humid interior, where they had been wedged for the last 30 minutes.

The new girl, Bella, climbed out. She had arrived in the car park that morning in a vest top and shorts which clung to her ample curves. She was in her early thirties I guessed. Her hair was dyed blonde and cropped short, and her sparkly eyeshadow had begun to smear onto her cheeks from the heat.

I had met her in the car park that morning. When I asked what had prompted her to come along she said that her parents had heard about the group and told her to join. "I guess they want to get rid of me for the day," she said, laughing.

Now she stood in the clearing looking less certain as she hefted the heavy bag she carried onto her shoulder.

I led the way from the clearing, along a shady path, into the woods. Enchanter's nightshade danced at the path edge. The white star-shaped flowers floated in an aerial delight around the stems and the smell of newly crushed mint rose up from beneath our boots. In the spring, I had been told, this area was covered with wild garlic and herb-paris, a cosmic-looking plant, its single black eye surrounded by a nebula of tendrils that spun out like space dust. It was the woodland flowers that had brought us here.

"Gather round," I called to the volunteers, and the group hushed their chatter, ready to listen to the day's instructions. By now I felt the team accepted me as group leader. The new volunteers like Meg, Kay, Esther and Wayland had never known anyone else, and some of the long-term volunteers I felt had my back.

The previous week Val had come up to me during the lunchtime break and, with her usual candour, had said, "You're not the most practical leader we've ever had, but you do make it fun."

It was praise I really appreciated from a strong-minded person who, for many years, had been the only woman in the group and had carved out a role for herself that the men respected. Not, I suspected, that Val cared too much for others' approval – she was quite happy to let a tumbleweed of embarrassment cross the room if she felt that something needed to be said. If Val gave praise, you could trust that she meant it.

Our mission that day was sycamore bashing. Once again we were trying to create a balance between vigorous fast-growing plants and other species which had become scarce.

"Sycamore is a pioneering species," I explained to the volunteers. "It's not originally a British tree but was probably introduced by the Romans from central Europe, so it's been here a long time. Sycamore can be a beautiful mature tree and has lots of insects that live on it but again, it's a little too successful. It sheds loads of seeds which spring up and take over the woods, quickly shading all the light from the woodland floor."

"Do we actually bash it?" asked Bella.

"Well, we don't literally hit it," I said. "It's just called that, I guess because we batter the endless seedlings into submission by uprooting them on a regular basis."

Like many things in conservation, the terminology had been created by men and often seemed to involve words implying violence, or "putting nature in its place". On days when I wasn't running the volunteer group I was working with a local river board persuading them to manage our waterways more sensitively. The men doing the work talked about "pioneering", a term which to them meant cutting back the trees alongside the river, something they did to open up the rivers to sunlight and to give better access for the digger drivers who cut the riverbanks. The term always sounded to me like they imagined themselves on horseback taming the Wild West by subjugating nature to man's will. Dead tree limbs that had toppled into the river were a valuable habitat for insects and fish but were known as "trash" by the river maintenance team, and removing the water plants that grew in the centre of the channel was called "weed control". It was difficult, when faced with such language, to persuade men that the trash and weeds were valuable and maybe they needed to cut back a little on the thrill of pioneering and learn to leave well alone.

Sycamore bashing had been a staple of volunteer tasks when I was young and starting out in conservation and I had spent many a day sawing down 20-year-old sycamore trees. Nowadays, sycamore is not thought of as "enemy number one" in the same way and, in some circumstances, should probably be left to get on with it, but not always.

"These woods are really valuable for orchids," I told the group. "Come here in May and you will see lady orchids, fly orchids and even the rare bird's-nest orchid growing. If the sycamore seedlings are allowed to grow unchecked, then they will create too much shade and make it harder for these plants to survive. So we are going to try to keep the number of young sycamores down in this part of the wood by pulling out the seedlings."

I pulled up a seedling that was growing at my feet. "Each leaf has five points," I said. "They are about the size of your palm and the stalks are usually red. There are other trees that have similar-shaped leaves so take a good look before tugging something up."

The group dispersed and set to, working their way between the pooling shade of the trees. Laurie hadn't been in the car park that morning. I had waited for him to appear around the corner long after the others had loaded themselves into the minibus. Don't call him, I told myself firmly. *You wouldn't call one of the others if they failed to appear,* I thought, *so don't give him special treatment.*

"Time to go," Reuben had called, keen to be off.

Reluctantly, I climbed into the driver's seat and headed out of the town with the others.

I could feel the weight of disappointment heavy in my stomach, knowing it would now be another week at least until I saw him again. No one had explained the terms of his Community Service Order to me so I had no idea if he could just turn up or not as he pleased, but I missed his presence and the little zinging electricity that sparked when he was around.

I sighed as Jim walked past and he eyed me curiously; after all, what had I to be down about? The tasks were going well, it was weeks since I'd forgotten anything essential and all the preparation was paying off. The volunteers were a merry bunch that day in the woods. These were the task days many of us enjoyed best: a job that could involve everyone, the team together, the hum of chatter, the breeze wafting the scent of insect spray and sun cream towards us. It was August, the birds were furtive now, tucked away and concentrating on changing their feathers for the autumn. The great flush of spring song had been reduced to an occasionally wistful "seep" from a bird hidden in the undergrowth. Instead, the buzz of insects took centre stage, honey-faced hoverflies hung in shafts of sunlight and dragonflies patrolled the woodland tracks like reconnaissance planes, endlessly quartering the skies looking for suspicious activity.

The peace of the summer woods was shattered by Bella's laugh. It bounced off the beech trees, causing the wood pigeons to take fright and clatter into the air.

"I can't pull it up. I'm not strong enough," she cried loudly in a well-spoken voice as she tugged at a sapling with theatrical exaggeration, spiralling around as she tried to yank the plant from the ground.

Roy came over to help.

"Take my waist," she cried, "we can pull together. It's like the fairy story of the giant turnip." Bella laughed. "Come on everyone, we can form a chain."

Suddenly the seedling gave way with a twang, and Bella toppled over onto the soft earth, causing her to roar with laughter still louder. She waved the plant above her head as she lay on the ground, her legs pointing skyward.

"It's the wrong tree," she laughed. She righted herself by rolling on her front and clambering upward. "I'm a fool," she said, coming towards me waving the twig. "I think I've pulled the wrong thing up. I was bound to get it wrong."

"It's close," I said, laughing, "but that's field maple. The leaves are a fair bit smaller and rounder than the sycamore."

"Thanks," Bella said. She paused, wiping a trickle of the sweat that was pouring down her face and into her cleavage, and suddenly seemed more composed. "By the way," she said casually. "You may want to know, I've just come out of prison with Rose West."

For a moment I wondered if somehow I had misheard her. "Pardon?" I said.

"I've just come out of prison," Bella said. "Rose West was in there as well."

I was stunned, but it wasn't entirely surprising that someone with a prison record would turn up with no warning. The Kingsdown Partnership had an open-door policy when it came to volunteer recruitment. To join you simply had to turn up in the car park on a Thursday morning and find a seat in the minibus. You could then be ferried out to a remote spot in the countryside to spend the day playing with sharp tools. So far there had been no issues, but now here was a girl waving a field maple at me and telling me she had been incarcerated with one of the most notorious murderers of all time.

I looked at her. She had an open face, flushed crimson from her exertions. She grinned broadly. The twinkly eyeshadow had danced down her cheeks and had mingled with smudges of leaf litter from her tumble. She didn't look dangerous.

"Do you want to know what I did?" she offered.

Did I? If she had been in prison with Rose West, it was obviously something fairly serious.

"Are you on probation?" I asked. "Is there a form you want me to sign?"

"I am on probation," she said. "But I'm not here because of community service, I'm here as a volunteer."

"Then thanks for the offer, but I don't think I need to know," I said carefully. "All I want to know is if you intend to do anything criminal here?"

"I don't think so," Bella said.

"Good," I told her, "it's what you do here that counts. Fill in the medical questionnaire at lunchtime and we'll leave it at that."

Bella went back to pulling sycamores, and by lunchtime she was a firmly established feature of the group. There was no hanging back with Bella, she blasted straight on in. She was a big presence, our Bel, she just couldn't be ignored. She was that girl at school who is the class clown and everyone's friend.

In the afternoon we moved on to another part of the wood, heading along a path lined with the candytuft flowers of hemp-agrimony. They thrived in the wide sunny clearings, but the rest of the woodland consisted of densely packed stands of sweet chestnut and conifers that had been planted by the Forestry Commission to provide timber following the First World War, when Britain's forests had shrunk to 5 per cent of land cover. No orchids grew there, no light found its way to the forest floor and all was silent beneath the canopy.

Beneath the trees, pockets of heathland still survived; untouched fragments of the habitat which had once dominated this area. The remnant heath was a world of dry sandy soils, grassland which exploded in firecracker crickets, whizzing off in all directions, like spits from burning logs. Adders basked in bare patches, soaking up the sun before going hunting.

With such tiny fragments of habitat remaining, we were once again here to suspend the natural process of succession. That afternoon we were focusing on removing birch saplings, creating more open habitat for birds like nightjars – wide-mouthed moth hunters, the colour of the woodland floor, who relied on these patches of heathland for camouflage during the day.

The birch roots were harder to remove than the sycamore had been. Bella was red faced once again as she tugged away at the saplings and chatted happily to Alex. Alex, overjoyed with this rare shot of female attention, was puffed up like a courting pigeon and swinging the mattock at stubborn roots with such gusto I feared the blade would fly off. Splinters of wood and grass seed flew in all directions, showering Bella.

"Oi, oi, Alex," Bella said. "Keep that chopper away from me. I don't trust a man with a big tool."

Roy sniggered and Val glared at him with disapproval. She deplored this kind of banter and kept it sharply in check, upbraiding anyone who wafted around a bawdy joke or sexist comment. By doing so, she helped the group stay a place of respect where people were treated as equals. Bella, however, was oblivious to Val's disapproval.

"Any more of that and I may be overcome," she said, wiping grass seeds from her cleavage, much to Alex's delight. "That's what comes from being incarcerated with only women for twelve months."

Bevan's head shot up with curiosity. Jim looked across as if to say, *Do you know about this?*

"What's she done?" Kay asked later while I was making the tea.

"I don't know," I said honestly, "maybe it's best not to know. Let's just see how she gets on here."

Bees buzzed in the heather as the sun sank lower, lighting up the edges of the dark conifer plantations that surrounded the tiny islands of heather where we worked. Sweat ran down the backs of my legs and pooled in my bra.

At the end of the day Bella approached me. "I've had a lovely time today," she said, and squeezed my arm affectionately, blowing any preconceived notions about ex-offenders out of the window in one gesture. She was good at that, as it turned out. Good at surprising you and knocking your prejudices on their head.

It was in her third week that we saw a different side to Bella. Up until then she had appeared to be a very loud and very jolly girl who acted as if most things in her life were a great joke. That day we were working at the riverbank in the centre of town. For once we were not pulling the vegetation up but instead were planting little flower plugs to create margins of wetland plants alongside the river – a task that Bella seemed to love.

"I help my dad with the garden at home," she said, carefully teasing out the roots of a little plug plant from the holder. "I'll send you some photos of the frogs in our pond. I do love frogs. I have a frog tattoo."

At lunch she sank down under the shade of a tree with a book.

Esther came up to me. "Have you seen what she's reading?"

I looked across, but the cover of the book was obscured.

"*The Cherry Orchard*, by Chekhov," Esther said. "Not what you'd expect necessarily, is it?

"I guess it seems a bit of a serious undertaking, although I've never read it so I wouldn't really know," I said. "She is bright though."

"Yes, she is," Esther paused, weighing her next words. "I've realised who she is. Her picture was in the local paper. She held a girl in the supermarket at knife point."

It was the sort of detail that I hadn't really wanted to know. My impression of Bella at that point was of someone full on but likeable. A warm, enthusiastic girl, more inclined to chat than work, but a positive member of the group.

Still, I knew that Esther wasn't judging her. She and Wayland had met through social work with young offenders.

"She looked different in the paper," Esther said. "She'd shaved her head and looked really tough, but it is the same girl."

It was hard to equate the woman now sitting quietly under the tree, reading Chekhov, with a knife-wielding criminal. I hadn't met the Bella who had committed that crime. I had met this Bella; she was the person we were getting to know. I couldn't view her in any other way. I walked over to her.

"Is it good?" I asked, indicating the book.

"Not bad," she said. "I'm reading three others as well." She opened the massive bag next to her to reveal it stuffed with books. "I've got a bunch of others at home too. I'd have more but the library will only let me get twelve books out at once and I keep getting fined for not bringing them back on time."

Bella was clearly more than she first appeared and more than the newspaper article about her would suggest. Still, it turned out that, once she had settled into the group, Bella wasn't reticent about her past. It wasn't long before we were all aware of what Bella had done and heard jolly stories of life on the inside.

To hear Bella talk, you would think prison was one long creative spa. She regaled us with tales of make-up sessions and music nights. She had joined the creative-writing group, made friends and got good counselling. Prison, it seemed, was a place that Bella longed to return to, which wasn't all that surprising. On the inside, it seemed, Bella got the support she needed; on the outside she didn't.

Bella had anxiety and depression, and the medication she was on to control these things also tended to make her hyper, causing her moods to swing from one extreme to the other.

I am not claiming any great knowledge of mental health problems. I'm only going by my own experience of working and befriending people struggling with their mental health. My experience with Bel was of someone who yo-yoed between excitable and loud, and internalised and vulnerable. On the outside she was like a member of the *Carry On* cast, all innuendo and comedy winks but under the surface there was a dark melancholy. She was sparkly eyeshadow and comedy hats, which she bought regularly off market vendors in the high street. She was weeping sores which she scratched into her skin when she was feeling bad.

Over the last few weeks I had found out that Bella had trained as a nurse but hadn't passed her exams so she ended up working in the local supermarket. She fell into a relationship with another store assistant. I don't know this guy but I am imagining some oily oik who thinks himself a stud because he's working in a store full of women without much male competition and therefore his ego has been amplified. When the relationship began to cool, he moved on to her friend. When Bella discovered this she felt betrayed and it pushed her to one of her extremes.

According to the newspaper article, Bella had gone into work to confront the other woman and, once in the shop, had picked up a knife from a display, unwrapped it and brandished it at the girl in question. I can imagine Bella at this moment, red faced, hair shaved, needing someone to pay attention to what was going on in her head. I can imagine she looked pretty scary. She was wrestled to the floor by colleagues as she called to the girl, "You have ruined my life."

This act changed Bella's life to be sure.

After a short while of knowing Bella, I would have sworn that she would never do such a thing again, she wasn't that person. Later still, I could see things weren't so black and white. When Bella felt supremely low or supremely high she acted in ways that can only be summed up by the words "reckless endangerment", mainly to herself.

Bella was one of many women, brought before the courts, who struggle with mental health. Eight in ten women entering prison report a problem, according to a report by the Prison Reform Trust.

Around 26 per cent of women entering prison had been given treatment for a mental health issue within the last 12 months. I don't mean to say that having a mental health problem is likely to lead you into crime, just maybe that, if someone is convicted of a crime, their mental health should be more of a factor in sentencing. People given Community Service Orders, subject to a mental health treatment requirement, are less likely to reoffend compared to people who are given no mental health support at all.

Neither am I making excuses for people involved in knife crime. I guess, I am making excuses for one person because I knew that person and came to see the whole picture.

I also couldn't escape the irony that Laurie's loss of control had caused physical harm to another person and yet he had been given a Community Service Order. Bella caused no injury, had no previous convictions and got two years. The law is not neutral: the judge wanted to make an example of her, show that knife crime was being dealt with.

"Knife crime is out of control," he was quoted as saying in the local paper. "A significant custodial sentence [is needed] so that members of the public can feel assured that the courts are trying to protect them."

Bella made a good, if atypical, example – she served one year.

She went home to her parents. She tried to find work as a carer, a role she would have been brilliant in. She tried to help out at a local kids' group. She got turned away from everything. She was seen as a violent criminal with a sentence that would take ten years to be spent. I saw a vulnerable woman who needed good continuous support to restart her life.

Bella got through life doing what many of us do: hiding our troubles from the world behind a larger-than-life exterior. Trying so hard to prove that we are fine, happy, just like everyone else. Who are we all trying to fool? What is this template of a "normal" person we are working so hard to portray? I was doing this myself, trying to appear as a totally together woman who was successful and had the answers when really I was riddled with insecurity too, especially when it came to relationships.

Laurie hadn't been around for the last four weeks and I had almost begun to fear that I wouldn't see him again when he reappeared in the car park one Thursday.

"Hello again," I said as he clambered into the front seat, elbowing Alex across.

"I've been job hunting," he said as way of explanation for his absence. "I've almost finished my community service hours so I thought I'd get out there and look."

"How's it going?" I asked.

"There's not much I'm qualified for," he said. "I saw a job dancing in a gay bar, thought I might audition for that."

"What's your dancing like then?" I asked.

"I'll give you a demo sometime," he said and winked.

It was good to have him back.

We were down by the river again in the water meadows with the wind tracing a story as it rushed through the leaves of the black poplar trees, softening the noise of the traffic on the motorway bridge that spliced the meadows in two. We were here for our long-awaited Austrian scything workshop. The meadows had recently been purchased by a local woman to protect them from a developer getting their hands on them and a trust had been set up to inform the management. Unsurprisingly Esther, Wayland and Val were all on the board and busy fundraising and organising events.

The meadows held a special place in the minds of the local people, as they featured in the paintings hanging on the walls of the town's art gallery. In the paintings, wild-eyed cattle roamed the fields, but nowadays the fields were open to the public and their dogs to roam across and I had struggled to find any modern-day farmer willing to graze his cows there, so it had been decided the group would have a go at scything the grass. I was doubtful if the volunteers could complete such a physically demanding task, after all most of them were retired but Kirk had found some funding for a trainer and all the volunteers were curious to learn a new skill.

"The scythe has been used in Britain for more than two thousand years," the instructor told us as we sat around on hay bales in the meadow.

"That's amazing," said Esther, which it was when you thought about connecting with all that history.

"They were still used right up until the nineteen fifties," the man said, "and then someone invented the power strimmer." He looked sad. "Now though people are rediscovering the scythe. It is quiet, environmentally friendly and you smell cut grass as you use it, not petrol fumes."

"A very good thing too," said Reuben who hated the rare days when we used power tools.

"The Austrian scythes, which we will be using today, are a fair bit lighter than old English scythes and are easier to use and sharpen," the man said.

Roy sighed. Our ancient implements stored at the farm were bound to be English scythes.

"How much can someone cut in one day?" asked Val.

"Well, they used to reckon that one man could cut about an acre in one day," the teacher said.

"And what about one woman?" Val said pointedly.

"Twice as much," Bella called and the others laughed.

Laurie was sitting alongside me on the hay bales. I could feel the pressure of his thigh against mine; the little warm thrill of it shot through me. It was probably the most physically charged contact I'd had with a man for a while.

Laurie shifted as the group rose and the scythes were handed out.

I took hold of the long straight wooden scythe handle and placed my hands on the two smaller handles, which stuck out at right angles. The long blade curved away. I looked just like every image I had ever seen of the Grim Reaper.

"You don't wave it around slashing things down," the instructor called as Wayland immediately began attacking the hay with gusto. "Done correctly, scything shouldn't use up unnecessary effort."

The man set off across the field, rocking from side to side, drawing his arms across his body in a gentle sweep, the grass tumbling in front of him with a clean swish. The long blade skimmed just above the ground safely. It was more akin to mopping the floor and appeared easy.

Soon it was our turn. Half the group spread out across the meadow with the scythes while the others raked up the cut grass, waiting for their turn. I took hold of the two small handles and set off into the grass. The sharp wind drew on the rising heat and caught the seed heads so the hay shushed in the breeze. Flocks of linnets and goldfinches were twittering across the fields, hanging from thistle heads like exotic fruits.

Rock and step, rock and step. I tried to copy the gentle rhythm of the instructor, igniting ancient muscle memories passed down from the ancestors. It was meditative; even the destruction of the late summer flowers, still blooming, felt Zen-like. The flowers fell before the swishing blade, laying down in a gentle rhythm, seed being scattered; we felled the old and spent to make way for new life. No wonder the Bible was so full of harvesting symbolism, it is hard not to feel allegorical with a scythe in your hand.

The scythes we were cutting with were box fresh and sliced the hay cleanly. I couldn't imagine our ancient blades doing the same, but even with the sharp blades it didn't take long for my muscles to start protesting from the repetitive swinging action. I stopped and looked out across the field. It was the school holidays. In the next field I could see children racing through the meadow catching crickets with vivid blue nets, pursued by grandparents and floppy meadow brown butterflies; teenagers, lost in first romances, strolled hand in hand along the paths, stopping to kiss copiously.

"Love is in the air," a voice sang behind me.

I stopped the blade swinging, turned and smiled at Laurie. "Summer's a happy time," I said. "We all feel a bit more open to new possibilities."

"Quite true," Laurie said. He paused. "So have you been?" he asked suddenly. "In love, I mean?"

I was taken aback. He had never asked such a personal question before. Quite the opposite; at times he seemed to force himself to appear disinterested in finding out more about me. "Yes," I said. "I was in love, for many years. And you?" I asked.

Laurie faltered. "I don't know," he said. "I'm no good at things like that. I've never been able to look into someone's eyes and really trust them before." He looked at me, searchingly. "It's so important isn't it," he said, "trust, even in friendship?"

The cricket song seemed to grow quiet. "Yes," I said. "My ex lost my trust but long after he deserved to."

Laurie looked confused and opened his mouth as if he wanted to ask more but stopped himself. "So you won't trust anyone either," he said finally.

"No, that's not true," I said quickly. "I can't judge everyone by the way one person acted."

We were both silent as the crickets began around us once again. He took a deep breath. *Now,* I thought, *now he's going to ask me out.*

"So, how are you finding the scything?" Laurie asked, and the mood was broken.

My mind whirled through the conversation over and over as the blade swished and the grasses fell before me. The afternoon was muggy, and hot pockets of vetch burst their twisted black seed pods with audible cracks. A million old gentlemen grasshoppers pinged out of the way as the grasses fell, but at least the slow pace of the blade allowed them to escape in a way they never could have if faced with a tractor and flail. *What did it mean, this sudden candidness?* I thought. *Had he been about to ask me out and I had somehow said the wrong thing?* The rules of dating were still a complete mystery to me.

After a few false starts, the internet dating had fizzled out and this was partly because I just didn't understand the rules. For a while, I had carried on being polite and answering everyone who contacted me, until one man had somehow sussed this out. "Are you actually interested on going on a date with me," he said, "or are you just messaging me to be polite?" At which point I caved in, stopped the pretence of being a carefree woman who just happened to be single, and told him that I'd just come out of a long-term relationship and didn't really know what I was doing on an internet dating site. He was clearly a lovely man. He told me to stop pushing myself before

I was ready regardless of what friends told me to do and give myself a bit of time before I tried to move on.

The problem was I just didn't feel like I fitted in with the world of internet dating. The other women looked free, easy and modern, and in contrast I felt like a knotty problem. Laurie was a knotty problem too. Two knotty problems are unlikely to live happily ever after, but it took me a while to figure that one out. All I knew was that I felt, with him, like I didn't have to pretend.

That afternoon, I watched Laurie surreptitiously behind my dark glasses as he scythed away, bare chested, the rising breeze cooling the sweat on his glistening shoulders. He was singing again, his voice echoing across the fields. Prince in his little red Corvette spun through the hay dust with a girl in a red beret.

A patch of water mint tumbled before my blade, the sharp smell of it taking me back to Sunday lunchtime at my parents' house. I had escaped there regularly throughout the winter months before getting my job with the Kingsdown Partnership, when the loneliness had been most acute. I had felt ashamed of being lonely. It was like admitting that I was unlikeable, so I tried to hide this label from the world.

"Got any exciting plans this week?" my dad would ask and sometimes I would lie and invent social engagements rather than admit that I sometimes spent Friday night wandering around the shopping centre, not shopping (I had no money to do that), but just walking around – anything to be out of the flat and surrounded by other people.

When I had got the job at Greengate Farm I had thought that would change. For the first time in years I had female colleagues and, I felt, we were bound to get on, once we got to know each other. But Gemima was in a serious relationship and Mel had a big circle of friends she had known for years. Like many women of their age, they were busy with their own lives and really didn't need to fit an extra person into their packed social diaries. Solo loneliness made me ashamed, but I had known loneliness within a relationship too and that had made me sadder. Over the years I felt I had poured so much energy into keeping my relationship afloat, compromising who I was and putting off what I wanted to do in life in order to stay connected to a man who was so central to my world. Now there were occasional moments, swimming in the sea perhaps, dancing to music in the flat or laughing with my oldest friend, Karen, when I thought, *Oh, hello Carol, that's you, isn't it? The person you were at 17. That independent, sassy woman who had the stuffing knocked out of her by spending years with someone with a roving eye and a different set of dreams.*

My relationship with the ex had begun when I was still very young. It was the only serious relationship I had ever known. It was hard to imagine ever sharing the same level of intimacy with another person. The thought of doing so filled me with fear, but those weekend nights were still lonely and I didn't want that to go on forever. I looked across at Laurie. The wind was rising, scattering hay dust into the air. Maybe it was time to be brave.

CHAPTER
SIX

Surprisingly, it was Kirk who gave me the perfect opportunity to ask Laurie out.

"I've got a new job for you," he said one day at the end of August.

I groaned inwardly. My to-do list was already overflowing and I expected Kirk to tell me about some tedious admin task I had to get on with straight away.

"I want you to do a water vole survey across the county," he said. "We had one commissioned a few years ago and we need to repeat it. This is to be your priority for the next couple of months."

"OK," I said. Now that was more like it. Water vole surveying was something I felt confident that I could do well. After all, I had written my dissertation on the furry rodents, which had involved surveying an entire river catchment. What was more, this task would allow me more time away from Greengate Farm, something which appealed.

"You can't do it on your own, though," Kirk said. "It's too dangerous to do river work alone. Ask one of your volunteers to go with you."

"Great," I said. "I know just the person."

I phoned him that lunchtime. "Hello," he said, his deep voice sounding extra polished on the phone.

"It's Carol," I said. "You know, from the volunteer group," I added, in case he knew lots of Carols. "I wonder if I might ask for your help?" I was nervous and garbling, my voice caught in my throat. "I need to do some water vole surveys which involves wading down rivers and I can't do it on my own, so I need some help and I wonder if you would like to come along and help me and we can add it to your community service hours or something." I finished in a rush.

There was a pause. "I'd love to," he said. "I'd love to."

I hugged that to myself, the way he said it twice.

"Great," I stammered. "That's great. I'd like to do it with you, because I think we get on." My heart gave an extra loud thump at admitting this. I quickly arranged the details and rang off before he had second thoughts.

Nothing could touch me for the rest of that day, not the boss's admin or Marley bringing in a half-chewed rabbit to lay at my feet. I walked around in a little bubble of happiness, reliving that "I'd love to" in my head and giddy at the thought of a day out of the office alone with Laurie.

I drove into town to meet him a few days later, part of me expecting him not to appear, but there he was, slouched up against the wall of the boarded-up pub at the end of his road, wearing his usual T-shirt with the arms cut off and broken boots.

Laurie came from a world of landowners and private education, but now he lived in a part of the city populated by the unemployed and recent immigrants. The city, in general, was a wealthy place, full of tapas bars and university students drinking cappuccinos while frantically tapping into iPads. It was hard, I knew from experience, to be poor in a town geared towards the rich. Laurie saw my car and grinned. It was going to be one of his sunny days.

We drove out of town, into a day full of promise, the kind of day where everyone steps out in summer clothes and feels frivolous knowing that autumn is on the horizon. Laurie sang us down the motorway, opening the windows, letting the breeze in.

"Look, cows," he said, as the last urban sprawl left us and the fields opened up. "Hello boys," he called from the window.

"They've got udders," I said.

"Sorry, ladies," he shouted.

Today his enthusiasm for the world shone as he revelled in the simple joy of being out in the sun and whizzing in a car past fields of cows.

His happiness in the small things made me pause and realise my own luck. In the long evenings and lonely weekends, I spent too long dwelling on what I didn't have and not enough time appreciating my fortune. In the last few months I had got a job, which meant that I could not only keep my head above water with the necessities of life but could afford such luxuries as a car. This gave me the freedom to escape from the office to play in the countryside with a man whose company I found fun. Life was really not so bad.

"That's where I used to be a choirboy," Laurie said, pointing out of the window as we whizzed past a church, "before I got thrown out."

I laughed. Laurie's stories were often like this, a brief moment when he might have triumphed in some upper-class and conservative environment before he misbehaved and it all fell apart.

Laurie was the son of a teacher and had been brought up to be a good Catholic boy. When he was six, his father died in a car crash and, sometime afterwards, his mum met a new man. The man was wealthy, owned land and was keen to take Laurie under his wing in the ways of hunting, fishing and generally being Davy Crockett; a world, I was sure, Laurie would have loved and excelled in. His new stepfather, however, was a strict disciplinarian who, according to Laurie, frequently hit him with a belt. This was a boy who had tragically lost his father, had a new man move into his mum's life and was being violently abused – it was small wonder he went off the rails.

After getting into trouble at several local schools, Laurie was sent the way of many troubled boys of strict, wealthy backgrounds: he was packed off to boarding school. It didn't end well; according to Laurie, he had broken into the school buildings and attempted to set fire to them. Was this true? It was hard to tell. Laurie's stories, it seemed to me, were as much about showing me he was bad news as telling the literal truth but, either way, his academic career had been cut short, and he took himself off to France to "teach English, smoke pot and drink too much", as he said.

After this the details were a little vague. He'd spent time on a kibbutz and at some point had returned to England, become estranged from all his family and transformed into the angry, disillusioned man he was today. There was no denying he was this man – even with my rose-tinted spectacles I could see the darkness – but there was also this hopeful innocence and joy that occasionally bubbled up to the surface like air escaping from muddy waters. I held on to those moments and delighted in them.

Today, Laurie's past seemed forgotten as we spun off onto a side road and dropped down into the valley. Lacy branches of oak trees dipped us into pools of shade. The road petered out to a track and dust clouds rose behind us. I pulled the car off the road beside a farm gate.

"This is as close as we get to the river," I said. "We walk from here."

Opening up the boot of the car, I pulled out two pairs of rubbery waist-high boots from the tangle of objects and held the black pair out to Laurie.

"Kinky," he said.

If only, I thought. Chest waders had to be the least glamorous item of clothing ever invented. They were massive wellies held up by braces, which ballooned around my middle, sagged in folds around my crotch and gave off little farting noises when I walked.

Laurie took off his battered boots and looked for a spot to store them in the car. He moved items around, pulling out waterproof trousers and folding them neatly, taking out a coil of rope and tying it with precision. He saw me watching him.

"It's my OCD," he said. "I tuck labels into people's clothes in the street."

"And how's that working out for you?" I asked.

He grinned and pointed at his missing tooth. "Not so great."

I knew by now that wasn't the story of how he had lost his tooth as he had already told me about the fight. How he had got into an argument in the street with someone he knew a little, got punched in the face and then lost his fragile restraint and hit back with so much fury he had landed himself in court. This was one story, unfortunately, I knew was true.

We clambered over a gate and the marshes opened before us. The fields were known as Fowler's Marsh after the duck hunters or wildfowlers who had once crouched on misty mornings in the fens waiting for the whistle of widgeon flying overhead. The wet meadows had long ago been drained, and now a yellow haze of wheat fields stretched across the horizon to the distant blue line of the sea. Every now and then, a little two-carriage train would rush by, taking tourists to the coast. I imagined the passengers looking out with curiosity at us, wondering what we were doing slogging across the fields in waders on a hot summer's day.

We came to a wide wooden bridge crossing a channel, where silver fish schooled in the shadows beneath.

Laurie looked down, "Dace, I think," he said. "My stepdad used to take me fishing."

"I'll take your word for it," I said. "I'm no good at fish IDs. What are your knots like?" I asked, handing him the rope. "I need you to tie this round my waist."

Laurie took the rope and leaned in to tie it. I could smell spicy aftershave and see the little nicks where he'd cut himself shaving that morning.

Was that for me? I thought. *The shave, the aftershave?*

He looked up and our eyes met, inches from each other.

"Water voles," I said hurriedly. "I'm going to tell you about water voles. Basically they are chunky rodents with really yellow teeth and eyes like burnt currants. If you squeeze them too hard their eyes look like they may just pop out of their heads."

"Best not to try then," Laurie suggested, smiling at me in amusement.

"They are not very well equipped for a life in water either, as they aren't good swimmers," I continued. "They do a kind of frantic doggy paddle and their fur isn't even waterproof. They are not really meant to be water voles; in other countries they live in hedgerows, field edges and the like."

"So why do they live by water here then?" he asked, getting interested.

I relaxed. I was OK now. I could talk to him about water voles, I was back in the world I knew.

"They lost a lot of their habitat and became confined to the riverbank. All would still have been fine though," I said, beginning to get theatrical, "if they hadn't encountered a new enemy. The American mink."

"Blighters," Laurie said.

"Well, it wasn't really the mink's fault. They had been released from fur farms by animal rights activists and really, if we hadn't already pushed the water vole to the brink, they might have been OK. The mink were just the final nail in the coffin. They had two assets which our native predators didn't: the ability to swim really well, and the fact that they were also quite skinny, so could follow water voles into their burrows. The mink found a niche on the riverbank and there they found these chunky, poorly swimming rodents."

"So water vole are rare?" asked Laurie.

"Well, yes and no," I replied. "In some places they have been wiped out entirely but here they are doing OK because all the ditches are well connected. Even if a mink comes along and kills off one colony then others can colonise from elsewhere. That's why we're here," I said. "A few years ago an expert found that this area was one of the best in the country for water voles, and we are following up on his survey to see if anything has changed."

"Sounds good," Laurie said.

I showed him how to fill in the survey form, judging water depth and steepness of the banks. This, I explained, would provide useful information to anyone who did the survey in the future as it would give a snapshot of the habitat. On the reverse I asked Laurie to draw a map showing the location of any field signs I found.

"What do you mean by field signs?" he asked.

"Anything that looks like water voles might be occupying this stretch of riverbank," I said. "Sometimes these can be quite subtle. If the water is full of duckweed for instance, you can sometimes see parallel lines that show something has swum from one bank to the other, or you get little gaps in the reeds where something has pushed through to reach the bank. You can't be certain though that these things have been made by water voles. Other field signs give more concrete evidence," I continued. "Burrows in the bank, for instance, are good signs, or little piles of vegetation along the banks show that something has been feeding. The only field sign that is an absolute certainty though is poo."

Laurie raised an eyebrow.

"Water vole poo is quite distinctive," I said. "It looks like wild rice. If we find some it will all become a bit clearer."

Laurie laughed. "No woman has ever asked me for a day out to look at poo before," he said.

"Well at least I have novelty value," I answered.

Laurie smiled. "Yes, you are quite unique."

Was that a good thing? I wondered. "Let's get started then," I said.

I chose a spot on the riverbank, got down on my bum and inelegantly slid with a flop into the river. The cool water rose up around me, sucking the rubber of the waders tight round my legs. I found my footing on the narrow shelf that ran along the edge of the channel. Up on the bank Laurie held the rope that was tied round my middle and took up the slack. By holding onto the taught rope I could keep my balance as I pushed my face into the reedy depths at the side of the channel. I parted the vegetation and could see a little wet patch of mud paddled by starry footprints. *They're here,* I thought. The little patches of mud showed that a creature had sat beside the riverbank on a regular basis and the footprints showed they belonged to a mammal about the size of a guinea pig. The star-shaped footprints looked like water vole, but the wet mud blurred the edges, so that they could belong to any number of creatures that frequented the riverbanks. I needed something more: paddly footprints and sitting platforms were not enough to spell empirically "water vole". I began to work my way along the bank. A dark hole the size of a man's fist appeared at the water's edge, and the smooth wet sides showed that something was regularly moving in and out of the entrance. A few feet further along another one appeared.

"Burrow," I shouted, "burrow."

Up above I could see Laurie's feet and hear him scribbling on the map. Burrows were a good field sign, but it was not a certainty that water voles were using the river now; something else could have occupied an old burrow. I parted the reed at another spot and, this time, on the wet mud, there was a little pile of short strips of reed, each one about an inch and a half long and sliced at one end at a 45-degree angle. "Bingo," I called, "feeding sign." I plucked a blade off the pile and held it up to Laurie.

"That's magic," he said. "How can you spot that among all this vegetation and know it means something?"

"By the angle that each blade has been cut. It's almost always forty-five degrees. Other rodents are more likely to leave a straight edge. There's a little pile of them down here, all the same length. They hold the grass in their front paws," I explained, "and gnaw their way down before dropping the last bit."

"Wasteful," he tutted.

"I'll have a word, shall I?" I laughed.

"I wish I knew more about wildlife," he said. "I saw a caterpillar, back there. Can I show it to you?" He dropped the rope, ran back and returned carrying a furry caterpillar.

"It's a woolly bear," I said delightedly. "Didn't you ever collect them as a child?"

Laurie shook his head.

"I loved them," I said. "They turn into garden tiger moths."

"What fantastic names," Laurie said.

I smiled. "The hairs deter birds from swallowing them, but they can also irritate the skin so I would put it back."

He went and put the caterpillar back. I liked that, that he didn't just drop it on the ground, like something which had served its purpose, but he respected that it had a life to be getting on with too.

It was hard work wading along the channel, pushing through the waterweed and moving my legs through thick silt.

"It would make a wonderful workout," I said, as I attempted to clamber over an unseen log below the surface.

"Hard one to market though," Laurie said, "slime aerobics."

He pulled out his phone and took a photo of me.

"Something to remember the day I spent holding a rope with a pretty girl attached," he said, smiling.

I hid my delight by stuffing my face back in the riverbank.

"Is that about fifty metres?" I said, after a few more moments of searching.

Laurie looked back. "I guess so."

"OK, time to get out," I said. "After fifty metres we count the number of signs. Then we can calculate how many voles live in this section."

Laurie bent down and held out his hand. I took it and he hauled me out of the river, my belly sliding along the ground, my face in the nettles, my legs scrabbling to get a foothold on the bank.

Back at home I had a book a well-meaning friend had recently sent me, called *Superflirt*. It advised that to show you're attracted to a man, you should spend time flipping your hair about, wearing figure-hugging clothes and sucking on the end of a drink straw. I flopped onto the bank, exhausted and panting from the effort of getting out of the river. The waders ballooned around my middle. Really, none of this was what *Superflirt* advised.

Oh stuff the book, I thought. I was enjoying myself. I was enjoying the company of a man, not in a big flirtatious way, but just as a person who, when he wasn't talking himself down, was quirky and interesting.

He was a great companion for water vole surveying as well, I thought, as I slid into another channel and began working my way along the bank. Laurie took care to unsnag the rope when it became entangled in bushes and flatten down nettles so I wouldn't get stung at the entrance and exit points. He always seemed to be thinking one step ahead when it came to my comfort. When we stopped for lunch I noticed he had created beautifully neat maps and accurately recorded my shouted instructions, even when my voice was muffled by reeds.

"You're a top assistant," I told him, handing the map back. "I'm really glad I asked you to help me."

"I'm more than happy being your Sherpa and tea boy," he said.

By mid-afternoon though, I was exhausted, and each 50-metre stretch of river felt like a marathon. I clambered up out of another ditch and lay on the bank with my eyes closed, gasping like a landed fish. I could feel him watching me. He shifted a little.

Oh my God, he's going to kiss me, I thought. *He's going to kiss me, right here, while I'm covered in slime and nettle stings.* To be honest, I had lain on my bed after every task day with Laurie, imagining him kissing me, but now I tensed.

Of course he wasn't going to kiss me. Instead, he flopped back on the grass next to me. I relaxed. The wind rustled in the reeds, the smell of warming waterweed rose in the air, and a cricket buzzed a static song in my ear.

"I've got a stone under my back," Laurie said after a bit and moved to dislodge it. When he settled again, his arm rested against mine, a tiny weight pushed alongside me. I didn't move, and we lay there, in silence as martins cut the sky, every feather and flurry of me alive to that inch of skin. I could do this, lie in a field under a martin sky and enjoy this bright moment, because it wasn't going to lead to anything more.

"OK," he said after a bit, "my turn."

I opened my eyes. "Really?" I said, looking doubtful.

"You've shown me what to look for, haven't you?" he said. "What's the point of having an assistant if you do all the hard work yourself?"

He stood up and held out his hand to me. I struggled up. He untied the elaborate knot at my waist and then tied the rope around his own midriff.

"Lead on," he said, giving me the end.

We walked down to the next river.

"Are you sure? This one looks deep. Feel for the shelf," I told him anxiously, as he shuffled forward on his bottom and lowered himself down. "There should be a little ledge at the edge of the channel that you can put your toes on and walk along."

As the water level climbed up to the waist of the waders, he looked a little less confident, but his feet found the ledge and he gripped the rope.

"It's harder than it looks," he said, edging his way along. "How can you see anything?"

"You have to part the reed," I told him. "Look for the sitting places near the bank."

"What do they look like again?" he asked.

"Well, just, water voley."

He looked up and cocked an eyebrow. "Just water voley," he said with those round vowels. The next moment his feet must have lost their purchase on the muddy shelf as he vanished beneath the water.

Going underwater in a pair of chest waders is a dangerous thing. They fill up with water and the weight pulls you down. I pulled the rope as hard as I could and managed to grab hold of one of the braces as he came within reach. I hauled with all my strength and he came to the surface, gasping and flailing. I grabbed hold of him under the arms and yanked him towards the bank, tugging at any bit of him that came into reach, no longer self-conscious of touching him, just desperate to get him out. He found a foothold and clambered up to the bank, flopping face-first into the grass.

We lay there, both breathing heavily, sopping wet and covered in duckweed, and then he laughed, really, he laughed.

"I'm sorry," I said. "Are you OK? You almost drowned."

"Yes," he laughed, "it's definitely harder than it looks. So when do we do it again?"

I decided that was quite enough for one day, though. He was drenched and it was obvious that that section was too deep to wade along.

"I'll try to hire a boat to do it," I told him.

"Fantastic," Laurie said. "I'll row."

As I drove home later that evening, examining every moment of the day, I felt that really it was the nicest day I had spent out with a man for a long time. I wanted to do it again too, but this was Laurie we were talking about – the sunshine could disappear as soon as it had arrived. Sure enough he failed to appear for the next few tasks.

"I'm job hunting," he said when I texted him. "I've got an interview next week and I've got to prepare."

"That's great," I said. "What's it for?"

"It's not exciting," he texted almost apologetically. "It's a sales job."

"Good luck," I said. "It might not be ideally what you would want but it's a start." I was really pleased to see that Laurie was serious about knuckling down and working. "Does that mean you won't be free for any more water vole surveys?" I asked.

Two hours later he texted back. "I'd like to do more," he said. "I'll be in touch."

Another week went by. Laurie didn't appear for the task again and I heard nothing. I felt torn. I didn't want to look like I was chasing his attention but at the same time the summer was ticking by and I needed help with the water vole surveys. If Laurie wasn't going to do it, I would have to ask one of the other volunteers. I knew Roy would be keen to be involved and Jim had offered to help too. They both would have been more reliable and good company, but I had enjoyed my day with Laurie so much I wanted to give him another chance, so I called him one lunchtime while Kirk, Gemima and Mel were out walking the dogs.

As soon as he picked up I knew something had changed. This time his voice sounded disinterested.

"It's Carol," I said breezily.

"I know, your name came up on my phone."

"I just wondered if everything was OK?" I ventured. "How did the interview go?"

There was a long silence. "I didn't get it," he said.

"Sorry to hear that," I said, "but something will come up. So what have you been up to?"

Again, silence. "I've been busy," he offered finally. "I had to visit my probation officer, the dole office and the jobcentre."

"Oh." Here it was, the reality. On the task days it was easy to see what I wanted to see in Laurie: a man whose company I enjoyed. *Well Carol,* the voice in my head said, *here is the truth: he's unemployed and has a probation officer, BEWARE.*

If I had been going to write a checklist of a suitable partner then these two things would not have been on it but, come on, how often have you paid attention to the flashing warning signs above someone's head, when the person beneath made you feel quite twinkly? Yes, I thought so. My logical brain had taken flight because, well, I just liked him so damn much.

"Yes, oh," he said.

I ploughed on determinedly. "So are you still coming to do the water vole work with me?" I asked.

No answer.

"I really need your help. I can't do it alone," I said, which was true, although I failed to mention that I had plenty of other offers.

"OK," he said, sounding brighter. "I'll come. I won't let you down if you really want my help."

Laurie returned to the group and throughout the following month, as well as seeing each other on the task days, we regularly headed out into the countryside in my little Micra, taking turns to wade down the river as hobbies hunted the skies above us for dragonflies before heading off on migration to tropical Africa. Some days he was a delight, funny and helpful, carrying all the survey equipment and suggesting we go for a beer or an ice cream after work. On other days his mood descended into sarcasm and anger.

"Every relationship I ever had has ended badly," he would tell me. "I've decided I don't need anyone. People are bad news. They bring you down."

Laurie was hounded by the black dog of depression, a soul-sucking demon to be sure. It could paint the sky black above us both, smothering me too, if I let it, with a weighty blanket of gloom which, in my own sensitive state, I fought hard to dig myself out from under. Some days he would let me down at the last minute with flimsy excuses: his teeth were hurting, his kitchen cupboard needed mending. Some days he would come along on a survey and seem quiet and withdrawn, on others he would talk solely about himself, a monologue of failure which didn't need a response.

That's the problem with trying to start a relationship with someone in the throes of depression. Depression can draw all attention to it and, unless you're careful, the person on the other side of the relationship ends up getting very little attention themselves. That's not a healthy, balanced relationship, but then what did I know about being healthy and balanced? He was joy, he was darkness but, in spite of it all, I still wanted to be with him. The good times were good, my days with him were lit by that unspoken thrill of mutual attraction and yet, still nothing happened. No certain move, no obvious sign that he wanted anything more from me than friendship. It was frustrating in the extreme and surely another woman, one whose self-esteem hadn't been so battered, would have cut her emotional losses and moved on, but I wasn't that woman. The sexual chemistry was addictive and my instinct remained that, despite some of the surface appearance, deep down he was a good guy. The something and nothing of our relationship also meant that it felt safe. It was like having a crush on someone famous – a fantasy with no risk of being engulfed. As autumn closed in, however, and things failed to move forward, the frustration grew. I needed for him to make a move or at least make his interest so clear it would spur me on to be brave. Maybe he would have said the same.

Thankfully, on Thursdays I was distracted from the complexity of Laurie by the rest of the volunteer gang. Bastian had been dropping hints about the "summer jolly" for weeks, but now he was more determined.

"We always have one, Carol," he insisted. "One year we went all the way to Kew Gardens."

When I asked Jim for details he was less enthusiastic.

"One of the previous leaders did organise a day out for us a couple of times," he said. "I'm not sure it's that important."

But Bastian was the social diarist. He knew that a jolly was due and in the end he won. After all, I figured, the team had worked hard all through the spring and summer, so why not arrange a day out to thank them?

I decided I would raise the matter during my appraisal with Kirk, something which I was not looking forward to.

I mused on this aloud to Alex as we drove home from the day's task.

"Bugger him," Alex said, when I confessed I was worried about Kirk's opinion of me.

I laughed; Alex's speech may have been hard to understand at times but his meaning often came through loud and clear. With far fewer words, the ones he did say had to be worth saying.

I repeated Alex's words silently to myself as I sat in Kirk's office the following day. Marley chose that moment to lay his great hairy head in my lap and gaze at me adoringly. I had his seal of approval at least. The boss was a funny one: on the one hand he acted like "his" staff should know their place, he gave the orders, you carried them out, a management style that was never going to work for me; on the other hand, I suspected he liked it when I stood up to him and fought back. We'd had our fair share of clashes over the last few months. Kirk would agree projects on my behalf, add them to my to-do list and expect them to be completed by some unrealistic timescale. I kicked over the traces and resented his control, often ignoring his priorities and doing things the way I thought best. Like I say, I am not a model employee. However, when it came to the big tasks, the water vole survey, the volunteer group, the boss left me to my own devices and consequently I threw all my energy into the work.

Kirk sat down and shuffled his paperwork.

"Maybe we should just focus on my positive points," I laughed nervously.

Marley shifted his head and gazed up at me lovingly. Kirk looked down at his dog and, to my amazement, decided to do just that.

"Well, you're doing a really good job with the volunteers," he said. "You organise the tasks well, you're getting really good numbers of new people joining. Your timekeeping with them is excellent."

A few weeks before, the volunteers had been asked to complete an anonymous survey, rating the tasks. Kirk looked down at the results. Wayland had already told me he'd given me a rating of 11 out of 10 as group leader.

"The volunteers seem to enjoy going out with you," he said.

I smiled.

"Your predecessors didn't always put the same amount of effort into that part of the job," Kirk added.

I almost fell off my chair at such rare praise from a man who was normally hyper-critical. Whatever had caused this change, I wasn't about to miss the opportunity, and I quickly told Kirk that I intended to take the gang out for the day to reward them for their hard work.

It was a blistering hot day in late September when I pulled into the car park for our day out. All the volunteers had taken the opportunity to put on their "going out" attire and we were all a little self-conscious in our "fancy" clothes. Even Roy was dressed in shorts and a smart T-shirt with no hint of gaffa tape. It didn't seem quite right. Still, I must have looked the strangest of the lot, having taken the opportunity to wear a skirt, knowing that, for once, I wouldn't be wading through brambles.

"You look pretty in your skirt," Laurie said, smiling at me as he climbed into the minibus.

"Well it is so hot that it was either this or my shorts," I said.

"That would have been nice too," he said and winked.

We headed out to a nature reserve run by the local Wildlife Trust. It was carpeted in purple marjoram and alive with silver-spotted skipper butterflies. Following a tour by the warden, we sat in the shade of an oak as I passed around home-made biscuits and elderflower cordial.

"This is lovely," Bel said. "I never get out of town normally, it makes such a change."

"I know what you mean," Kay agreed. "I'm going back to full-time hours at work soon so won't be able to come out regularly any more, and I will miss it so much."

"Poor you," Bella said, "stuck inside all day. I know how that feels. Have another biscuit."

The two women had struck up an unlikely friendship. Where else would a solicitor and an ex-convict have met? Nowhere good that was for sure. Nowhere they would have been on an equal footing, but the volunteer group was good for stripping away labels.

Roy had said something similar a few weeks previously. "It is a great leveller," he'd said. "We all set off for the tasks from different parts of the city but once we are in the car park, waiting for the minibus to round the corner, we are all on the same starting block."

It was true. In the group no one was a solicitor or an ex-prisoner, everyone was simply a member of the team.

After a cup of tea at the reserve we piled back into the minibus.

"Where now, Carol?" said Bastian from the back, where he was squished between Jim and Bevan.

"A surprise," I called.

"I like surprises," he said. He was glowing from the exertion of climbing the hills at the nature reserve but also because he was in his happy place, in the thick of things with the team.

I drove the bus up and down hills and lanes.

Laurie began singing "The Long and Winding Road". Esther joined in and Bella added a chorus of howls which caused Reuben to wince in horror.

"Are we almost there?" he asked.

"Almost," I called, also suffering from Bella's decibels. We turned another corner and there it was, a whole field of poppies covering the hill in a scarlet cloak.

"Beautiful," breathed Bella, suddenly becoming the quiet, thoughtful girl we all knew she could be.

"Sublime," said Reuben in agreement.

"I'm going to bottle this view," said Kay. "I am going to take it out when I'm stuck in my office during the winter and can't be with you all."

We climbed out and stood before the sea of poppies. "The farmer must have ploughed the soil too deep," said Val, "disturbed the old seeds that lay dormant. That's why they are all flowering."

"I don't want to know," said Esther. "Don't tell me all this beauty is a farmer's mistake."

Laurie sidled up to me. "Well done," he said quietly.

"Yes," Bastian said overhearing him. "Well done, Carol. It's a lovely surprise for our day out."

"Well you've all been great," I said, "putting up with all my early mistakes and working extra hours when a task needed finishing. This year would have been a lot harder for me without all of you. When I passed this field the other day I knew I wanted to bring you all here."

"It's like a gift," Alex mumbled.

"Yes, Alex, that's exactly what it is, it's a gift."

For lunch we headed to a pub by the river, where we crowded onto picnic tables and chatted and joked as I told the group about my belly dancing classes.

I had signed up to the classes a few weeks previously. I was proud of being an outdoorsy, practical woman, but I seemed to spend my whole life in combat trousers and walking boots. I felt it was about time I aimed for a bit of balance and embraced my femininity.

I had bought a long, flowing gypsy skirt that trailed on the floor, and had joined a gaggle of other women down at the local gym on a Monday night. Everyone seemed to feel self-conscious, but soon we were laughing as we tried to snake our hips and camel-rock in a way that resembled the double-jointed Cypriot woman teaching us.

"Show us your moves then," Laurie said now.

"Yes, go on," chorused some of the others.

Blushing, I got up and did a little shimmy before sitting down quickly. "Now your turn," I said to Laurie. "You promised to show me your dance moves too."

Laurie grinned and to my amazement he pulled up his shirt and revolved his stomach in and out like a pro.

"You win," I said.

It was what I had wished for in those dark early days in the flat: sitting in a pub garden with a crowd of people whose company I truly enjoyed, with the added bonus of a handsome man who, as I walked towards him eating an ice cream later that day, held my gaze with such intensity that it made me want to sink to my knees.

Towards the end of the day the group and I took a walk beside the river. Laurie fell into step alongside me.

"So have you found a boat to do that final water vole survey?" he asked.

If I was ever to survey the channel Laurie had almost drowned in, a boat would be needed.

"I'd love to row you down the river," Laurie said now. "You can sit under an umbrella and drink Pimm's. In fact, forget the water vole stuff, you can sit under a parasol in your skirt and read a book while I row you along."

I laughed. "Well, I'm not sure that was what the Environment Agency had in mind when they said they would lend me their skiff," I said, "but it does sound jolly nice."

We smiled at each other.

"It's a date," he said.

I arranged it for the following week, but when I called, his voice sounded flat.

"I can't make it," he said. "My boots have fallen apart."

I laughed, there were so many excuses when he was in one of these moods.

"OK," I said, "I'll give you a pair from the workshop. What day are you free?"

"I'm not," he said shortly. "I think I am going to be busy for some time. I have to look for a job. I can't be a volunteer all my life."

"Oh," I said, "oh OK."

He was silent. I was dismissed.

I put the phone down, the sun having gone out of my own day. I just didn't understand what had happened. He had been so keen to do it and yet there had been something so final in his tone. Was I even going to see him again? He had finished his community service hours a few weeks previously but I had felt certain that, even if he left the group, we would stay in touch. After all, we had become friends at the very least, hadn't we? Now I wasn't sure.

When I had found out my ex was having an affair, my confidence had taken a nosedive. My flirtation with Laurie had helped me feel attractive and hopeful that my love life wasn't over, but now it felt that the door on that future had been slammed shut. Had I misread things? I didn't think so. All those looks and comments that had passed between us could only add up to someone who was attracted to me too, so what had happened to make him drop out of something we had planned and looked forward to?

That evening as I wiggled away in my belly dancing class, I felt sad. It seemed my summer with Laurie was at an end and the dark days of autumn lay ahead. Then I looked up into the brightly lit mirrors and was amazed. The woman gyrating and shimmying along with the others looked OK, in fact she looked pretty damn fine. If Laurie couldn't appreciate that I was an attractive woman and worth making the effort for, then maybe he wasn't worthy of me – at least not yet.

CHAPTER
SEVEN

Autumn at Greengate Farm marked the beginning of months of wet trouser bottoms, rain-blasted visits to the loo and fingerless gloves until 3 p.m. to combat the chill in the porta cabin. Inside, the air was ripe with soggy dog smells, and heaters propped on bricks buzzed with electrical fizz. A season of growing gloom was upon us. Hours confined inside the office, writing up the results of the summer's survey work or management advice for landowners with the oppressive silence, broken only by the tick of the clock.

It was a time of washing up the volunteer's tea kit in the pitch dark of the unlit kitchen, of swollen doors, and buckets, buckets everywhere. New leaks appearing every day, despite Roy's best efforts with the bitumen paint. Puddles on the floor and on the desks, water spray blasting across your face as you typed before a leaking window with rain hammering on it.

The countryside sector was struggling through waves of government cutbacks. That year national park authorities reduced their staff by a quarter. Natural England had its budget slashed by 30 per cent and most of its experienced staff left. In the face of such change, we knew we were lucky to still be in a job at all. Kirk's boss, a severe-looking woman who rarely made an appearance in our dilapidated office, suddenly arrived and told us there would be no pay rises, no new porta cabin but maybe, maybe, they could erect a giant tent around the current building to keep out the rain. The tent never arrived and I was glad – the atmosphere in the office was claustrophobic enough without the loss of natural daylight.

Life began to feel flat again. My fledgling romance with Laurie had been a useful distraction but now, with no word from him, the sadness returned. As the evenings drew in, it was harder to resist the temptation of Facebook stalking the ex and his new girlfriend.

There they were, out together on Saturday night, laughing into a camera, while I curled up on the couch and felt sure that every other person in the world was having more fun than me. On these nights, I would feel my life hadn't moved on at all. It was almost a year since the split and here I was still, in a cold flat, in a low-paid job, still lonely.

I called Graham. I often turned to him when I was feeling low, not to offload my troubles but just to remember who I was. Graham was someone who made me feel I was all right and should trust in myself. Once, during my time working at College Lake, I had confessed to Graham about my history of altercations with bosses.

"Well there must be something wrong with them," he said. "Who wouldn't want to employ you? You're the first woman I've ever had as a summer warden and you're the best one of the bloody lot."

The truth was that I became a different person at College Lake, a person I liked much better. Under the kindness and encouragement of the volunteers and Graham, I became someone who was relaxed, friendly, generous. I was allowed to emerge as myself, without censure, and began to feel that maybe I was OK.

"Come and stay," Graham said when I spoke to him and told him that I had been feeling a little low. "We'd be delighted to have you."

I took Graham up on his invite and went to visit him at College Lake. In the years since I had left, the Wildlife Trusts had begun to take over the reserve. They had always been there, in the background, but Graham's health had begun to deteriorate and now they were keen to steer the reserve down a path more closely aligned with their way of doing things. Consequently, much of the individuality of the place had been stripped away. My old home, The Lodge, had been condemned as unsafe and what had once been my view across the lake was now dominated by a giant car park and visitor centre. Nowadays, it was best to walk around the reserve with blinkers, trying to spot the small elements that still made the place unique. Thankfully though, many of the volunteers who I had worked alongside were still there, beavering away, trying to keep the College Lake we all loved alive. The volunteers suffered the changes but really we knew whose vision we were following. I spent the morning working alongside the others, repainting the old shepherd's hut that was in need of a touch-up. At lunchtime the College Lake volunteers and I locked ourselves in the Bothy, the tea room which we had all helped to build, and Graham sat on his customary chair. He was frailer, that was obvious, but he was back, once again king of a kingdom he had created.

It was at College Lake I had first discovered the sense of family which can arise between a group of ragtag misfits who care about the same things, and despite the changes to the reserve, that feeling still existed. I didn't know if it was Graham or the reserve that wove the magic but I drove back home down the motorway on Sunday evening feeling calmer and happier than I had in weeks.

Back at work I realised a little of the magic of College Lake had permeated down into my own volunteer group too. Within the confines of the porta cabin I often felt weighed down by the gloomy atmosphere and a sense that my colleagues didn't feel my face quite fitted but on the task days I felt liked for who I was, rain splattered, tatty clothed, mud smudged and vitally alive, with the wind whipping the autumn leaves overhead and the bonfire singeing my eyelashes. Life was not on Facebook, it was out there, in the elements, with a gang of people who laughed and chatted and passed cups of tea back and forth across the benches as we huddled in the back of the minibus during wet lunch breaks, misting the windows up with our breath. For those few hours the world was in perspective and, like at College Lake, I came away from each Thursday feeling clearer and more certain about who I was.

The group soon forgot about Laurie. The long-term members had seen many such young men come and go, but I missed him. Despite the occasional text message telling me he planned to come along to the next task day, he never appeared and really I had given up expecting him to show. However, there was one person on the group who was more than happy about Laurie's departure: Alex.

Alex was tall with a thatch of now greying hair and bright blue eyes. I suspect when he was young he had been quite the man. Alex still thought he *was* quite the man.

"Come to my home," he had said on week two after my arrival. "I will send a cab for you. We will go out for dinner." Except the whole sentence came out jangled and rushed in excitement at the thought.

"Thanks, Alex," I had said "but I can't. I have to keep things professional."

When Laurie had arrived, I guess my attraction to him was obvious to everyone. Alex competed for my attention and wasn't going to let someone he saw as an upstart public school boy stop him fighting for my hand. I admired him for it; I liked that, despite the fact that he was living in a care home, his movements monitored night and day, he was still willing to take the risk and ask a girl out. I wished Laurie had been equally brave; I wished I was.

"I would fight the bull for you," Alex would tell me.

Inside this misfiring brain was very much the man I suspect he had always been. A swaggering, wealthy, fast-driving man, with a woman in every camp. He had told me about these women once, the ones he had been dating when the car accident happened which had robbed him of so much.

Alex was still living in Zimbabwe when the accident happened. In the days following the crash, his girlfriends had visited him; they had sat at his bedside and then, slowly, when they realised that the man they had dated wasn't coming back, they had left – all but one.

"She stayed," he said. "She came over and over again to the hospital."

Maybe she also saw that the man he had been was still inside, and hoped that, one day, a key would be found to unlock him.

However, the reality was that Alex now had little control over his life. For the last few weeks, unbeknown to me, his doctors had begun trialling new drugs to help improve his condition. We had next to no contact with the home he lived in, and no one gave us any idea that Alex's behaviour was likely to change as a result.

Alex was probably in his late forties when I met him. He had been coming out with the group for years before I arrived. I hope my arrival was not a contributing factor to the way things ended. I will never know for sure.

Alex was waiting at the gate of the farm as usual on the morning that things changed for him. I unlocked the gate and he headed straight to the barn to help me load the vehicle, as he did every Thursday. If I'm to be honest, Alex's help normally consisted of wandering around by my side talking while I tried to remember what I had to pack. That day, however, we didn't need to pack.

"Not today, Alex," I called after him, as he strode away across the site. "We're getting straight in the minibus today and heading to town to collect the others, then we are coming back here to work."

The plan that day was for the group to come to Greengate Farm to build bird boxes. We spent the morning holed up in the leaking barn, working in pairs, hammering and sawing. I liked these tasks, when we all worked together, it was a fine old craic, but Alex struggled to get involved.

"Hold the ruler straight, will you," Jim said in frustration, as he tried to measure a length of wood to cut for a bird box and Alex jiggled the ruler around.

"Bugger you," Alex said and threw the ruler across the workbench before storming off.

I ran after him. "Come back, Alex," I said. "Jim didn't mean anything by it."

"Bloody bugger," he muttered, but followed me back to the others.

It was a full house that day and I was kept busy making sure the production line of bird boxes was running smoothly. It wasn't until we began packing up that I realised Alex had gone missing.

"Have you seen him?" I asked everyone as they tidied away the leftover sections of wood and dropped nails.

"I think he wandered away, Carol," Bastian said. "He seemed in a bad mood again. I think he's gone out towards the road."

I walked out to the country lane and found Alex sitting on a chair he had dragged out to the car park.

"What are you doing out here, Alex?" I asked.

He folded his arms across his chest. "I'm waiting for my cab," he garbled. His speech had become more erratic over the last couple of weeks.

Alex was an adult man; if he wanted to sit in a chair in a car park and wait for his cab, it was up to him. I had no training in how to work with people with brain injuries, so I treated him like everyone else, but I could see he was upset – and I wouldn't have left one of the other volunteers by the side of the road feeling down.

"Your cab's not due for ages, Alex," I said. "It looks like it's going to rain. Why don't you come back to the barn and wait there?"

He came, moodily dragging the chair after him. I made him a cup of tea and left him sitting in the kitchen next to the office. I knew if he needed anything then the other staff were on hand. I returned to the barn to find the rest of the volunteers had already tidied up and were sitting in the minibus waiting for their lift back to town.

I was just driving out of the farm gate to drop the others back to their home town 10 miles away when I saw, from the corner of my eye, Alex leaving the kitchen and heading back out to the road.

I leaned out of the window. "You need to stay on site," I said. "Don't just wander off. Kirk's in the office if you need anything."

"Bugger you," he said, his blue eyes glaring at me.

I stopped the vehicle, got out and walked over to him, leaving the others sitting in the back watching out of the window.

"What's wrong, Alex?" I said. "That's not like you."

I wasn't expecting it, the punch. A punch aimed not at me – thankfully not aimed at me – but at himself. Alex punched himself in the face with full force, leaving a red glowing fist shape on his cheek. He lifted his fist and punched himself again, and this time the blow landed on his eye, the white reddening on impact.

"Stop it, Alex!" I shouted, but he didn't. He raised his other hand and smacked himself around the head, the force sending his head ricocheting to one side.

"I hate myself," he shouted, as spit flew from his mouth and hit me across the cheek.

I was stunned at seeing a man hitting himself with full force. To be so close to such violence sent my mind reeling. I didn't think, I reacted.

I grabbed hold of his wrists. "Alex, don't," I said. "You're frightening me."

He was. This was not the man who made me laugh in the minibus, who would fight the bull for me; this was a mad man.

"Alex, stop this," I said. "You don't want to frighten me, do you?"

He looked at me, his eyes bloodshot and wild.

"No, no," he said. "I don't want to frighten you."

He grabbed me in a hug so tight it pinned my arms to my side.

"Care about you," he said. "I don't want to frighten you." Then the mania seemed to take hold of him again. "Can't help it," he said. "Can't help it," and he released me to punch himself again.

It was then he saw the metal bar. It was a rusty handhold that led up to the kitchen, attached to the wall. The metal tube ended at waist height in a sharp circular hollow where it had rusted through. He grabbed the tube with both hands and swung his head back as if he intended to ram the metal into his eye. I can still picture that moment now; the jagged edge of the metal pole. It seemed that Alex and I both looked at the jagged metal at the same moment and my mind went black around the image of the sharp iron and the yawning dark "O" at the centre of the pole. It was like time stopped and in my head I had a premonition of Alex smashing his face against the pole, the metal gouging into his eye. I groaned involuntarily and pulled back as if the act had already taken place.

Maybe it was this sound, this movement that stopped him. Maybe Alex's head was just buzzing too much to follow through, but he let go of the pole.

"Get me a knife," he shouted instead. "I want to kill myself."

The next moment I sensed Roy running from the minibus into the office. I hadn't been aware of the other volunteers until then, just caught up in Alex, in his face, red and bruised, and the complete lack of reason in his eyes, in holding his hands down and the spit flying. I guess they had been as stunned by what they were seeing as I was.

The boss appeared, laughing casually, as if the whole thing was an amusing joke, but for some reason, the sight of him seemed to diffuse Alex.

"Come with me, Alex," Kirk said. "We'll have a chat and a cup of tea."

Alex slackened and allowed himself to be led into the kitchen.

I stumbled back to the minibus and drove into town through the horrendous rush-hour traffic. I could hear the others discussing what had happened in the back. I could see the stop–start of the traffic, red brake lights flashing on and off in front of me as I drove on autopilot.

It was dark when I arrived back at the farm, but the lights were still on in the office. I felt so exhausted I could have just lain down to sleep in the minibus, but there was still the vehicle to offload and the washing up to be done. I kicked open the door of the porta cabin; the boss and Mel were huddled around one of the computers and didn't look up.

I knew how it was by then. I would often come back from a long, difficult day, wanting to tell someone what had happened, only to be met by a wall of silence. Even so, tonight I had expected something, someone to say, "That was awful. How are you?" Nothing. The boss and Mel talked on as I wrote up the day's task report.

Finally, I could bear it no longer. I walked into the boss's room; only Marley looked up from his basket with interest.

"How's Alex?" I asked.

"Oh, he calmed down," Kirk said. "Then his cab turned up and he went home." He turned back to the screen.

I wanted more. I wanted to tell someone how I felt, discuss why it had happened, what was going to happen now. I tried again.

"I hate to think what he would have done if he had been in the workshop with the tools," I said.

The boss gave me one of his "stop making a fuss" looks. I couldn't believe it. They were acting as though nothing special had happened, as if this was just a routine part of the job, holding volunteers' hands down while they tried to punch themselves in the face.

"Did you tell the cab driver or Alex's home what happened?" I asked Kirk.

"No," he said. "I didn't feel it was necessary."

I went home to my flat and thought about calling someone, but I didn't want to worry anyone so I watched TV as a distraction and took nothing in. I didn't sleep well that night. Every time I closed my eyes I could see Alex's face as he punched himself. I kept reliving the moment when he grabbed the metal bar and I thought he was going to take his eye out with it.

I told myself I was overreacting, it was a one-off, but two weeks later it happened again. This time we were cutting scrub on a hillside, working to keep a patchwork of open space and dense bushes. It was bonfire season, and Roy was working hard to keep the fire going, swiping side branches off the trees with a billhook, a handheld tool with a short curved blade. He laid each branch onto the fire in the same direction, in order to keep it from growing too large and unwieldy. The sky was hammer dark, the wind brushing the trees, the motorway roaring nearby. My boots were slimy with mud.

It was one of those days when a female conservation volunteer finds it tricky to pee. I had struggled to find cover under fast-balding trees and avoid the attentions of the loose dogs squirrelling through the undergrowth, free of their owners. Having wiggled out of layers of long johns and waterproof trousers, I was crouched down, bare behind exposed to the damp air, when I heard Bevan call from a discreet distance.

"Carol, you'd better come quickly, I think Alex is about to go again."

I walked into confusion.

"Alex has threatened Roy with the billhook," someone said.

Roy was looking shocked and Alex's face was growing red. The billhook lay on the floor between them.

I tried to take charge, smooth things over. "What's happened, Alex?" I began and then I looked into his eyes and froze. It was there again, that same look, and this time I knew what could happen next. A bubble rose up in my mind; *I can't deal with this,* I thought. I was out of my depth and could feel panic starting to rise. My body was telling me danger was coming and I wanted to flee.

"Let's call it a day," I said, my voice too loud.

There was a slight nod of agreement from Bevan. The volunteers understood the need for an early finish.

As the others began to gather the tools around me. I could feel myself rushing, just wanting to put as much distance between Alex and sharp instruments as possible. As I instructed Roy to turn the fire in and I dumped the loppers into the wheelbarrow, I felt a growing anger at Alex's care home for sending him out when it must have been obvious to the staff that Alex's behaviour was currently unpredictable. Just who was responsible if Alex took it into his head to injure himself or someone else? The care home? Kirk? Me? Alex certainly couldn't be held responsible. As far as I was aware he had never shown any aggression before.

However, as we were slip-sliding in the mud back to where the minibus was parked, Bevan came up alongside me.

"He did it once before," he said. "When he was frustrated on a task, he stuck a spade through his foot. No one knew if he had done it on purpose or if it was an accident. I think now that it wasn't an accident."

I drove the others back to town and reluctantly said goodbye. My heart was hammering at the thought of being alone with Alex for the 10-mile drive through pitch-black country lanes to Greengate Farm where his cab would be waiting.

It wasn't that I was scared for my safety, not really. I was fairly sure Alex would never intentionally hurt me. I was scared of my inability to cope. I worried that Alex would have another outburst while I was driving or alone in a remote spot with a vehicle full of sharp implements and I wouldn't know what to do. I tried to picture all the lay-bys along the route. *If anything happens,* I thought, *I will just have to pull over, get out of the vehicle, lock him inside and call the police.* I knew this situation couldn't carry on. In the last two weeks I felt I had grown stiff around Alex. I hated myself for it but I had lost my nerve.

Thankfully, Alex seemed to have forgotten that anything had taken place and didn't notice the change in my behaviour. He chatted away as normal and we made it back without any incident. After packing him off in his cab, I took the folder marked *Accident and Incident Log* off the shelf in order to find out more about the episode Bevan had mentioned. The log was empty; in the 20 years of the Partnership's existence, no one had felt anything was serious enough to make a note of. I wrote an account of the day and recorded the first "incident" in the book, then I presented it to the boss and clumsily tried to explain how I was feeling.

"So you don't want Alex to come to the tasks any more?" he said.

"It's not that easy," I said. "This is one of the few things he does independently. I don't want to take that away from him when he has so little else to look forward to."

"So you do want him to come out?" the boss said, confused.

"I don't know," I said. "It is a safety concern."

Kirk sighed loudly; he didn't deal with subtleties, he dealt with certainties. We were chalk and cheese, the boss and I; he a man of figures, spreadsheets, black and white, me a person of theories, ideas and a need to discuss how I felt.

"You're spending way too much time thinking about this problem. It's stopping you doing your job," he said. "It's a simple decision. Carry on as normal or tell him to go."

It didn't feel that simple to me. I agonised about it at home later that evening and the next day I phoned the care home and tried to find a middle ground.

"Could you send one of your staff along with Alex?" I asked. "Someone who is trained in dealing with this kind of behaviour."

"We don't have enough staff for such things," the manager said shortly. "No one else has complained, only you. I will tell Alex he's not welcome in your group any more, if that's what you want."

This is your fault, not mine, I wanted to say. *You must have known he wasn't acting himself and yet still you sent him out without warning us.* But instead I put the phone down feeling like a totally heartless person. *If you were a kind person, you would still take him out,* I told myself. But I knew I couldn't, not alone.

Kirk walked through the office and caught me staring at the wall, trying to decide.

"I hope you are working," he said.

"I need to get some cement for next week's task," I said on the spur of the moment. I needed to think and I couldn't do that in the hotbed of the office. "I'm just going to pop down to town to pick some up."

"Are you eating the stuff?" the boss said sceptically. "You seem to use a lot of it."

"I'm putting in a lot of waymarker posts," I snapped. "You don't want them falling over, do you?"

The boss snorted but I grabbed the Land Rover keys from the cabinet and walked out before he could call me back.

In town I bought the cement and then headed over to the steamy workman's café on the edge of the industrial site.

"Sticky toffee pudding and a mug of hot chocolate," I told the waitress.

I ate the pudding, hoping the sugar rush would help my brain come to a decision. I was just writing out a list of pros and cons on a notepad when the phone rang.

"What's taking you so long?" Kirk shouted down the phone. "Come back to work this instant."

Back at the office, the others were having lunch, crowded into one room, with the dogs. They snapped into silence as I opened the door. I pulled a chair in from the other room and sat down with my sandwiches. The boss stood up and left. The two women turned their backs on me, pulling their chairs closer to each other. I longed for colleagues to discuss this with, to say, *What would you do? This is how I feel,* but, instead, I only felt more alone.

I got up and took my cup into the tumbledown kitchen to wash it under the slow leak of the furred-up tap.

The boss came in. "What were you doing in town?" he said. "I know you didn't spend all that time buying cement."

I looked at him. "I went for a coffee," I said firmly. "I didn't find your attitude to the situation with Alex very helpful so I needed some time out to think about my decision."

"I've made the decision," Kirk said. "I've phoned the care home and told them he can't come out again."

I thought for one moment of acting outraged at the boss. How dare he? It was my volunteer group and I would decide what happened with its members. But then I felt a wave of relief. I am ashamed to tell you I felt a wave of relief that I would no longer have to deal with my fear about managing Alex. I realised that it was what I wanted all along. For someone else to make the decision for me.

Alex never came out again. I think about him still from time to time. I hope he's still stealing spoons and asking girls out. I hope they worked out a combination of drugs that restored a little of what he had lost. I hope most of all that he is still Alex, rebellious, lazy, cheeky, funny, stubborn and really quite the man.

CHAPTER EIGHT

The path through the woods smelled damp with leaf mould but, as I emerged into the orchard, the valley opened up. The flat tops of the old Bramleys gathered in the pale light, their trunks bloated into elephantine forms. These were great-grandmother trees, spreading interlocking knitting needles across the path towards each other. Here the air was rich with the warm scent of rotting apples while the apples that were yet to fall swung from bare branches, like decorations waiting to be removed.

I had survived my first Christmas as a single woman – secretly, I had been dreading the confinement indoors, the family's questions. As the holiday approached, I would drive to work along the road, listening to the radio telling me it was "the most wonderful time of the year".

"Not for everyone," I shouted at the singers.

The drive through the woods was a salve that rescued me each morning. Turning off the main road, I would tip over the edge of the hill and descend through the trees. The woods felt real to me, the earth and the bare branches, the cold and death of winter were more solid and true than the tinsel and lights of the town. I wanted to hole up in the woods, bury myself in the leaf litter and resurface on Boxing Day. This wasn't depression, I knew that – it wasn't the extreme blackness that could eclipse Laurie. It was the opposite. It was a love of life, wanting a closeness to the earth. Amid those trees I felt, with utter certainty, that there was nothing to fret over; it was all being taken care of.

In the end Christmas Day was fine. It probably helped that I had been rescued from pity by an event which could have come straight out of my parents' 1950s dating-code book.

I had gone to a quiz night with a friend and a man had spotted me across a crowded room; we had mutual acquaintances, they told me he wanted my phone number. *Why not?* I thought, after all, Laurie had vanished and this was a real-life man who, from what I remembered, had looked easy enough on the eye.

When he called, he sounded more nervous than I was, but we arranged to meet for a date. The dates were polite: a game of pool here, a walk by the sea there, a peck on the cheek in the doorway. I thought about Laurie, all that tucked-away passion, how I had fantasised about kissing him till he popped. I ended things with this man, but it was also a beginning, a first step into the real world.

Now it was the 6th of January, life was carrying on again and I was back at work; back to the leaky office, to the mud around the porta cabin, to the dogs, wet and breathy and begging for my lunch. The boss was off sick, so I took the opportunity to head to the orchard in order to mark out the locations for the new fruit trees the volunteers and I were to plant out the following Thursday. The 6th of January happens to be the traditional day for people to wassail in the orchards.

Wassailing is an old pagan tradition: villagers would visit the orchards on Twelfth Night to drive out the devil by creating a bit of a din and to appease good spirits by making offerings to the tree to ensure a good harvest. The word "wassail" is thought to be old English for good health.

Today the orchard was empty. I selected the largest tree and reached into my bag for the remains of my lunch as the sun briefly burnt through the fog. I stuffed the bread crusts into a bowl-shaped hollow between the main branches and poured on the remains of my apple juice. Not quite the toast and cider that wassailing traditionally called for, but the best I could muster.

I took a deep breath. "Wassail," I yelled.

A few fieldfares chuck-chucked overhead. The yelling felt so good, I did it twice more, something about that holy trinity of threes.

"Wassail, wassail," I yelled.

The short day was coming to a close already, the sun was going down and, for one instant, I felt that old connection with a long line of people who worked on the land and stood in orchards and yelled down the demons of winter in the hope of a bountiful new year. After all, I worked the land, I was the protector of this orchard, and the volunteers and I were going to plant new trees, putting faith in the coming of spring and the future.

There is a connection with the earth you can only feel with working on it, working with it, getting your hands in the soil and tending it to produce for you without depleting it for all other creatures. Some moments working in the woods over the last few months I had felt this, the peeling back of layers, the woodsmen of the past watching from the trees. No, that's not quite right, not watching, not conscious of us but there all the same, working alongside us. I had felt their shadows throughout that winter as we coppiced in the woods. They had been there as we bundled up the hazel poles to be used by hedge layers and the twigs into long sausages tied up with string called, officially, faggots. These had been used by our ancestors to light their bread ovens, but we were to use them that summer for river work.

The ancestors had been there as we created a holy blaze from bramble, and they breathed into the bonfire alongside Roy; the smell of the smoke held in their ghost hair and clothes, as it lingered in ours. They had moved among us as the afternoon progressed, understanding the bite of the cold, the chatter of the volunteers, the hot-ear-cold-ear effect of walking past the bonfire.

These figures understood our tiredness, that particular brand of outdoor, airy dog-tiredness that came from a day working in the woods. They had followed us as we packed up our tools and headed back home.

The volunteers and I were part of the essential life of the English countryside as they had been. It was as if the Industrial Revolution had not yet happened, wolves had not yet been exterminated, we were still part of nature. It was in that feeling that a deep calmness came over me. Being human can be such a tiresome burden, and being a human who cares about nature, it was easy to feel frayed, wired and guilty in your very blood at what your species had done and is doing to the earth. However, in the woods, I felt part of the cycle of life, I was in harmony with it all, part of the dirt and the fire and nothing else. The self-doubt and to-do list ceased to matter.

I packed up my bag and walked away from the orchard. The yelling was cathartic, a crying out of the old year, a calling in of the new. On the way back up the path my phone buzzed. It was Laurie.

"Hey lovely girl," the text said. "I have applied for another job and I wonder if you could give me a reference as no one has anything good to say about me other than you?"

Typical Laurie, but it seemed his life was moving on, too.

That night the country became blanketed in snow. The next day I fought my way along the lanes to the office, my little Micra valiantly sailing down hills, passed only by four-wheel drives. I arrived at the office to find it empty, none of the other staff having attempted the journey. Another message arrived from Laurie.

"I want to build a snowman but I feel a fool doing it on my own. Come over and frolic in the snow with me."

I would have loved to go and frolic in the snow with him, but there were miles of country lanes between us and thick flakes were falling again. I told him so.

"Come tomorrow, bring a tea tray," he said. "We can go sledging."

I remembered this was what I had loved about him, the simple joy in life. He reminded me of my ex in the early days of our relationship when he too had wanted to gambol and life seemed new. My ex had grown up, as he would have put it, but I hadn't. I wanted this man who found pleasure in building snowmen.

"The thought of sledging down a hill on a tea tray makes me feel very happy," I told him. "If I'm not snowed in tomorrow, I will try to come."

"It's been a long time since I've been responsible for making a beautiful woman happy," his text shot back, sending a little glow of warmth lighting up my afternoon.

However, this was Laurie, and the next day he sent a message saying he couldn't make it back until the afternoon as he had visited a friend, got drunk and had just woken up on the friend's couch. That morning the snow thawed and the boss recalled everyone to the office to work.

Laurie got his job, as a barman in a local hotel. It was a beginning, a step back into employment and away from the fight and Community Service Order. I knew how hard it could be to start again on square one of the snakes-and-ladders board of life. He had confided in me once that, after the fight, he hadn't left the house in weeks, scared rigid by his own actions and fear of reprisals. In front of the other volunteers, Laurie had sometimes appeared to be a cocky, educated man, swaggering around with his shirt off, singing Elvis, but I appreciated those moments when he trusted me enough to reveal that, deep down, he had felt far from home and out of his depth in the world of court appearances and probation officers, which he had faced alone.

It was for these moments, when he let me in, that I waited.

"You need to know one way or another," my oldest friend, Karen, urged when I confided to her that he was back on the scene and, once again, blowing hot and cold. "Ask him out on a date."

But Laurie got there first.

The text arrived as I coppiced in the woods with the other volunteers.

"Don't laugh," it said, "but I had to get a new haircut for the job or they wouldn't take me on."

I felt momentarily sad at the loss of Laurie's long hair that I liked so much, but he was trying to make a good impression with his new employers and I knew it was hard for him to show he cared what others thought of him.

"Send me a photo?" I suggested.

"I'm too embarrassed," he replied, "but why don't we meet for coffee and you can see the results for yourself? I'm waiting until I get my first pay packet, then I can take you out properly."

"A coffee would be nice," I said. "I'm interested in you, not your bank balance."

"For the record," he said, "I am interested in you too."

Thank God, I thought. I couldn't have stood much more of that guessing game.

But then I heard nothing more for days. It was always this way, a bold move forward followed by a complete disappearance. I found the silences frustrating but I knew if I chased him and appeared too eager he would bolt entirely, so I waited and tried to get on with my own thing.

Ten days later he reappeared. The text pinged across as I was being driven to Norfolk by my friend Karen for a weekend away.

"When you say you are interested in me," it read, "is it A) that I've led an interesting life and you want to get to know me better? Or B) that you sometimes picture me naked, just getting out of the shower? Best to know for certain early on and save any embarrassment on my part."

I laughed out loud, causing my friend to miss the exit of the roundabout. It was typical Laurie, precise, surprising, formal and the bravery tinged with doubt.

"Can I say yes to both A and B?"

"Good," he said. "Just so you know I have also whiled away many a moment thinking of you in the shower. I hope you don't mind."

Mind? Not at all. I needed to know that I was thought of in that way. Not just as one of the boys, good for sharing a pint with and not much else. Karen was less enamoured. "He doesn't seem like a very solid option," she said. "Take it for what it is, friendship with someone you fancy but maybe not someone for a committed relationship." I knew it was good advice.

But, in the week, Laurie had second thoughts about a conventional date.

"Let's do some work together," he suggested when he called. "Less pressurised, more us."

I didn't want him to feel pressurised, I knew by now it wouldn't bring out the best in him, so I agreed.

We met on an icy winter's afternoon with the temperature falling fast. He was propped up against the hoardings surrounding the dilapidated pub at the end of his road when I pulled into the lay-by. He looked so different – I had only known him in the summer, with cut-off T-shirts, tanned muscles and long fair hair. Now his hair was cut short and he was cold, bundled up, not just in layers but in himself. The plan to spend the day working together had seemed a good idea at the time but, as we planted hedgerow trees outside a farm, it couldn't have felt less like a date. We fell into our roles of the previous summer, me the boss, him the volunteer. Afterwards we drove back through the darkening woods.

"I know these woods," Laurie said. "I used to play here when I was a boy. There was an old mansion. We used to sneak into the grounds and play on their tennis courts. Maybe we could look for it."

"I'd be up for finding it," I said.

The country lane was potholed and littered with branches from winter storms. We rattled around inside the Micra, pheasants skedaddling across the road, as the countryside grew dark. In the end we gave up and parked in a lay-by to drink the hot chocolate I had prepared in a flask. We sat in the car as dusk fizzled in and the last crows crossed the sky. The motorway hummed in the distance as he talked at high speed, in a Laurie-like way, spewing information to keep intimacy at bay. He talked about quantum physics. I had no idea what he was on about but I knew enough to know that black hole theory doesn't lend itself to kissing. The monologue moved on; all his previous girlfriends had cheated on him, he told me, but then he had cheated on all of them too and his parents had cheated on each other. I guess, looking back, that what he was asking was, was I different? Could I be trusted? Problem was, I was so different that I just didn't understand. Black woods, black night, black thoughts. The wind buffeting the car, a little owl quipping, night crawling in from the edges, leaves scuttling down the lane, I shivered.

"Do you want to go home?" he said flatly.

I did, I was confused. Just what had this day been about?

I drove him back to town.

"Drop me at the end of the road," he said. "My flat's crummy, I never invite anyone inside."

I pulled over and he was out of the car before I could even turn off the ignition.

"Well, let me know if you need any more help with work," he said, leaning back in the window but, before I could answer, he was gone. *Aren't you going to kiss me?* I thought. *Was this a date or wasn't it? What happened to naked showering?*

I was left more confused than ever – after wishing he would ask me out for so long, I now wasn't so sure I wanted to see him again. It all just felt such hard work. In the end I sent him a message, not sugar coated. The date had been weird and there was no point pretending it hadn't been. "You puzzle me," I said. "I like you but I feel I get mixed signals over how you see me."

"Maybe I wouldn't be such a mystery if I had more self-confidence," he said.

I warmed to him again. "My confidence has also taken a beating," I told him. "It's been a while since I chanced my arm with someone new, but my instinct tells me that you are a good guy so if you want to meet up again let me know."

This time I knew better than to expect a quick reply.

I went back to the woods, back to the coppicing and faggot creation, as watery spring sunlight burst through the trees and the first wind-blown blast of wood anemones blushed up from the warming soil. Woodpeckers drummed a tattoo amid the branches as we worked with intricate, face-fixed concentration at the complex puzzle of a coppice stool.

Coppicing is an ancient woodland management technique that has been carried out for centuries in lowland woodlands. It involves cutting trees down at the base to leave a ground-level platform called a coppice stool. Coppice woods are divided into blocks and each block is cut on a rotation of anything between 7 and 25 years, and generally some trees will be left alone to reach maturity. Cutting trees down to the ground sounds and looks super drastic, but many trees respond by sending up lots of shoots from the base that then create dense bushy growth. Managing the trees in blocks creates a tapestry of habitats: some open areas flooded with sunlight, some with light tufty stems and a low canopy and some with darker thickets. It is a highly controlled environment but it is one that benefits many scarce species.

It should be pointed out though that coppicing does not benefit all woodland species as it provides very few mature trees and little dead wood, which is necessary for beetles, fungi and hole-nesting birds, but opening up the woodland floor to light creates a rush of flowers such as early purple orchids, primroses and violets; this in turn creates an abundance of nectar which benefits scarce butterflies like Duke of Burgundy and heath fritillary. Numbers of these butterflies decline when coppicing ceases. Birds such as spotted flycatchers can feed on the flush of insects and, as the trees begin to regrow and create a denser canopy, nightingales and warblers move in to nest.

Coppicing may have developed when Neolithic man noticed the regrowth sprouting from trees gnawed by beavers. Academic and author Oliver Rackham, who wrote *The History of the Countryside*, suggested that the Neolithic causeways crossing the marshes were created from coppiced trees. All kinds of trees will coppice, including hazel, ash, lime and oak trees. Once the trees have received a first cut, the new stems grow into long straight poles which can then be cut down and used as a sustainable source of timber.

By the time of the *Domesday Book*, coppice woodlands were widespread across the country. They would create wood fuel to fire the furnaces for potteries, glassworks, brick making and metal work, as well as providing pliable poles used for hedge laying, walking sticks, besom brooms, sheep hurdles and practically every domestic item used in a labourer's cottage. What a marvellous, sustainable, waste-free world it must have been.

However, from the nineteenth century, Britain became increasingly dependent on imported wood and later on barbed wire fencing and plastic. By the 1950s many coppice woodlands had been converted to conifer plantations, which were heavily subsidised by the government. The remaining coppice became neglected, or "overstood" as it is sometimes called when the poles, which should grow straight, begin to twist and fuse together, making cutting them down difficult.

To coppice a mature stool involves unpicking a puzzle, working round the spiral, communicating with the tree to decide which pole to fell in which order. Ideally each pole is cut at the base to leave a cut that slopes outwards from the centre, allowing the rain to run off. That's the ideal that we all aim for but in reality it is hard to achieve as the fused trunks, dense poles and inflexibility of a bow saw make it fiendishly tricky. You invariably end up with saw blades wedged, poles ripping and splitting and calling in your neighbouring volunteer to lean their weight on the tree to help things along. However, a well-coppiced stool is a thing of beauty and something to be proud of. You are entitled to walk past it discreetly several times admiring it until your neighbour notices your achievement and comments positively but with a hint of envy.

Since the 1980s most coppicing had been done to benefit wildlife, but now times were changing and the volunteers and I coppiced with a purpose.

The Water Framework Directive was an EU initiative which hoped to restore the health of our rivers and, all over the country, faggots were in demand for river work. A faggot held in place on the riverbed acts in the same way as a dropped tree limb, making the current work around the obstruction and form riffles and eddies. In doing so, it changes the riverbed, creating shallows and deeper pools. These are good news for invertebrates and fish who thrive in the varied habitat pockets created, while the twiggyness provides nursery areas for fish fry. The volunteers and I cut the trees, not only for the benefit of woodland wildlife, but for use to restore our rivers as healthy habitats too.

Faggot making was a good task to do with volunteers, as everyone could play a part and use their individual skills. Reuben could cut perfect coppice stools, the stems low and golden like fat penny coins spilled on the woodland floor. Bruno, our oldest volunteer, selected the biggest coppice stools and still possessed the strength to cut through the thick trunks with just a hand saw, a feat which never failed to astound me. Bastian bundled the branches together and Esther teamed up with Meg to grasp the bundles and wrap them with natural twine, while Wayland produced a fancy way of knotting the bundles which even Esther had to admit worked well.

Joggers and dog walkers using the forest would weave in and out of the bundles of twigs we left lying all over the path. We scarcely noticed them. We were in a separate world. We, the woodland workers; they, the recreationists.

Together, we became a crack team, producing up to 70 4-metre-long bundles of wood a day, which Jim and Bevan would load onto the top of the minibus while I lay on top attempting to strap the load in place with an elaborate cat's cradle of haulage straps. We became so good that I was able to sell the surplus faggots to a river restoration company for good money.

Back at the office, I argued that the money raised should go towards something that would directly benefit the volunteer group. I wanted to save up and buy a defibrillator. The volunteers still spoke about the time when a former group member had had a heart attack on a task, and the then group leader had tried and failed to save his life with CPR. I wondered how I would feel, deep in the woods, trying to save the life of someone I cared about, as Val ran up and down with the cheap mobile, trying to find a signal to call an ambulance. I knew that, in this scenario, the chances of saving a life were tiny and a defibrillator could make all the difference.

"What is the point of buying a defibrillator when we might never use it?" the other staff argued.

"I hope I never do use it," I said, "but it would be nice to know it was there if I needed it."

I was outvoted.

It wasn't just the volunteers' lives I feared for in the woods. It was a risky business loading the faggots onto the minibus so they could be transported back to Greengate Farm for storage. I would stand perched on the roof of the bus, shouting "tips, butts" at the volunteers, depending on which way I wanted the giant bundles delivered up to me. It was an art, the stacking: get it wrong and the load would sway alarmingly and threaten to block the ring road as I drove it through town back to the farm. As the twiggy nest grew upwards, I would lay flat on top of the faggots, hanging precariously over the sides of the tall vehicle, as I attempted to feed the haulage straps through the roof rack struts and around the load, in such a way that it would be secure. Jim was always there, special advisor, on the ground, making sure I kept myself safe.

These were good days, the days in the wood. At the end of each task I walked with a swinging confidence that came from being outdoors and having done something physical, working my muscles in a way they were meant to be worked. The confidence came with the tatty layers and some unconscious understanding that real human value is not held in the outer layers but within. When I worked in the woods, no one worried how I looked, if my make-up was in place or my clothes were making me look attractive. On the tasks I had something else, a physical confidence in myself, a languid, loose confidence that comes with being accepted for who I was. For those few hours, after a task, I knew my own worth, I liked myself and if someone had popped up then telling me that I was a failure for not having a man in my life, I would have told them where to get off.

I didn't need a man but that didn't mean I didn't enjoy their company or appreciate their help. So one day, after a task, when the confidence was beaming out of me, I called Laurie again. I knew the man I had seen on our last date was not the whole story and I had liked him so much the previous summer, I figured it was worth giving it another go.

"Do you fancy getting out of town," I suggested. "Come cook some bangers over a campfire with me?"

I knew the idea would appeal to Laurie and it was a delight for me finally to have a friend living close by that I could suggest this to and who wouldn't think my ideas were weird.

"I know just the spot," he replied. "We can build a wee fire, cook some food and if I can dig a hole, climb a tree and build a dam, it will be a great day."

How could I not fall for him when he said things like this? Laurie was, in so many ways, the man I wanted, an intelligent, cultured, nature boy. However, I became a little sceptical about his chosen campfire location as we drove through the silent streets of mock clapperboard cottages on the edge of town. This was glossy brochure living, the sort of place where neighbours are strangers and people walk no further than the few steps between their front door and their car as they "live the dream". We passed a large sign saying, "No Access, No Fishing, No Fires. Police Will Remove Trespassers." I looked at Laurie doubtfully.

"Makes it more fun," he said. "I used to come here to fish when it was just a mill but they are going to destroy it all soon and build flats along the river. We should enjoy it before they do."

Two channels met under the old mill house, one slack and oiling out of the city, one bubbling over the weir. A pike rested in the eddies, water crowfoot fanned in the currents. We stepped over a low gate and into a meadow of red clover and white-flecked plantain; bumblebees buzzed in the nodding heads of borage flowers, bats were flitting around the dead elms in the evening light. We stepped onto a dirt track leading into a little copse of old trees, creepered with ivy, a blackbird alarmed away. The path wound beside the bank and we emerged to a spot where the two rivers met again to fall away in a still water channel. The light was beginning to die, the dark waters cast a mirror for the sky. The trees shushed the earth and all was still. In the shallows, water forget-me-nots trailed and the tall spikes of purple loosestrife framed the river.

"It's beautiful," I said. "The city feels miles away."

"I know, I come here sometimes, when I need to," Laurie said enigmatically.

"And they're going to build along it?" I asked incredulously.

"Of course," he said.

Laurie built a fire, he did this stuff so well. He laid it perfectly and it lit quickly. We cooked sausages, drank beer and watched the fish jump, creating little golden stars as the water caught the last glint of the sun through the trees. The fire died down, and Laurie stood up. There was an old piece of tin laying to one side of the path, someone else's litter, I guess. He got a stick and swept all the embers of the fire onto the tin and picked it up, holding on with one corner. He flicked his wrist and the embers flew out across the darkness. We stood, our hands slack by our sides, on the spot where two rivers met and watched as the embers floated on the water, each little organic red star burning on the water and floating away from us, winking out one by one. He reached out and for a second I thought he was going to take my hand, but at the last moment he stopped himself and we watched the last stars go out until there was only us, in the darkness, on the pinnacle of land and all the rush of the city was somewhere else.

It couldn't go on, this endless romance with no consummation, just the frustration of wanting and not having. In the end something had to give. Laurie invited me to a party with some new friends from his workplace who were mainly from eastern Europe. The women taught me Bulgarian belly dancing, the men sang songs. We drank under-the-counter whisky that made us both forget ourselves. Laurie took his shirt off and joined in the belly dancing, wiggling around as the others cheered until he dived for the couch in sudden embarrassment.

I lay on the couch next to him, my head propped up against his arm and listened to those public school vowels. Sometimes, it has to be said, Laurie talked a lot of crap, but those vowels could make everything all right. *Say something, say something, anything*, I thought. It didn't matter what, he made it all sound like honey. I fell asleep and when I woke, an hour later, everyone else had gone to bed.

"Come back to mine," he said.

I followed him back to his flat, the place he never invited anyone, through a council estate in a part of the city the tourists never saw. At the end stood a municipal building, two storeys high, that looked like an old school building with pale yellow – probably flammable – cladding. Single-glazed windows were barred with metal grids, the grass outside was littered with old beer bottles and broken kids' bikes. A sign told residents that "anyone found setting fire to the grass will face eviction". He pressed a code on the security pad and the door buzzed open. We walked along a glaring white corridor, past identical doors with tiny windows glazed with unbreakable glass. It smelled of stale urine and, even at 3 a.m., the air was thick with pot smoke and the sound of televisions.

Inside Laurie's flat, the smell of damp grabbed hold of me. Black mould grew in spider webs along the walls. The flat consisted of one main room that served as bedroom, dining room and living room. The furniture was of the kind that other people leave outside their houses for the bin men, but this was a world as familiar to me as it was to him. I was in no position to judge; I might have been working full-time but my living conditions were little better, my rented flat was all black mould and furniture rejected by charity shops too.

We stood in his living room facing each other, and he took a step forward. *He's going to kiss me,* I thought, but he didn't.

I was confused. The sexual tension had been crackling in the air. Was it just me? Hadn't he felt it too? Was I doing something wrong, sending out the wrong signals?

"Let's get some sleep," he said.

His bed dominated the room.

"My rock-star bed," he said. "A charity gave it to me."

It was the biggest bed I had ever seen.

We climbed into his rock-star bed and he turned off the lights. We lay there in the dark, neither of us making a move.

"This is a little unexpected," I said, to break the silence.

"I didn't expect you to come back," he said.

"And now?" I asked.

"Do you mean alternatives to going to sleep?"

I paused. I didn't want him to think I just jumped into bed with men I had gone to parties with on a regular basis, but he had been in my life for over a year and I couldn't be in this moment, lying next to him, in bed, in the dark and not want more. I summoned up all my courage. "Yes," I said.

There was silence. Why did we talk? Talk was danger with Laurie. Talk would lead him down a dark alley and away from me.

"It's no good," he said. "I just can't have a relationship."

It felt like a bucket of cold water had been poured over the moment.

"So what does that mean?" I asked. "That I'm never going to get to kiss you? I like you," I said, the drink making me brave. "I want to kiss you. You need kissing."

Laurie lay staring up at the ceiling.

"I need to know if you are still interested in me in the way you said you were?" I squirmed with embarrassment at asking, but I had to know.

"You mean, do I still think of you in the shower?" he said. There was a long pause. "Yes, I do but I am no good at relationships," he repeated. "The moment I kiss you, we are no longer friends, and I don't know how I would deal with that."

I felt awkward and deflated. All of those moments of looks and touch had led to this? Nothing? But I tried to console my wounded feelings by telling myself that at least it sounded like he valued my friendship.

"We wouldn't stop being friends," I said, but really I knew that I couldn't handle an endless unconsummated friendship that was never going to lead to more. It wasn't what our relationship was naturally meant to be. The fact that he wanted my friendship was flattering but it also felt deeply unflattering. I didn't want to be only his mate, I wanted to be his girlfriend, with all that entailed.

"I am trying," he said. "I saw a psychiatrist recently but she told me my depression was caused by smoking pot. The pot smoking is a symptom of my depression," he said, "not the cause."

It probably isn't helping, I thought but it wasn't the moment to argue this.

He sighed. "I'm no good at this relationship bullshit. I like you, you're here because I really like you, but I can't put you through what I would do to you if we were in a relationship." Then all the black thoughts crept into his head and I tuned out this monologue of negativity because, once it began, it would suck me in, too. I lay in the dark, trying to process what he had said. In many ways I felt clearer than I had in months. All the promise with no fulfilment had left me permanently on edge, hoping and not getting. Now at least I knew where I stood: I was flogging a dead horse. He liked me, he was attracted to me, but he was in no fit state to have a relationship and maybe, by falling for this man, it showed that I wasn't either. At least I now knew his lack of action was no reflection on me. The conversation made me sad but I had plucked up the courage to ask for clarity and now I had it. Somehow that felt positive. With that thought, I drifted off to sleep, in the rock-star bed.

I woke to sunlight leaching through the thin curtains and Laurie beside me, his leg pushed against me, his hand touching mine. For so long I had thought that it would feel strange to find myself in bed with any man other than my ex but, with Laurie, it felt the most natural thing in the world. I watched him breathing and occasionally he would mumble something and push closer to me. I wanted to reach out to him but I knew that if he woke, woke properly, the spell would be broken, so I waited for his breathing to change, and then very slowly climbed out of the bed, got dressed and left.

That wasn't quite it, the end, but after that there were few places for the relationship to go. There were other lovely moments, lovely days, but he wasn't ready and there was little I could do to change that. Ultimately I wanted companionship and support and a full fun physical relationship and he couldn't provide that. Eventually Laurie vanished again, and this time I didn't stay in touch.

I am grateful for that time: Laurie helped me step forward. He had appeared in my life at a time when I needed a boost to my confidence and a local friend to confide in. He had given me hope in those early days that there was a future following the break-up of my long-term relationship. That other men would find me attractive and want to spend time with me. I firmly believe that, when it comes to relationships, you get what you're ready for. At that moment I had been ready for Laurie, all that he was and all that he wasn't. The lack of physical involvement may have driven me nuts but at the same time it had provided a safety zone. I could try out being with a man without the intensity or vulnerability that sex would have brought. But it couldn't continue. We both had to be ready to take that risk and move things forward and maybe it just wasn't the right time for us. I felt very sad about this. It seemed a real shame that two people who genuinely liked and respected each other, had loads of stuff in common, enjoyed each other's company and were attracted to each other couldn't make a go at things, but Laurie just had too much baggage piled up around him and, if I were to be honest, so did I. It was hard to close the door on Laurie but I knew it was the only thing to do, the only way to ever get the relationship I really wanted and deserved. It was time to move on.

CHAPTER NINE

I threw myself into my work, which was easy as that summer we had a big task ahead of us: creating an erosion barrier in the river.

Kirk had long championed the idea of a cycle route running from the city centre along the river. To set this up had been a challenge as the route involved crossing land owned by aggregate companies and fishing interests, two groups not renowned for their love of public access. Eventually though, Kirk's determination had paid off and the cycle path had opened the previous year. It was an immediate success.

On a sunny weekend, cyclists, people in wheelchairs, parents pushing prams, joggers, dog walkers and kids on scooters could all be found weaving in and out of each other along the narrow strips of Tarmac beside the river.

It was still a remarkably wildlife-rich river, gravel bottomed and feathery with waterweed, like long mermaid tresses; trout laid eggs in the gravel bed, and otters were said to come exploring after dark. Once upon a time, the river had frequently flooded the water meadows outside the city, providing a backdrop for paintings of wild-eyed cattle. Once, the Romans had crossed it en route to slaughter the British in their hill camp. Once, Henry VIII had travelled alongside it, on his way to visit the home of one of his countrymen in order to eat his food and probably bed his daughter.

With the coming of the Industrial Revolution, the river had been blocked by giant weirs built in an age of British confidence and engineering prowess. It was forced through mill workings which stopped the migration of fish, slowed the current and created sluggish silted pools where once the salmon spun. In the ancient city the river had been contained between concrete banks; buildings and bridges hung over the water, tidal gates controlled the flow, restricting the water to a tightly managed channel.

We have long thought we have beaten our rivers into submission, tamed them to do our bidding. We have long thought we have tamed *all* nature to do our bidding. Nature has other ideas. Climate change was creating more turbulent weather. A month's rain could fall in one day and the chained and urbanised river, along which the tourists were punted in the summer months, could suddenly become quite a different beast altogether and create floods which almost marooned the city on an island.

We had built all over the flood plain, deforested the uplands, trampling the banks with too many cattle and sheep, which then caused the banks to collapse and bloat the river with silt. We had Tarmacked our front gardens, which caused the rain to run off quickly into the drains instead of absorbing into the earth and swelled the rivers at high speed. We had removed the trees which would have slowed the currents and allowed the river to top out in places where it was safe to do so.

A river is ever-changing: a tree limb dropped in the winter creates a sandbar by the spring, pushes the water to the far bank, a meander forms, leave it alone and, given time, the meander loops to an oxbow. A river is a poem, a dialogue between water and gravel, earthen banks and tree roots.

In this case the river wanted to rewrite the boss's work and eat up the cycle path, undercut the Tarmac and send the mums, prams, cyclists and wheelchair users on a lovely water ride downstream. Our job that summer was to protect the cycle path from the erosive forces of the river.

The erosion barrier was a typical Kingsdown Partnership task. Kirk took me to the river one morning for a meeting with some people from the Environment Agency. They talked at length about the problem while I listened in.

"So," Kirk said, turning to me, "you need to create something that will stop the path eroding."

Everyone nodded wisely, as if the problem was already solved, while I was left thinking, *Where do I begin?*

In many ways the boss and I were not a dream team when it came to work but in other ways his approach suited me just fine. I liked a challenge, I liked to learn, I was happy to be left to my own devices. Just point me in the right direction and then get out of my way was all I asked for. I scoured the internet for similar conundrums, made phone calls to organisations that did this kind of work all the time, asked questions and thanked people profusely for their answers.

With all the free information I gained I came up with a design for the erosion barrier. This involved creating an underwater fence of hazel faggots topped with a giant hairy sausage called a coir roll made from coconut fibre. Behind the fence we would build an earthen bank by stacking hessian sacks filled with soil into the gap and then plant wetland plants into that soil. Eventually the plants' root systems would hold the structure in place.

Would it work? That was anyone's guess. Much of the time I was just shooting in the dark and trying things out and, to be honest, I liked that. In a big organisation, like the RSPB, such a project would have been designed by a team of experts; computer models would have been created to see if it would work, a funding application would have been submitted to pay for materials and contractors would have installed it. At the Kingsdown Partnership I drew a design on some paper by hand, submitted it for approval to the Environment Agency, sourced coir rolls and sandbags and then set the volunteers to work. The design wasn't perfect and later on I learned better ways of doing things, but the barrier is still there.

It was a July day when we headed past the paper mill along the riverbank to begin work on the barrier, passing the old whitewashed mill cottages, boarded up and sitting idle. Cycle-path users stopped to stare as we carried the long sausages of coir rolls over our heads.

"Is it an art project?" one man called.

Bastian stopped. "Carol," he called. "This gentleman wants to know if we are making an art project."

"No," I called back under the weight of a post driver. "Bastian, tell the man what we are doing."

Bastian swelled with sudden importance and began to explain.

When I had first known that the group would be working by the river for weeks on end I had been worried about Bastian. His agility was limited and he was nervous around water. I thought I would struggle to find him a job he could safely do. I shouldn't have worried – Bastian found his place.

This is the thing I learned from working with people with brain conditions like Alex and Bastian: a difference in mentality is just that, a difference. It doesn't have to mean a lack of comprehension or that someone's brain is not functioning extremely well in other areas. I soon realised, for instance, that Bastian had a fantastic memory, which I came to rely on.

"What task are we doing in three weeks' time?" someone would ask.

"Gawd knows," I'd say, but Bastian would know.

"What was the name of that man we met at the farm gate in June, Bastian?" I would ask, and Bastian would tell me. He was like Alexa but with more useful information and a less annoying voice.

The volunteers were a happy team that summer. The riverbank was a shady place to be and on a hot day the water was a liquid delight to slip into. Water babies like Reuben donned waders and took to the river, to bang in chestnut stakes. We slithered down the bank on our bottoms and the water sucked at our rubber-clad legs. Suddenly we were transported to another realm where demoiselles danced at eye level and, less magically, wasps flew from bank-side colonies to sting you angrily in the face if you got in the way of their desire to reach the tangle of blushing pink bramble flowers on the far bank.

Those who didn't fancy being in the water become "bank gophers", as we christened them. Their job was to keep up a steady stream of equipment to the people in the river: scissors, faggots and sandbags constantly moved between one team and the next. Esther and Meg worked on the bank retying faggots so they could be slotted between the stakes. Our fly fisherman, Trevor – a long-term, occasional member of the team – invented a technique he called frapping, which involved a complicated cat's cradle of natural twine, tied in a way to keep the whole structure in place until the plants established root systems.

Up on the bank I was in my element. My job was to organise the team to create something that none of us had any prior experience of making. The trick was to keep everyone working efficiently and happily. I loved it; more than that, I felt I was good at it. I was on my game, working to the best of my ability and finding pleasure in a job well done.

Mihaly Csikszentmihalyi, a Hungarian psychologist working at the University of Chicago, might describe this feeling as an "optimal experience". In a paper he wrote with Judith LeFevre, "Optimal

Experience in Work and Leisure", they suggested that an experience was most enjoyable when a person feels that their environment contains opportunities for action or challenge which can be matched with their own level of skill. This creates a feeling they called "flow".

I love that expression – flow – because it was exactly how I felt that summer, sailing up and down the riverbank in my tattered layers, keeping the work on track and having a laugh with the team. I was bobbing along like a cork in the current. Csikszentmihalyi felt that, when challenges and skills are high, a person is not only enjoying the moment but stretching their capabilities and, at the same time, learning new skills, increasing self-esteem and personal complexity. In such an experience, Csikszentmihalyi and LeFevre said, people feel active, alert, concentrated, satisfied and creative. That was me, high and buoyant with how good life could be.

Maybe for the same reason, Bastian loved the work too. Since we were alongside such a busy cycle path, passers-by couldn't help but notice our work.

"What is it?" they asked repeatedly. "What other work does the group do? Are they on probation?"

"Some of us," Bella called merrily from the river as she held a stake for Bevan to bash in with the post driver.

Bastian talked to everyone, explaining the work and the group. He retained information really well and was very sociable, so his skills were more than a match for the challenge of being group spokesperson. In between answering questions, he was supremely helpful, tying up faggots in the sun, filling sandbags full of soil to stack behind the coir roll and delivering items to people in the river.

"Bastian, Bastian," the volunteers called every time they needed something. His name rang up and down the river. On so many tasks

Bastian's lack of agility had kept him on the sidelines. I hope I did my best to include him and make him feel useful but sometimes, I admit, it had been easier to hand Bastian a rake and leave him tidying up after the others. Now, however, Bastian was an essential cog in the wheel.

Bastian longed to be useful. Despite the fact that he had both physical and mental disabilities then, as far as I know, he didn't receive any kind of disability benefit. Instead he looked for work. He was a well-known figure all over the area because he volunteered anywhere that would take him. Bastian contributed far more to society than many people with far fewer excuses but, instead of being rewarded for this work, he was punished. Bastian was forever applying for jobs in garden centres and animal-care facilities, anywhere that his wealth of volunteering experience qualified him for, but with no luck. People were being made redundant all over the country; young, fit men couldn't find work, let alone Bastian, who was 58. Instead Bastian was forced to go to the dole office each week, sign on and run the gauntlet of steely young women with boxes to tick and little bits of power to wield.

One week Bastian turned up by the river visibly stressed after a visit to the dole office.

"I can't come out with the group for a while, Carol," he said sadly. "I have been told by the lady at the jobcentre that I have to go on a maths course instead. She told me that I shouldn't be volunteering with you. I should be looking for work." He was close to tears.

Esther, noticing something was wrong, came over. "Sit down while we make you a cup of tea," she told Bastian.

"Maths course?" Esther whispered angrily at me over the teabags, squishing the one bag in Bastian's mug so hard in her annoyance that I feared it would burst. "It's ridiculous. What is the point in making him go on that? They've already sent him on an English course. There's nothing wrong with his English. As if a lack of a maths qualification is the reason that Bastian can't find work."

"What was the woman's name who said this to you, Bastian?" I asked.

"We'll go down to this dole office, find the woman and give her a piece of our minds," Esther said.

But Bastian, probably sensing that a fuss was going to be made on his behalf, uncharacteristically couldn't recall the woman's name.

There was little we could do. Bastian got sent on his maths course and went off sadly, returning a few weeks later with a piece of paper, and carried on his volunteering. The woman at the dole office had presumably been placated by ticking that box on her form.

It was typical of Esther to wish to go the extra mile to help someone. She and Wayland were people of action. They had always been Greenpeace members, signing the occasional petition, going on marches, but now, in retirement, they felt the time was right to get more involved.

A few weeks previously Esther had been arrested, along with 50 other protestors, after climbing on board a coal train as it attempted to deliver a consignment of Russian coal to a power station. They had stopped the train – well, technically it was a giant mechanical polar bear positioned on the tracks that had stopped it, Esther had just prevented the train moving again. Once on board she began shovelling the coal into bags and laying them alongside the track to return to Putin.

"That way we couldn't be accused of stealing it," she explained the following week. "At first it was exciting. The adrenalin sweeps you along and you know what you want to achieve. The prime minister has just been at a climate change conference in New York and we wanted to raise awareness of the damage coal-fired power stations were doing. Later on though, when we were arrested, it was awful as the police kept us standing in the rain, kettled together while they processed us."

Eventually she had been rescued by Wayland, who used his years of experience as a social worker to negotiate with the police, provide welfare and afterwards find everyone a bed for the night. "My knight in shining armour," Esther said, squeezing his knee.

"I'm due in court in a few weeks," she told me. "Would you be able to write a character reference for me?"

"It would be my absolute honour," I said.

It was. They were brave, braver than me; good, ordinary people who had tried to peacefully make the government listen to the facts and stop us all walking into a climate apocalypse.

"We're not planning on getting involved in things that disrupt ordinary people," Wayland said. "We want to fix the blame right back on the people causing the destruction."

The character reference was the smallest thing I could do to support them.

The sociability of the task that summer drew us together in new ways and we all began to get involved in each other's lives outside the group. Problems and worries naturally came to light when you worked alongside each other week in, week out, and we began to look out for each other. Esther and I realised that living with her parents wasn't helping Bella's mental health, and tried to find her a place to live independently in an almshouse. Jim and Bevan's walking group always included an invitation to anyone they felt was having a hard time. We all knew when someone was not themselves and either gave them the space they needed or gently asked, "What's up?" The work was good for that. It was easier to talk about what was troubling you when you were waist deep in water, wrapping strings around fence posts. Conversation flowed as I stood in the river, with minnows circling my legs, having long discussions with Reuben on literature and travel or getting advice from Bevan on the art of polite conversation, to assist Bella and me, who were debating whether to go speed dating.

That summer we also got a new group member, Josie. She appeared in the car park one Thursday morning, hiding behind long hair, and for the rest of the day I worked hard to get more than two words out of her.

It must have taken a monumental amount of bravery for Josie to join us in the car park that first day, but over the years many of the volunteers must have also struggled to take that first step. Laurie, telling himself he needed nothing and no one, had braved it. Bella, used to being judged, had braved it. Josie, fearful of talking to people, had braved it. I think of this sometimes, when I am scared of taking a step in my life which could lead to being exposed to ridicule or hurt or heartache; I think of my youthful gang and how worried and fearful they must have felt at taking that step, how easy it would have been for all of them to stay at home and never try to change things. I think how brave they were and feel buoyed up by their courage. *If they could do it,* I tell myself, knowing how they felt at that time in their lives, *if they could take the risk, then you can too.* I feel sometimes, if I don't take that brave step, then I somehow let them down, diminish their bravery – and that I am not willing to do.

Josie was probably the shyest person who ever joined the group.

"I had been stuck inside with just my parents for company for so long I didn't really know how to talk to people any more," she told me once, years later. But, before too long, the river worked its magic. Bevan was a master of drawing people out as well. It was those lullaby Welsh tones, I'm sure. They hypnotised you into revealing your innermost secrets, but I never found Bevan's questions intrusive, he was just naturally curious about people. After a morning of working alongside Josie, tying the cat's cradle of string around the faggots, he discovered that she was 24, had been to art college, dropped out because the course hadn't met her expectations and was now living with her parents in a village where the chances of a social life were zero.

The following week I teamed her with Bella. Bella nudged her with her arm as they tied bundles of twigs together in the sun.

"So, what are you reading then?" she asked, and they discovered a shared love of the same author and a passion for computer games.

No one could be shy for long with Bella, she had personality enough for two, but she was sensitive as well.

"She's had depression," Bella said to me at lunch. "She's barely left the house in the last few years. She is really keen to help wildlife but she might get some bad days too.

Bella knew what a bad day felt like.

The bad days came and Josie would vanish and be found sitting further along the riverbank with her head in her hands. Bella would go to find her and sit down beside her, dangling her legs over the edge of the bank. She knew enough not to say, "What's wrong?" Not just then. Instead she would point out the moorhen chicks and make a joke and before long they would both get up and come back for tea.

Other days it was harder to get her to move on from the crisis in her head. Once she started shaking so badly, while I was driving the minibus to a task, that I had to pull over, offload the others and try to talk her back into the present, saying whatever sprang to mind. I had no training in dealing with such things and often I found it hard to summon up some magic words that would get the show back on the road. At times it felt hard to balance the practicalities of the job with the mental health needs of the volunteers.

However, despite people's differences, unlikely friendships blossomed in the group, across age groups and social spheres. People who would never have met each other in normal life found common ground. Bella, our loud and bright jailbird, had laughed alongside Kay, before Kay had returned to full-time work as a solicitor. Meg was a keen artist, had been to art college and exhibited locally. In Josie, she saw a shy and anxious young woman, struggling to find her place in the world. When she found out that Josie was also a keen artist she went out of her way to encourage her.

"I'd love to see some of your art," she prompted Josie.

It was weeks before Josie appeared with her portfolio.

"I've brought along some of my paintings," she mumbled as we sat by the river during our coffee break.

I knew it had taken a lot for Josie to put that trust in us and show her artwork. She handed the paintings round. Fantastic oils of mountain goats caught in shafts of light, bears fishing on salmon streams. The family dogs, working spaniels, eager to please.

"These are really good, Josie," Meg encouraged her. "You should approach some local galleries, join an art group."

Josie smiled uncertainly. "I don't know if I am really up to that," she said.

But Meg persisted and, with her encouragement, Josie entered a local art show. She won, of course, but still it was an uphill struggle to get her to do more.

There should be more of this in society. More opportunities for young people and older people to work beside each other and find the things they share. We have a habit of sticking with our tribe if left to our own devices. It is unhealthy. It breeds inward-looking mentalities where the other, the unknown becomes the enemy. There need to be more opportunities for age groups to mix in a natural way, to understand and build sympathy; the volunteer group was good for that.

It was around then that I began to need the support of the group too. That autumn I became unwell: a mystery illness crept up on me, which caused swollen glands, sore throats, pains in the joints and such all-consuming tiredness that I sometimes could not, just could not, keep my eyes open.

The doctors were sceptical. "Eat a healthier diet," one barked.

"But you don't know my diet isn't healthy," I said. "It is, actually."

"Well, get some exercise then. Take up squash."

I thought of the hours of walking and the loading and offloading of heavy tools and materials I did for work every week and sighed.

Even sympathetic doctors were perplexed and, in the end, I gave up bothering them and just tried to battle on, but there were days when I struggled to get out of bed, overwhelmed with a mental and physical tiredness I couldn't explain – a complete lethargy and a worrying inability to even think. Sleep, sleep was the only thing on days like that. I hated having to cancel the task day at short notice but the volunteers were predictably lovely.

"I'm coming round and making you some soup," Esther texted me. "I'm getting you some ginseng."

It was harder to explain to Kirk what was happening. After all, I had no diagnosis and I didn't think he would have the patience to listen to me describing how my random symptoms were making it difficult to work. In my experience people involved in conservation don't get sick, or at least, if they do, they don't give in to it. This, I guess, is a hangover from the days when the profession was dominated by hardy, outdoor men. It was a badge of honour at the RSPB, when I worked there, never to take a day off work. I tried to push on through the bouts of exhaustion but it was tough. Sometimes, while doing a survey, I would have to stop, wherever I was, and nap on the side of a riverbank just to summon up enough energy to walk back. After a long day out with the volunteers I was too tired to do anything in the evening. "Even if Keanu Reeves asked me out on a Thursday night I would have to say no," I told Bevan.

"Maybe this illness is a reaction to all that uncertainty over Laurie," my friend Karen suggested when she came over one weekend for a stroll.

"I don't think so," I told her as I climbed over a stile. "I'm sad about Laurie, frustrated that all the energy I put into thinking about him came to nothing, but it hasn't floored me." I paused mid-step and considered. "No, I think this is more likely a delayed reaction to my break-up with the ex. Laurie was a year of flirtation, not a fourteen-year relationship with someone I thought I would grow old with."

"But you seemed to get it together so well after that break-up," Karen said, following me along the footpath.

"I think that's the problem. I prided myself on ploughing on, not slumping into depression, getting a job, getting on with things. Maybe I just pushed myself too hard."

It was true. I hadn't allowed myself to fall apart, not even for a moment. *Pull yourself together*, I had commanded myself. *You can't let their actions defeat you.* I felt I had side-stepped the fall-out of the break-up, but maybe you can't dodge a bullet like that.

"Maybe instead of dealing with it, I just stored it up," I said. "Too much stress hormone in the blood or something. I just pocketed it away and it's seeping out slowly now, when I thought it was behind me."

Website browsing revealed that I was suffering from everything from glandular fever to multiple sclerosis. Internet diagnosis is not good, but the websites did give some sensible advice. "Pace yourself," they said, "realise your limitations." Of course, instead of listening, I did the exact opposite: frustrated at my lack of energy, I decided to defy my illness and continue on the same path. *You just need the right mental attitude*, I told myself. *You will feel better once you get out.* Sometimes I did but I always paid for it later. It just seemed so dull and bloody annoying that I should be knocked by this just when I was feeling ready for life again.

That summer the group began to break out of the confines of the Thursday task. It began one lunchtime. Bella, Josie and I were sitting under the shade of the old willow as the wasps flew in and out of the hollow above our heads.

"Got any plans for the weekend?" Bella asked.

"Not likely," Josie said. "I'll be sitting in my room trying to avoid the family as always. What about you, Carol?" she asked.

I opened my mouth to give my normal response to questions about my social life – to claim that I had plans with friends when the truth was that, since Laurie's departure, my weekends were back to being a yawning blank. But, maybe with these women, I didn't need to pretend or be ashamed. After all, they weren't living Instagram lives either.

"I've got nothing on," I said. "I will probably spend all weekend filling my time up with useful projects to prevent myself from feeling lonely."

Bella grinned. "I've seen an advert for night-time punting trips around the city," she said. "With ghost stories. Whooooo," she cried loudly, startling Roy, who had dozed off, propped up on one of the faggot bundles.

Josie and I laughed.

"So do you fancy booking one this weekend?" Bella asked.

"Booking what?" Esther called.

"Night-time ghostly punting trip," I said.

"Count me in," Esther said.

Being honest about my loneliness opened a door and, suddenly, I was rescued from Saturday night in front of the telly in the mouldy flat.

That weekend we went punting. Bella wore a comedy hat, and Esther brought hot chocolate and told Wayland to stay at home. We drifted beneath the low bridges along the river, wrapped in blankets, listening to tales of gruesome murders and the walking dead.

At the end of the night, Josie asked, "Do you want to go surfing with me one day? I really fancy it but don't want to go alone."

When she finally emerged from her shell, we discovered that shy, timid, Josie was actually an adrenalin junkie and up for anything. Later, we went down to the beach to catch a wave, wedging ourselves into wetsuits so we could frisk around on surfboards.

Josie and I waded out into the water to wait for our wave. "What do we do when we see it?" I asked Josie, who had bodyboarded before.

"We paddle like hell and then kind of leap up onto our feet."

"Are you up for that, Bella?" I asked. "Leaping onto the board while riding a wave?"

There was no reply. I turned round but couldn't see her anywhere.

"Where's she gone?" I asked Josie. "She was right there."

Then we saw her, halfway up the beach, surrounded by lifeguards. We raced back out of the surf, dragging the unwieldy boards with us.

Bella was being given oxygen by a young lifeguard who was loosening her wetsuit. "It's nothing," Bella said when she saw us. "I tripped over a little wave and the wetsuit was so tight I couldn't get up, so the waves kept battering me in the face."

"I think she's had a panic attack," the lifeguard said. Bella was looking red and flustered. "We've given her some oxygen to stabilise her breathing but I think she should be OK now."

"Are you OK, Bella?" I asked. Bella gave a thumbs up and a grin from inside the oxygen mask. I was relieved to see she was looking OK and smiling again.

"He's gorgeous," Bella said, as the lifeguard walked away. "I was hoping for the kiss of life."

A few weeks later, Josie had another water-based idea. "Let's go canoeing," she said. In spite of her recent mishap, Bella was up for coming along too, so we joined a local group and ploughed along the river as dusk came on and bats flitted overhead.

Towards the end of the evening, the wake of a cruising boat caused Bella to capsize in the dark. She had to be rescued by some fellow kayakers who hauled her back on board. Poor Bella, Josie and I must have used up her nine lives in near-death experiences but still, she always came up laughing, wet and red-faced but willing to try again.

Before long there were regular trips to the pictures along with Roy, Meg and Val. Roy hosted a firework party for his birthday. We all learned line dancing on Esther and Wayland's lawn. Roy it turned out had been taking lessons, and Reuben was a funky dancer. We began theme nights with exotic food, where we wore outfits inspired by the country the food originated from. Bella and I, fully tutored in the art of polite conversation by Bevan, went speed dating. "Do not mention your stay in prison," I told Bella as we headed for the pub. It seemed that Bella always wanted to tell people she had only just met about her crime.

"It's the only interesting thing about me," Bella said. She was still inclined to define herself by this one act. I wasn't ashamed of Bella's past, but I wanted her to start believing she was more than this one moment.

"It's not," I told her. "You have loads of interesting things about you. Tell them about your poetry writing instead." I wanted the speed dating to be a positive step for Bella and, with only three minutes for each date, I feared our potential suitors wouldn't discover the real person if the whole conversation got dominated by this "interesting fact".

"Would Bevan say that divulging your criminal record is polite conversation?" I asked. "I'm not about to tell them my ex ran off with another woman and I have a mystery illness I can't shake. It's chit-chat, not life histories."

Bella grinned. "OK, I get your point."

In the end it turned out that the men at the speed dating weren't half as interesting as Bella, but we had a laugh and she wrote an excellent poem about it which she read out to the group the following Thursday.

Kirk noted this at my next yearly appraisal. "It's good of you to organise all these social events for the volunteers." But it wasn't good of me at all. The volunteers may have been 10 years younger than me or 20 years older but what did that matter? With them I had fun, I was happy, and happiness was a thing I knew could be fleeting and precious.

Summer wound on and the erosion barrier began to snake its way through the waters by the mill. We worked in the river as it shivered in pools of sunlight, as the yellow bobbing wagtails plucked flies from the air beside us, as the sunlight broke into slivers of silvered glass, as the blue bullet kingfishers whistled past, as the minnows gulped and the mayflies rose, and the water rolled and foamed down the weir.

Somewhere in the midst of cyclists and string and lunch breaks under the willow tree, we stopped being a group of people who came out to volunteer and we became a community. We might have arguments, a week when so and so drove us nuts. We might moan about a member's peccadilloes or feel wounded at a sharp comment but, if one of us was in trouble, we rallied round.

It wouldn't work like this with all volunteer groups. I can't say to you, go and join your local conservation group and you will find an alternate family to care about you. I had been involved with other groups that weren't like this. It was just alchemy, the right mixture of personalities at the right time in their lives. It was the right time in my own life too. If I had been a happily married woman with a family of my own, I doubt if I would have had the time or the need to gravitate to the volunteers in the way that I did, but I wasn't. I was lonely, bruised, needing friends and support, and there they were.

With Laurie gone, I needed the group and maybe it's in that space between relationships where we have the most chance to grow. Maybe this was especially true of me, who was prone to taking a back seat and putting others' needs before my own. In this space I learned things about myself. I learned that I wasn't flaky, I was a super organiser. I wasn't hopeless at practical things; I could bang a nail in straight even underwater and I didn't have to apologise for that ability. I wasn't a selfish person just because I was single and without children; I was a decent woman who cared about her friends. I wasn't bossy, a term forever being levelled at me by my mum. It just so happened that, when it came to the volunteer group, I was a natural leader. In order to get the job done someone had to be in charge and, as I was the one that was being paid and was responsible should anything go wrong, then I felt strongly that the person in charge should be me.

On that one day in the week the confidence shone out of me and I knew that, if only Laurie could see me now, then he would have liked this version of me. I was a capable woman and, I realised now, that was who he had liked all along. I was not and never would be the kind of woman who acted coy, who played games, who flattered a man for the sake of his ego. I had spent too long trying to turn myself inside out and be someone I wasn't. Not to please him, Laurie never asked for that, but to appease society with its outdated ideas of what a woman should be in order to be seen as attractive by the opposite sex. I had at times tried to act girly and soft in front of Laurie, believing that this was how women should act to win a man and yet, if I had opened my eyes, I would have seen that Laurie had liked me most when I was being true to myself, up to my waist in duckweed, imparting my knowledge about nature. Strolling across a field with a pack on my back and a big pair of walking boots. He liked the woman who was self-assured, capable and practical. From now on I was going to have faith that a man worthy of me would want the person I naturally was, not some watered-down, insipid version of me.

The summer passed and the barrier grew until we ran out of supplies.

"That's it," I called from the back of the minibus. "We are out of faggots and sandbags. We will have to stock up again this winter."

I don't know who spotted it first, the bag floating down the river. Josie was the only one in waders still and I asked her to go in and pull it out. Our good deed to end the day.

"It's heavy," Josie said. "I don't think it's rubbish."

"Treasure," Bella said, and took the bag off her to open it.

Inside was the oddest collection of objects. A flower arrangement, a little terracotta pot, a piece of agate with a silver shell attached, an oven glove, a plate with a ship on it, some Greek sweets and an unopened bottle of good quality Merlot.

"What's that all about?" I said.

"Maybe it's been lost, from a picnic," Esther speculated.

Reuben, our Cambridge scholar, picked over the contents, "I think it's an offering," he said. He looked at the Greek sweets. "Maybe from a Greek wedding."

"It's meant for us, Carol," Bastian said. "The river has sent it to us, to bless our barrier."

"Well it is all vaguely nautical," I agreed, picking up the ship plate.

"We should keep it then," Bastian said.

I picked up the Merlot. It was firmly corked and seemed fine. "We will, Bastian. When we come back and plant the barrier next spring we will have a toast with this wine."

We were sad to finish the barrier that day. It was one of those last days of summer when the sun is still hot but the birds have gone quiet and the light is slanting low and you know it's soon to go. The earth had turned again. I had found happiness with my gang that summer, our friendships had ripened under the sun, and I hoped that would sustain me for the winter months that lay ahead.

CHAPTER
TEN

I parked the minibus on the cliff top, finding a spot between the rows of cars lined up on the strip, which looked out to sea. Retired men sat behind the steering wheels, escaping the house, reading the newspaper or enjoying the cricket on the radio. It was a beautiful September day, everything cut and glistening with that sharp autumnal light, the last hurrah before winter. Walkers had been caught between seasons, unsure whether it was a day for shorts or jumpers. The gentle slap of flip-flops sounded on the Tarmac path, which led down the cliff face to the beach.

The volunteers tumbled out of the bus, attracting curious stares. We were incongruous in such terrain, the battered layers like moth plumage. In the woods we slotted in against the bark, but here, our cover was broken. We were exposed among the public, medieval woodsmen appearing in a seaside town. Late swallows zipped along the cliff top in gangs as we headed down the path towards the beach. They followed us as we waded through the tussocky grass, towards the bramble bushes that clung to the steep slopes.

Patches of coastal scrub are invaluable as resting places for birds blown in on autumn storms, but here the scrub was threatening to shade out a plant called hog's fennel. The floppy hog's fennel was a subtle beauty; the blue-green summer foliage had now faded to teabag brown. If you took the trouble to really look at it, the plant resembled the spokes of an upside down umbrella but, en masse, this late in the season, it just looked a bit of a mess.

Hog's fennel had none of the eye-popping delight of the lipstick red hips of the dog rose, which covered the slopes leading down to the sea. It didn't have the beer flavouring and mildly hallucinogenic properties of the mugwort that grew alongside it. It didn't have the cultural resonance of the brambles we were here to cut down, ripe with childhood memories of stained fingers. We do struggle, us people, to recognise the value in nature when it has no obvious practical or aesthetic value to us. We struggle to recognise that we are just one component of the natural world. The web of life sucks in and out and we are just one strand. Sometimes we forget this and think we are the spider and the whole damn thing is just there to serve our appetite.

Although we haven't invented a use or have a great cultural affinity with hog's fennel, that doesn't make it valueless. It is extremely valuable to the Fisher's estuarine moth, whose caterpillars eat this and nothing else. Without the hog's fennel, they can't survive. As it is, the moth only exists in a narrow band of habitat on the coast, most of which is vulnerable to sea-level rise. The coastal cliffs, where we were working, were one of the few places that moth and plant were not threatened with being drowned.

I understand though that hog's fennel doesn't have instant appeal for people, and therefore it was not entirely surprising that some of the people walking along the seafront that day struggled to understand why we were cutting down their favourite blackberry bushes to make way for it.

"Stop that now," a smartly dressed woman bellowed at Roy, as he attempted to fork a pile of bramble onto the small fire I had instructed him to light on the beach.

Burning the bramble on the beach had seemed the safest option, as the cliffs were a protected zone where no fires were allowed. Leaving the giant prickly tumbleweeds of vegetation to blow around the cliff top and ensnare passing tourists had seemed unwise. However, what I had failed to consider was how sick the locals were at holidaymakers lighting fires on the beach.

The woman came pounding up to Roy.

"Stop that now," she shouted at him again. "You are going to burn the beach groyne."

Roy stood poised with his fork in the air, the bramble mass swaying on top of it in the breeze. I skidded down the slope to see what the problem was. It was hard to see how our tiny fire was going to engulf the beach groyne in flames, as it was sitting in the middle of a wide shingle beach, with a ready supply of salt water to hand to douse any rogue embers. However, I struggled to make myself heard above the woman's strident voice. She was determined to have her say and was not willing to hear about the plight of the hog's fennel or the tiny moth that relied on it for survival.

"I am going to call the authorities," she said.

"But it's the council that have asked us to do this," I explained.

"A likely story," she said. "My husband is a magistrate. You will be hearing from him. I will see you in court."

I took off my sunglasses and gently touched her arm. I was used to these scenes by now. For the most part passers-by were positive about our work, but with so much vegetation bashing underway, it was inevitable that, occasionally a member of the public would see our work as destructive and take exception to it.

"I admire your passion for the countryside," I told her. "We are on the same side."

But it was no good. She marched off, presumably to rouse the magistrate from his chambers, and everyone got back to work. Thankfully, that was the last we heard from her.

Cutting down the bramble was difficult enough without these problems. We crawled over the hill, lopping or bundling together the prickly vegetation and hauling it down to the shingle beach, where blue smoke was still rising from the bonfire. The air specked and popped as the black pea pods of kidney vetch burst in the warmth of the sun. By lunchtime the sky was so blue you wanted to reach up and grab a handful of it and bottle it for winter. We could resist the lure of the sea no longer.

Pulling off our sweaty and itchy layers, Val and I stripped to just T-shirts and pants and ran between the cockles and slipper limpets to the hush rush of the sea edge, where it raced to meet us over the pebbles. The sea flipped in green curls, and gulls with the black spots of winter plumage behind their eyes sat on the beach groynes, watching us as we bellyflopped into the waves, our feet digging into the wet pebbles, salt water healing the fresh bramble scratches. The air was heavy with the high iodine of warming seaweed. The sun beat on our bare necks. I flipped onto my back and felt cold fingers of icy water run through my hair, letting all the everyday stresses of life go. The sea could do this, make all the worries of day-to-day life go away with the currents and leave you anew. I backstroked away from the beach, swallowed up by the immensity of sea and sky with mountainous cumulus clouds gathering overhead. It was harder getting out than in, and harder still to get back into our wrecked and reeking layers. The swim was so impromptu that neither Val or I had a towel. We writhed around on the wet pebbles trying to dry ourselves with sweat-stained shirts and pull jeans back over our still wet bodies. Still, it was worth an afternoon of scrub cutting in soggy underwear for the feeling of being centred that I always came away with after a swim in the sea.

As I pulled my damp, burn-hole-ridden T-shirt over my head, I noticed Bastian was still sitting on the hill by himself. That was odd in itself as normally he loved being in the thick of things.

Now I thought about it, he had struggled more than usual to get down the steep hill that morning and had spent the day leaning on his rake, not doing much. I couldn't remember seeing him eat his lunch.

Scrabbling up the hill, I plopped myself down next to him on the grass. "Are you OK, Bastian?" I asked.

"I'm sorry, Carol," he said. "I'll do more work in a minute."

"Never mind that," I told him. "What's wrong?"

"I've been having some problems," he said reluctantly. "Some problems eating. The doctor has sent me to the hospital for some tests."

"I'm sure it will turn out to be nothing," I said, not sure at all. For Bastian to raise any issue affecting himself meant he must be feeling very ill. I looked at him properly and saw that he had lost weight, and quickly. Back in the summer I had struggled to get the seat belt across Bastian's spreading middle, literally moulding his stomach so I could strap him in; now, it would fit easily.

"Bastian, I don't think you are feeling at all well today," I said. "I think you should go home and talk to your dad and tell the doctor how you are really feeling."

"Yes, maybe you're right," Bastian said. "Maybe I should go home."

I knew things were wrong. Bastian loved the group, loved being part of the gang, and now he was willing to leave.

I rounded up Wayland, who had brought his car along.

"Would you and Esther take him back home?" I asked. "Right home to his door?"

Wayland agreed.

"Come on, Bastian," I said. "You've got a lift."

I helped him up and looked up to where Wayland was waiting by his car at the top of the hill. It was a long way up. We walked slowly, oh so slowly, up the cracked Tarmac path, between the cricket buzz. The shush of the sea mellowed out behind us, and the chatter of the others faded away. The slope seemed like a mountain; Bastian stopped every few steps. I was worried.

"I'm sorry," Bastian repeated. "I'm sorry, I'm so slow, I'm sorry I'm taking up so much of your time, I'm sorry I am a problem."

"Bastian," I said. "Of all my volunteers, when have you ever been a problem for me? You are never anything but helpful and useful to me."

Bastian smiled. It wasn't strictly true but I'm glad I said it.

Slowly we continued, stopping every few paces as the clouds built and rose up to black-bottomed cumulus towers. The light was suddenly too hard for this, the heat too intense, the cricket song an electric static without cease. It all mocked our progress, step by slow step up that hill. The shiny-cased beetles crawling along the edge of the Tarmac outpaced us with ease.

Wayland and Esther were waiting at the top of the hill. We bundled Bastian into the car and they took off. I turned to face the sea; the cloud shadows had crept in. Something was wrong.

Cancer is a powerful force; at its most virulent, it is a hurricane that sweeps in and takes the body away before anything can be done. In Bastian the hurricane had arrived before anyone knew. By the following week, he was too ill to come out with the group, and his sister arrived to care for him and his elderly father, who he lived with. Over the next few weeks we visited him at home, little gangs of us, sitting politely, sharing tea in his dad's living room while Bastian looked embarrassed and apologetic for the trouble he was causing.

This wasn't us; us was bundling Bastian into the minibus among the laughter and muddy boots of the others; us was tying faggots in the sun or watching the embers of a dying bonfire. Us was a big bundle of dirt and rags and wood smoke but, for Bastian, that was gone, so we sat and sipped tea and told him about our exploits.

As the darkness came on for Bastian it began to affect me too. The mystery illness, coupled with the physical work of running the tasks, left me exhausted. Some days, after dropping the volunteers off in town, I would drive back to the farm, only able to keep my eyes open because Val had given me a supply of sugary toffees as an energy boost. The thought of offloading the minibus and setting foot into the office, where I was expected to work in silence for another hour, seemed an impossible feat.

I was burning the candle at both ends. My friendships with the volunteers were a lifesaver but it meant that there were few boundaries between my work life and my downtime. Neither Josie nor Bella drove, so I would taxi them to our social nights and sometimes let them stay at mine afterwards. After a long day at work I would find myself cooking meals, making up beds on my couch and washing up. It was my choice but, at times, it did feel a little as though I was parenting them.

Conditions in the porta cabin had deteriorated even further until it seemed in imminent danger of collapse. One morning I came in to find a mini waterfall had erupted over my filing cabinet. The ceiling had sagged and water was cascading in. Someone had stuck a bucket under the waterfall, but no one suggested how the leak could be fixed. It was my office space, my problem. At times it felt that the other staff would rather pretend that the office was not so bad and maybe for them it wasn't – as long as it wasn't too far from their homes and they could have their dogs with them during the day, then it worked for them.

I thought about suggesting to Kirk that I work from home part of the week. I had read that some staff in city firms were beginning to do this but couldn't imagine that this idea would go down well within the archaic management structure of the Kingsdown Partnership. In Kirk's mind, it seemed, if he couldn't physically see you at work then you were probably slacking. My days out of the office doing river surveys were punctuated with messages from Kirk wanting to know why I was taking so long. Despite the fact that the survey work often involved walking many miles across country, scrabbling up and down riverbanks and jumping fences while carrying a bag full of heavy equipment, Kirk seemed certain that I was somehow taking it easy. He would have done it all so much quicker, he felt, forgetting that he hadn't done a physical job like mine in years. Several times I almost discussed the idea of home working with him, but then I'd imagine his incredulous stare and chicken out.

On top of this, Kirk was still accepting every piece of work that came our way, in order to keep us afloat. As well as managing the volunteer group I was now out of the office several days a week doing river surveys and writing reports on restoring the habitat. I was giving talks to digger drivers on sensitive river management and reporting back to local drainage boards on my findings. I was running guided walks for festivals, organising community tree-planting schemes, undertaking surveys for landowners and providing them with advice, and occasionally running school-holiday clubs for kids and parents. Taking on this amount of work was Kirk's strategy to survive in difficult times, but an easier one for him to decide on than for his staff to implement. He was accepting work like he had a team of ten, not me and two part-timers. Overtime became the norm and I sometimes came into the office on a Saturday to finish a project on time.

"I can't take any more on," I said to Kirk in despair, as he outlined yet another project which had to be a "priority".

"Well you don't have as much on as me," he said.

"I do," I said. "I'm finding the workload overwhelming."

"Well, it's a busy time," he said. "You'll just have to cope."

But I couldn't. I felt like if I was asked to do one more thing then the whole house of cards would collapse.

I began to think about leaving for another job or even going freelance. I knew I had learned some valuable skills in the last couple of years but wasn't sure if it was really enough to set up on my own as an ecologist, a title I struggled to identify with. To my mind, ecologists were bespectacled fungi experts who spoke Latin, not Essex chancers getting by on a bit of cheek and a childhood of nature study. I just didn't feel I knew enough to award myself that title.

On the Monday, Roy came in as normal and set about fixing the leak in the roof. He noticed that I was not myself.

"It's getting to me, Roy," I confessed when he asked. "The office conditions and the workload are beginning to weigh me down. I wake up and have to really force myself to come in and deal with it."

"Have you thought about using the free counselling service?" he asked.

"I didn't know there was one," I said.

"Well, theoretically, you're a council employee, aren't you," Roy said. "You are entitled to six weeks' free counselling. Why don't you call them if you are struggling to manage? There's no shame in asking for some support."

Roy made it sound a logical step whereas I still felt that asking for mental health support carried a stigma. Despite the fact that – or maybe because – I had witnessed the struggles of Laurie, Bella and Josie, I didn't feel justified in saying I was finding it hard to cope. After all, I didn't think I felt the way they sometimes did.

However, on Roy's urging, I made the call in my lunch hour and was shocked to be offered an appointment the next day. I sat in the counsellor's room and told her how I was feeling about my job and the conditions in the office.

"That's appalling," she said. "You need to get a new job."

I wasn't so sure that counsellors were meant to give such cut-and-dried advice, but it made me feel justified.

"I think you are someone who hides everything behind a show of coping," she said. "But how well are you coping?"

"Not well," I said. "To be honest I feel that if Kirk gives me one more piece of work then I am going to pop."

"Take sick leave," she urged. "Go to the doctor, take time off."

"There is no way that I can hand Kirk a note saying I am taking time off with stress," I said. "No one in the real world goes off work with stress. At least no one I know has ever done that." I thought about the guys at the RSPB or Graham at College Lake. These were the men I admired, and they didn't take time off work with stress.

The counsellor looked at me seriously. "How much longer can you go on feeling the way you do?" she asked. "The conditions in that office sound appalling and your boss sounds like a bully."

I was shocked to hear her use such blunt language. Kirk was controlling, but a bully? Not intentionally, I thought; a lot of the time I think he was genuinely unaware of how his management style made me feel, but the counsellor's summary of the situation did make me feel justified in complaining.

On Monday I confided in Roy about the counsellor's advice. "It sounds like an excellent idea," he said. "Take time off, get away." He showed me a photo taken on his recent holiday to the Northumberland coast. "A trip here always clears my head. How about heading to Holy Island for a couple of weeks?"

"But I've no holiday due," I explained.

Roy looked serious. "Take the sick leave," he said. "None of us want to see you leave for good, you've had more impact on the volunteer group than anyone else but, if you're unhappy and it is affecting your health, you must take a break. Instead of jumping ship entirely, why don't you take some time away and consider your options?"

I thought about Bastian. I couldn't possibly leave while Bastian was so ill. Who was going to rally the volunteers to visit? Who was going to run the volunteer group while I was away? Who was Bella going to talk to about her relationship troubles? She had met someone on one of our speed dating nights, which was great, but she was still going to need her wingwoman. Who was going to give Josie her driving lessons? I wanted to help her move on in life and have the independence to leave the village where she lived without relying on a sporadic bus service. I had volunteered to give her a few lessons to kick-start things. If I didn't take her out regularly I felt her resolve would waver.

It was thinking like this of course that had made me ill in the first place. I deluded myself that my help was indispensable, that without me, the whole thing would fall apart. Only I could keep everyone's lives on track. It was an arrogant presumption. I tried to fix everyone's problems, dispensing advice and support to Bella and Josie while pretending to the world that I was coping fine. I wanted to give, give, give, to show the world what a success I had made of my life when really I was the one in danger of going under. I thought about Bastian again. Bastian had a catchphrase, one that he called to me every time I was rushing round fixing things for the group.

"Take a little break, Carol, you deserve it."

I looked at the picture of the Holy Island of Lindisfarne again; it showed a wide and deserted beach. The two words "island" and "retreat" sang out to me – each word represented something I dearly wanted, to be cut off from the world and disappear from my daily life for a short while at least.

"I can get you some maps. I know a place you could stay," Roy prompted.

"OK," I said.

When I got home that evening, I found the photo of the island stuffed inside my bag – clearly Roy had slipped it there when I wasn't looking.

Still, I did nothing. Kirk loaded more work on, Bella and Josie stayed in my house, I ran myself in circles making sure every volunteer task ran smoothly and everyone enjoyed themselves, and my illness got worse. Finally, I psyched myself up to ask Kirk for one day a week working from home.

"Put it in writing," he said.

I did, and waited for a reply while Kirk piled more work onto me, making me feel that he wasn't listening to my request at all.

"I'm considering it," he told me when I pushed, but still I heard nothing.

Roy came into the office and waited until Kirk left for a meeting before sheepishly standing by my desk.

"I've brought in some things for you," he whispered so Gemima and Mel couldn't overhear, and then pulled from his bag maps of the Northumberland coast, bus timetables and a list of B&B numbers.

I wanted to cry.

I went to the doctor's feeling a fraud, like somehow I was play-acting in order to get time off. "I'm feeling a little stressed with work," I said and, much to my surprise, burst into tears. The tears shocked me – until that point I believed I was making a fuss about nothing and should just toughen up. After all, I was still functioning. Mind over matter was what I needed, but the tears were genuine. Crying in a doctor's office was so out of my comfort zone that I finally accepted I was running on empty and had to stop.

The doctor offered me three choices.

Antidepressants, which I didn't think I needed.

Counselling, "Although there is at least a six-month waiting list," she explained.

I walked out with option three: a sick certificate for two weeks.

It was an enormous relief for a medical professional to say to me, "You're not coping," – words I had struggled to tell myself. Now I had a piece of paper that gave me permission to fall apart. I could check out for a while. It was exactly what I wanted to do but, first, there were still things that needed to be done.

On Monday I arrived at the porta cabin an hour early. I went through the dozens of photos I had taken of the volunteer group over the last few years and selected ones to create a card for Bastian. I photocopied the sick certificate and put a copy on Kirk's desk and then put the out-of-office message on my emails.

I was just putting the final touches to Bastian's card when the boss walked in.

"Morning," he said and headed for his office.

I followed him. I had prepared a speech which I had practised in front of the bathroom mirror that morning. I planned to look resolute but calm as I explained my reasons for taking sick leave to Kirk. I opened my mouth, Kirk looked up and my heart leapt into my throat.

"I've been given a sick note from the doctor," I garbled, waving my hand in the direction of the note on his desk. "I'm finding the workload overwhelming. I tried to speak to you about it but you wouldn't listen."

Kirk looked flummoxed, as well he might when he had just walked in on a Monday morning to find a member of his staff had already gone into meltdown.

"You've never mentioned that you are finding the work too hard."

"I did mention it," I said.

"In my opinion the work is not too hard," Kirk countered.

"You continually deny that we are overworked and it is not helpful," I said. "Besides, the conditions in the office are awful." I swept my hand around the buckets and the stained carpet. "I can't bear another winter in this office. My doctor thinks it's partly the conditions here that are making me ill."

"Well I don't know what I can do about the office," he said. "We just can't afford anything else."

"I'm not prepared to work in these dangerous conditions any more. There is such a thing as an employer's duty-of-care," I blurted out, not really knowing what this was or how it worked. It sounded impressive though, and besides, the office conditions were something solid, and blaming my need for sick leave on them, instead of stress, made me sound less of a weak link.

Kirk looked a little pale.

"I'm going now," I said and walked out.

Outside, I sat in my Micra, my hands shaking. *What have I just done?* I thought. I was supposed to look professional and instead I'd acted like some mad confrontational woman. And what was all that stuff about the duty-of-care act? It was true, the conditions in the office were awful and the doctor *had* suggested that they could be causing the mystery sickness, but I hadn't intended to mention that. It sounded like I was giving some ultimatum: fix the office or I am leaving. Was I? I'd certainly thought about leaving, but I hadn't meant it to sound like I was resigning. I had just panicked as I didn't know how to talk about my feelings with a man who didn't seem to understand emotion.

"Well, it's done, Carol," I said aloud. "It can't be undone. Turn on the ignition and put your foot on the gas before the others appear."

I zoomed off down the country lane into town and, by the time I reached the hospital, I had calmed down.

Bastian had been transferred into hospital a few days before. It had only been a week since I had seen him last but the cancer had found its mark. He was diminished, a loose skeleton of a man, and even worse, he seemed visibly distressed at seeing me there. The cancer in his throat had robbed him of the ability to speak but it was obvious he was agitated by my visit, upset that I was seeing him like this, in his pyjamas, not at his best, not fit to be helpful and work. I felt I had done the wrong thing by coming, but I was there now and I couldn't just turn tail, not when his dad and sister looked so relieved that I had arrived to break up the long hours they had sat by his bedside.

A nurse brought in an extra chair and I sat down beside him. "I've brought you a card from the group," I told him, "and some pictures of us all together on our days out."

Bastian looked down at the pictures.

"Remember this one at the jolly, Bastian?" I said. "Remember how we saw the field of poppies and we all sat under the tree and drank the cordial I made? Do you remember how sweet Reuben liked his drink?"

He smiled and seemed to relax.

I went through each photo and talked about his favourite tasks, reminding him of all the good times.

"Thank you so much for coming," his sister said as I left. "He is missing the group very much."

The next day, Esther called to tell me Bastian had died. We all knew Bastian's cancer was terminal, it had become obvious not long after the diagnosis. On each visit to his house to drink tea we could see the change, the sudden loss of weight which hollowed out his jolly face and seemed almost to shrink the very essence of him. Even so his death was still a shock. He had looked terribly ill when I had visited him in hospital the previous day, but still very much alive. How could he be dead today, gone, no more Bastian in the world? I couldn't get my head around how things had changed so fast. One month, October, was all it took for cancer to eat away at this big man and kill him. Four weeks ago, Bastian had been out with the volunteers, ill, yes, but still Bastian; now he was dead. Cancer was a disease so powerful I was left quaking at its ability to destroy. In front of this disease, I felt tiny. Bastian was a humble man and it was his very humbleness that took him. He hadn't wanted to make a fuss, draw attention to himself, put his hand up and say, "I'm not feeling well." By the time anyone noticed, it was too late.

"His sister said he died looking at photos of the group," Esther said down the phone. "We've got to do something. Kirk has cancelled the task because you're on sick leave. He told everyone that you've got a bad back, but we must meet up and do something."

I felt the pressure load in again. I thought of my island retreat. I so, so wanted to turn my phone off and run away, but I was the group leader; even on sick leave, that was still my role. It was my responsibility, I felt, to lead the group in this thing that affected us all. I spent the day sending emails, phoning volunteers, making a plan to have a makeshift memorial service, and all the time I could hear Bastian's voice in my head.

"Take a little break, Carol, you deserve it."

Thursday came and the volunteers and I met in the car park by the river. It was a day when the damp filters into your bones and the sky bunches up, leaden and pregnant with rain. We were awkward with each other, standing in our smart clothes, caught between my meltdown and Bastian's death.

Roy took me to one side. "I won't tell a soul about your problem," he said. "I won't breathe a word of why you've really taken time off work."

I smiled, while inside I thought, *Tell them, Roy, please tell them. I want them to know that I am struggling but I can't tell them myself.*

Bastian's sister and dad arrived and we walked down the path to the spot where we had all spent the summer building the erosion barrier. The river was khaki coloured and swollen from the rains; not the sparkling, wagtail river of summer; now it ran bloated alongside the abandoned mill cottages, the banks overhung with the skeletal and mossy boughs of dead hawthorns. We walked beneath the old weeping willow, the trunk darkened by rain. The wasps were quiet now, tucked down inside, chewing on papery dreams in their winter slumber. The yellowing branches of the willow fountained out across the river like a Roman candle. We gathered at the start of the barrier; a few rain-darkened stakes rose up above the water surface but the rest was submerged. That was OK – beneath the water, the roots had begun to knit the soil in place, stabilising the bank.

The cold was burning my hands as I turned to face the group.

"Bastian was a man of great determination," I said. "Always positive, whatever task he was asked to do. He gave all that he had to the world."

"Yes," his dad said. "That was Bastian."

I told them how Bastian would send me a weekly email, telling me how to improve the tasks, which made them laugh. "What will I do without his amazing memory?" I said. "He never forgot a name. How will I know when you're all due a day out, if Bastian doesn't tell me?" I felt tears well up. *I should have been kinder to him,* I thought. I shouldn't have always made him rake. I should have noticed he was ill before that day beside the sea. Why did none of us notice? There must have been some sign I could have spotted. Maybe if I had, the cancer could have been caught quicker, he could have been treated, he could still have been here. I knew it wasn't true. There had been no sign. Bastian was robust and well and then he wasn't. No one had noticed.

We cracked open the bottle of wine the river had sent us.

"To Bastian," we all said, and we raised a toast.

We tossed the last glass of wine into the river. It mixed into the water and slipped away, past the tangled roots of ash trees, clinging to the banks, down over the weir where the river bubbled, under bridges, past the marshes, past kingfishers and herons, into the city, where Bastian had spent his life. Filtering through the driftwood it travelled on, where beavers swam and egret fished, and out to sea. An offering for one of our own. An offering to the boatman for safe passage.

Afterwards we headed to the village hall, where the farmers' market was in full swing, and someone bought tea and someone bought cake.

"You did well," Jim said. It meant something to me, Jim's praise, it always did, but the day had taken more out of me than I could admit.

A few days later I took Roy's advice. I packed my bags, closed my front door, turned my phone off and drove to Holy Island.

CHAPTER
ELEVEN

It was late when I arrived, gone 10 p.m. I sat in the car looking out at the dark causeway that led to the island, trying to judge if it was safe to cross. There was nothing to be seen, only the blackness and a strip of Tarmac heading out to the water's edge. My mind was addled from the 10-hour drive up north. Curlews flew low across the road, briefly illuminated by my headlights before vanishing back into the pooling darkness. I drove across the mudflats and entered the village, but I had lost my bearings.

In the days before my departure, my two weeks of sick leave seemed to take on a life of their own. Kirk's boss had phoned me at home on Friday night after Bastian's memorial. I had taken the sick leave to give myself a break from the pressure of work, yet now it felt that work was forcing its way into my home, into my evening. It didn't feel right. I had only met this woman a couple of times when she arrived for a board members' meeting which, unsurprisingly, was held somewhere other than the dilapidated porta cabin. To the best of my memory she had never directly spoken to me but, from appearances, she didn't look like someone who would be sympathetic. Still, I was surprised at her tone.

"You have to come into head office for a hearing on Monday," she barked down the phone. "You must sign a risk assessment immediately."

"Why?" I asked.

"It's not a choice," she snapped. "If you don't sign the risk assessment it will be a case for a performance review."

A performance review? I thought, my stress levels rocketing. This was getting out of hand. What had I done to deserve that? My work was good. Years later, I learned that there are certain words that you don't say to your employer, unless you are prepared to follow through. Claim you are the victim of sexism, racism, bullying or discrimination of any kind and all hell breaks loose. Organisations are so scared of the repercussions they will go into overdrive and declare you unfit to work in order to shut you up. It seemed that "duty of care" was one of those expressions.

"You must read the risk assessment for the office and sign to say you understand the risks."

"But the office conditions are unsafe," I said bravely. "I think we should be allowed to work in a safe place or at home some of the time until they are rectified."

"You can't work from home," she almost shouted down the phone at me. "There is a business need for you to work from that office and you knew the conditions when you went to the interview and accepted them. Now you must sign to say you accept them."

But I don't, I thought. I don't accept mouse droppings in the coffee cups, or water dripping on the electrics. I don't accept fungus sprouting on the carpets or mould on the walls or an outside toilet you can't flush in winter because the water has frozen in the cistern.

I got off the phone, feeling shaken. I didn't want things to escalate, but my mentioning duty of care seemed to have lit a touchpaper that was burning out of my control. Later that evening I found myself reviewing environmental health websites and the law around whistle-blowing. The more I read, the more I felt justified in saying my working conditions were unacceptable and something should be done to make them safe, but this hadn't been my intention. I had just wanted to take some time out to recover from overload. However, I was not prepared to sign away my safety. I emailed Kay. Kay had left the volunteers a year ago to return to full-time work as a solicitor and I was beginning to feel that legal advice might be useful.

"The conditions in that office are horrendous. I've seen that for myself," she said. "I think you have a good case for asking to work elsewhere but it's not really my field. Let me ask around my colleagues and see if we can get you some help. Don't go to the hearing or answer any more calls from them before I come back to you."

I sent Kirk's boss an email. "I wish to take further advice before signing anything," I wrote and then scarpered.

Why had I got myself into this pickle again? I can count on one hand, well actually two fingers, the amount of times I have left a job with the conventional send-off of best wishes and a leaving gift. Now I had somehow become entrenched in a stand-off, from which the likely outcome, it seemed, was the sack, or a lawsuit, or probably both. In my twenties I seemed to be forever burning my bridges by taking some moral stand. It had been easy then to leave a job on a point of principle, do some creative CV work to hide the error and get another job in another part of the country a few weeks later. But I didn't wish to be that person now. My career was important to me. I had worked hard to do good work. I loved the volunteers, I cared about my job. I didn't want to leave, at least not this way. I owed myself more than that.

I was too tired to think of it any more. I drove through the darkened village on Holy Island, half of me already asleep and the other half still just about functioning. The directions had said to head to the priory but I had no idea where that was. The place seemed a ghost town, the only sign that life existed was the wood smoke hanging in the icy November air. Just as it seemed I would have to give up and sleep in the car, I saw a sign, the Open Gate Retreat. It was warm, it was bright, and two young, enthusiastic people met me at the door and showed me my room. I fell into my bed and slept.

The next morning I found myself having breakfast with a vicar. The accommodation was part of a Christian retreat centre.

"It can be cut off for days if the tides are high," Roy had warned.

Fine by me. My mobile showed no bars and I didn't ask for the Wi-Fi code. I hadn't come here to communicate. I excused myself from all possible social activities. The good thing about places like the Open Gate is that they are used to having people turn up who are on the run from something in their lives; who arrive looking frazzled and wide eyed, and they don't ask questions. They are there if you want to talk but, if you don't, it is OK to be by yourself. It was good for me, new for me, this not being polite. I had become good at looking in control, confident, upbeat and available for everyone else to lean on, but now I felt in need of turning off the smile and the chat and just being me – the other me, the one who was maybe a little quieter and more introspective than I first appeared. This was the me that I gave myself permission to be on Holy Island.

Tourists came to view the ruins of the priory created by St Aidan, to gaze at St Cuthbert's Island off the coast, to visit the Gertrude Jekyll garden and the castle, and to buy mead. The tourists were there the next morning, queueing on the causeway, stressing over parking spaces. They headed for a stroll around the village and rarely ventured further afield, fearful of being caught out by the incoming tide. Luckily for me, this meant that, when I walked out of the retreat centre after breakfast, I had the majority of the island to myself.

I had picked up a guided walk leaflet at the centre: *A Holy Wander*, the title read. Along with directions, it offered suggestions to use the island landscape to evaluate where you were in your own life. Clearly the people who wrote it understood that people came to a place like this for precisely this reason. *Don't know which way to turn in life?* the authors of the walk guide seemed to imply, *Then cast off to an island, view things from a distance. Maybe the answer will come.* Considering my current state of mind, it felt appropriate.

I set off from the village, through the dunes. The path headed through an abandoned hamlet. The guide suggested I should stand in the doorway of one of the old houses and think about whether it was time to step out from security to a new direction in my own life. I hadn't taken the sick leave intending to leave my job but, now Kirk's boss had come down so hard, I felt pushed into a corner. Did I really want to go back? Maybe this was the time to leave the security of this job and go freelance. After all, I was sick of Kirk making all the decisions, and of being told what to do. I was no good at being a cog in the machine, I wanted autonomy. I loved having a job that allowed me so much time outside and, as it turned out, I loved the practical physicality of the volunteer tasks, but on the other hand, the work could be exhausting and the commute took hours. I stood in the doorway, trying to feel which direction to step out in. It was impossible, I had only just arrived, the island had yet to work its magic. I walked on, through the dunes to the North Shore.

Surf rolled lazily onto the beach. Eider ducks, freshly arrived from their Arctic breeding grounds, rose and fell among the breakers. A seal checked me out from a safe distance, out-staring me with large, liquid eyes before performing a graceful descent beneath the waves, nose and whiskers held skyward. I walked and sat, watched the waves roll in, felt the calm of the island descend. I looked at the guided walk leaflet again. "During life there are many partings," it said. "These can be painful but, without leaving one place, finalising a situation, or letting go of a particular person, we may not be able to freely move on. Are you tied in unhelpful ways?" The guide asked, "Are there people you need to leave behind in order to walk into the next part of your life?"

Laurie sprang to mind. I hadn't been in touch with him in ages, but I still thought of him. Despite my efforts at the speed dating, no one new had come into my life that I felt the same way about. He was still the most interesting person I had met since the break-up but, if I didn't close that door on Laurie, then maybe they never would. I had the bottle top from the evening by the river with Laurie in my bag. It was just a bottle top with a dent in it where he had popped it off with the opener, but I had found it in my bag months after he'd vanished. It had been tucked in a split in the lining, and I had kept it there. Why? It was rubbish, really, but I couldn't quite throw away this memento of a beautiful evening as if it meant nothing, so it had stayed in the bag, which I had brought to the island with me.

I rounded the corner, and tucked away in the lea of the dunes was a little hut built of stones, with a roof made of driftwood. Laurie would have loved it. Inside the crevices of the hut, visitors had left behind mementos found on the beach or little offerings to whatever god they had found. Notes were stuffed into cracks and written down in a book, faded with salt spray.

I sat down on the little driftwood bench inside the hut and poured a drink from my flask. Outside, oystercatchers made their way up the tideline and the wind whipped the sand into dust devils but

I felt cocooned, miles from all the stresses and responsibilities of home. Here there was only me and I felt pretty proud of myself. I was the kind of woman who could jump in her ancient car and drive for 10 hours to stay in a retreat on an island. Some people would have thought me peculiar but I didn't feel lonely or scared or bored or in need of a companion. At that moment I felt a huge buzz at being an independent woman who didn't have to answer to anyone.

I pulled the bottle top out from the lining of the bag and thought of that beautiful evening by the river. I knew that, for all the rest of my days, I would be glad that I had spent that night with him but, if I was ever to reach another beautiful evening with a man by a river, then I needed to let it go. I pushed the bottle top into a crack between the rocks and walked away.

I'm leaving you behind, I thought, *I'm leaving you behind.* I repeated the mantra to cement the intention in my mind. I didn't look back. I crossed over a headland into another bay. I was leaving Laurie behind on Holy Island, a place where a precious thing could be sheltered. That felt OK.

The following morning, I was up early and heading back across the causeway to walk the Pilgrim's Way, following a set of wooden markers which led across the wide sands of the estuary. It had been the traditional route for pilgrims in the days before the causeway and cars. I felt slightly silly stepping off the road and plodding to the first marker. After all, this wasn't summer, when thousands of tourists head across the sands as a jolly holiday thing to do. This was November and I was a solitary walker on the route. I looked serious about this stuff.

Once out on the estuary I was glad I had made the effort. Skeins of geese drifted across the horizon, sounding like the approach of a thousand crazed cyclists with squeaky wheels, and the hopeful light of the morning painted a thin veneer across the wet sands. I reached the first of the refuge boxes, built to provide a safe haven for those who had failed to read the tide timetable and found themselves about to meet their maker in an altogether more graphic sense than they had bargained for as the tide came racing in.

I climbed the rickety wooden ladder into the box and looked out over the expanse of mud and water. Today's walk guide talked about places of sanctuary. For me, sanctuary was College Lake and Graham. It was the place I always ran to for shelter, but this time I hadn't, as Graham's health wasn't good. Though this time I had chosen the island for my escape, Graham was still a beacon. *What would he do?* I thought. Graham was a practical man. I didn't think he would advise me to chuck in the towel and quit, however tempting that might be. He kept negotiating with the Wildlife Trusts for the future of College Lake, no matter how much he disagreed with aspects of their vision for the reserve. He still attempted to find a middle ground, but he was no pushover either – if people didn't appreciate him I suspected he would have cut his losses and taken his talents elsewhere. This time my decision affected more than just me, though.

Beneath the Open Gate Retreat there was a chapel. It was a simple, quiet place in which to think. I had gone there that morning to light a candle for Bastian, and had been surprised to find a little statue of a group of people holding hands around the space where the candle should go. It reminded me of the volunteers and me standing around a winter bonfire. Over the last few years the volunteers had also become a place of sanctuary to me. A safe place where I could be most myself. When I pulled up in the car park every Thursday to meet them for the day's task, I knew I was arriving in a place where I was known and liked for who I was and was among people who cared about me.

Standing in the refuge box, I thought about the volunteers. Tomorrow was a Thursday: what were they going to do, my gang? Would they meet without me? Go for a wander of their own, perhaps? Some of them, maybe, but others would stay at home, wishing there was a task to go to, thinking about me, of that I was sure. I hated doing this to them; it felt selfish, it felt like throwing all their kindness and friendship back at them. I had received messages from many of them on the journey north. "How are you feeling?" "Are you OK?" Others maybe sensed that there was something else going on that I hadn't explained. "We're all behind you," Bruno said, "but stay calm, keep your temper." Bruno was a sensible man of few words, and it was advice I knew I needed to take on board.

If I left the job, then what? Kirk would find a replacement but it wouldn't be the same. The group needed the right elements to live: take an element out and we would lose our way a little. I wasn't irreplaceable, the group had existed before me and it would be there afterwards, but something would be lost, that moment, that feeling would be lost. Things changed, but not like this, not with all this drama and bad feeling. The story couldn't just end with me crashing out with stress.

I was also no good at being sick. I never had been. It was OK to retreat from the world for a day or two, but I soon got bored. I realised I was itching to get back to the volunteers, back to leading the tasks. I loved my job, and making the tea on a sunny hillside as the others gossiped around me, watching the last embers of a bonfire on a winter's day, experiencing the joy of being outside in sharp weather, laughing till I cried as I spun round in a boat on the river while trying to pick Himalayan balsam, I would realise how much I loved it. This was joy, this was life, this was as good as the world got. But the thought of returning to the office, to the filth and overloaded in-tray just made me feel weighed down. I didn't have all the answers, up there on the pilgrims' refuge box, but I had one: I wanted to do right by the volunteers. I knew that for sure.

My car was covered in sand by the time I drove back down the motorway. It felt like a coating of Holy Island, a little layer of protection to help deal with what lay ahead. Halfway home, while parked in a service station trying to catch forty winks, I received a call from a solicitor in Kay's firm. He gave it to me straight.

"You will need to issue a formal grievance against the conditions in the office," he said. "Ask for a grievance hearing and say that you wish to work elsewhere until the health and safety of the office is improved. If they refuse, you have a case for constructive dismissal. You need to think carefully about this route." I tried to take in everything he was saying. "I am confident you would win but I think you would only get around four thousand pounds in damages and you would have to pay your legal costs."

I thanked him for his advice. It made me feel justified in complaining about the conditions and it gave me a clear path to follow should I wish to go down it, plus a realistic assessment of the outcome of taking matters further. I spent the weekend at my parents' and got home on Sunday night to find a letter from Kirk's boss, telling me I was to attend a performance review the following Thursday. It was ridiculously heavy-handed considering my sick leave was only for two weeks. My stress levels shot up again.

I called Graham.

"I'm not sure I'm the best one to give advice on keeping a level head with authority," he said. "I've just had a row with the Wildlife Trusts about College Lake."

I knew what this was about. The Wildlife Trusts were changing things at College Lake. They wished to commercialise the reserve. The rustic world and quirky humour of the place didn't fit with the Trusts' professional image. Graham's ancient farm machinery had been declared unsafe, his chickens and guinea pigs unnecessary, his DIY hides too scruffy. They wanted it all gone. I was saddened over the loss of this little world that meant so much to me, Graham and his other volunteers. I also felt relief that I was not the only one in a tussle with authority. It made me feel justified in standing up for myself.

Graham and I were similar characters. Neither of us were good at being told what to do by people who hadn't earned our respect, but Graham's advice I did value. He was a man with vision who wanted to do things his own way, but Graham was also about 30 years older than me. He had learned to better manage his own fiery temperament and be practical.

"They sound like idiots if they don't appreciate what a good worker you are and accommodate you, but even so, I think you need to find a way of reconciliation. You like this job so don't be forced out by this. Don't chuck in the towel; you've come too far," he said. "If you want to go freelance then that's fine, but do it in your own time. Go back, be as charming as I know you can be, make a plan. Don't resign."

It wasn't what I wanted to hear. Fireworks I could do, a middle way was a lot tougher.

"I can't go back to that awful office with no change," I said.

"Then don't," he said. "Ask for change."

After I put the phone down, I got in the car and drove on autopilot. I needed to think and I couldn't do that within concrete walls.

I found myself at the RSPB reserve, where I had lived in a caravan under the willow tree. Why there? Because, in many ways, it was still home. More than that, it was the last place my life had been stable before the rug got pulled out from under me by the redundancy and the ex's departure. Sometimes going back to the beginning is useful to show you where you've come from. I parked the car outside the locked gates and climbed the stile.

The reserve had changed since I had left. The farmhouse where the wardens, Gordon and Mike, had lived was now occupied by interns. The rooms were clean and freshly painted and the interns were watching the telly as I crossed in front of the house and made for the reserve. Light spilled out from the farmhouse kitchen. I heard the bang of a door and froze. Here I was again, being weird, not normal. Did other women do this, wander across darkened reserves at night, in meltdown? I suspected not.

Away on the marshes, the geese called, lighting up the sky with noise. I walked the familiar path, hoping not to break an ankle in a rabbit hole. Planes and satellites criss-crossed the sky as I reached the hilltop, and I sensed the expanse of the marsh rather than saw it. Widgeons whistled down below. I sat on the bench but it was too cold to think, ice in the wind and in my blood. I returned to the relative warmth of the Micra and stared out into the blackness. The three points of Orion's Belt appeared slowly above the silos, next to where my caravan had once sat. My brain was fogged with cold and nervous exhaustion, but it is in that white place where your mind can become clear and the answers sometimes come.

Graham was right, of course. I had to be sensible. I couldn't just leave my job with no plan, and hadn't I been here before? Why had I come back to this place? Because here things had gone wrong, too, and I had reached that moment when I had wanted to tell them all to go to hell and leave, but I hadn't. Here I had stayed and worked things out. Here I had not flounced out, but found a way through. Here I had grown up, hadn't I? I was proud of having left the RSPB with a good reputation. It was the one thing I had been determined to achieve, leave cleanly without the mess of my previous jobs. What had I done differently at the RSPB? What could I do now?

Be careful, Carol, I told myself. *If you're not careful you will find yourself back sitting on that pillbox, with no work and no money. You could end up on the dole and missing your friends. Things could be a lot worse than they are now, you know that. Graham was right, I loved parts of the job. You can't leave a job you love because the office is cold and dark,* I told myself. What had Graham said? "Ask for change." *Maybe,* I thought, *some of the problems in the office could be fixed, a few outside lights, some better heaters, with timers that could turn on automatically before we arrived. Some rodent control would be good.* I was thinking clearly now, not panicking but formulating a workable plan. *What about the ridiculous workload?* my mind argued. *Well,* I thought, *maybe we can compromise on that too.* I could suggest getting a volunteer in to help, someone who was keen, who would provide another friendly face in the office on the days Roy wasn't in.

I began to see that the situation was not impossible. Maybe I could do the unthinkable, back down. No, not back down, but compromise. I could do that. *This could work,* I thought, *at least for now.* I would go back, bide my time. The truth was, if I left now, there was no plan – £4,000 would not last long, I needed a regular income. It didn't mean I would stay forever and, ultimately, if I wanted to go freelance that was fine, but I would do it properly, not just jump and hope for the best like last time. This time I needed to think it through, make contacts, look at those figures and only do it when I felt ready.

The next day I went to the doctor's to extend my sick leave and the following Thursday I attended the performance review with Kirk's boss and a woman from the occupational-health team, and asked for one day a week working from home and for the office conditions to be improved before I returned to work.

"The working conditions are perfectly acceptable," Kirk's boss said. "And you can't work from home as you need to be in the office to answer the phone and take deliveries."

I pulled a folder from my bag and laid the photos I had taken of the office on the table. They clearly showed the flies, mouse droppings, damp and mould, buckets balanced on top of photocopiers, pools of water on the carpet and the collapsed ceiling in my office with water pouring in. Kirk's boss went the colour of a ripe tomato and the woman from occupational health looked at her sternly.

"I'm not asking for too much," I told her, "but if I don't get it I will see you in court."

One week later I returned to work, where I found a surprising ally.

"I'm so glad you're back," Kirk said, and he meant it. He showed me the new heaters which had been installed. "I've set the timers to go on for an hour before we arrive," he said. "It's much better. I don't know why we didn't do it before."

I was amazed by his sudden change of manner. Before Kirk had been haughty and unapproachable; now he was friendly, understanding and keen to please. If only he had been like this before, it would have been so much easier to sit down and talk over my worries calmly, but instead I had felt that any attempt to discuss how the workload was making me feel had been rebuffed, causing me to store up my feelings until they had exploded.

He showed me the electric light in the kitchen and the torch he had bought so I could see my way across the site at night. "We've got a company doing rodent control," he said, "and I thought Friday would be the best day for you to work from home. If that suits you?" he asked.

We sat down and went through my to-do list.

"I can do some of these," he said to my amazement.

"Right," I said, "thanks." The change in his attitude was both gratifying and annoying. *Why*, I thought, *why couldn't you have been this way before? It would have saved us both so much stress.*

With Kirk it seemed you had to sledgehammer him over the head with your needs to make him pay attention. Kirk was to be commended for keeping the project afloat in difficult financial times and often found us really interesting projects to work on, but when it came to people-management skills he had often appeared unapproachable, patronising and controlling. Even in meetings with people from outside organisations he often said things that caused offence. I had begun to suspect that some of this was unintentional. He just didn't seem to appreciate how his comments could come across. The thing was that sometimes, just sometimes, Kirk surprised me. It was as though, if you shouted loudly enough, he suddenly got the message. It had taken walking out and threatening a lawsuit to do it but now he was listening. I hoped it would last but was sceptical that it would.

The following Thursday I headed out with the volunteers to plant apple trees in the streets around the city.

Bella handed me a pickaxe. "Take it out on the soil if you're feeling frustrated," she said. "I find it good stress relief these days."

We took it in turns to whack the mattock into the rock-hard earth. I laughed a lot. Val had baked a cake for my return. Roy gave my arm a squeeze. I was back.

Another winter of bonfires rolled on. Conditions in the office were far from perfect but at least for now it was warmer and drier with fewer rodents. The one day working from home was a huge help for dealing with the exhaustion of running the volunteer tasks and Kirk, true to his word, found me volunteer assistants. Firstly, a funny, irreverent guy called Danny appeared. He was clever, opinionated and hoping to get a job in nature conservation. Later, when he moved on, he was replaced by Hayley, a bright woman, just returned from travelling in the Far East, who was a great worker. Their presence helped enormously, not just by lightening the workload but because they provided friendship and support. Now there was someone in the office to laugh with, talk over the work with and roll my eyes at when Kirk came out with annoying comments, which he invariably still did. They helped put the world of the Kingsdown Partnership into perspective.

That winter my personal life moved on, too. My belly dancing class had suddenly packed up after the teacher became pregnant, so instead I learned the Argentine Tango, something I had long wanted to try. I loved the glamour of a week night in high heels with painted nails, in sharp contrast to the day job where I seemed to live permanently in soggy trouser bottoms with dirt-ingrained hands.

At the class I met people whose lives were very different from my own. Conservation is still a very white, middle-class profession and now I was meeting people from all over the world with day jobs I didn't understand. I met men. I flirted with men, men with foreign accents and aftershave, men with extravagant trousers and dance shoes. Suddenly I was getting asked out on dates in the real world by men that I got to meet for more than 3 minutes. I started dating a man who I met in the class. He seemed so very different to anyone I would have imagined dating. He was from a different ethnic background, he drove a flash car, he played golf. It wasn't meant to last, but that wasn't the point. He was what I was ready for. He took me to restaurants and spa retreats, he made me laugh, he celebrated our difference as something positive and exciting. He took charge and kissed me so effortlessly on our first date, turning the page on Laurie. When it ended I was briefly sad, but glad that it had happened.

Life was moving on.

CHAPTER
TWELVE

Time passed. The porta cabin at Greengate Farm deteriorated further, and eventually Kirk's boss admitted we could be housed there no longer and we moved to a soulless office on the outskirts of town. I was grateful to be working somewhere safe and dry but I missed the rolling views of the downs and the drive through the woods to work. Gemima and Mel were furious that the new arrangements meant that they could no longer take their dogs to work but really, within weeks of us leaving, the porta cabin began to sag and collapse without Roy's constant attention. The change of address made little difference to my Thursday morning routine, as the tools and the volunteers' tea things were still housed in the leaky old kitchen and tool shed, and I still visited Greengate Farm to load and unload everything each task day.

As my time signed off with stress became a distant memory, Kirk returned to his old nitpicking and critical ways, but the presence of Danny and later Hayley, my volunteer assistants, really helped me keep these comments in perspective. However, when Hayley left for a new job, I wondered where I was going to find another helper. That's when Kit appeared.

Kit walked across the car park one autumn morning, long black hair falling across his eyes. He appeared to be dressed for a morning pheasant shooting. He was wearing a long waxed jacket and a flat tweed cap, and his dark beard and moustache were neatly trimmed. I bounced out of the minibus driver's seat.

"Hello, hello," I called to the assembled gang. "Climb in. You must be Kit, my new recruit." I held out my hand. The young man looked a bit shocked at my direct approach and seemed to shake hands without thinking, before recovering his air of cool indifference.

He climbed into the front seat of the minibus and, as he sat there staring out of the window, he appeared to want to distance himself from the others. In Kit I felt the shadow of Laurie – he seemed angry at the world and had pulled up the drawbridge to keep people at bay, but those barriers weren't going to stay in place for long with me. On the journey out to that day's worksite I pummelled Kit with questions that must have made Bevan proud. By the end of the journey, I had discovered that Kit was living with his brother who was at university, had not long since finished a diploma in countryside management, and had come to the area hoping to get a place as a trainee with the local Wildlife Trust.

"I didn't get the placement," he said angrily. "They asked stupid questions and they didn't know what they were on about."

"I know who got that placement," I said. "He is a man mountain, about fifty and a former gamekeeper. They probably just took one look at him, all that life experience, and couldn't say no. You probably did fine."

He looked at me sullenly.

"They said I was second choice. What use is it telling me that?"

"Well I can't offer you a paid placement," I said. "The Partnership doesn't have the money for that kind of thing, but if you want some experience I could offer you a volunteer role as my assistant. It would mean coming into the office and helping with surveys and planning projects. Do you fancy that?"

He looked at me. There were so many things going on in that look that I couldn't begin to pick them apart.

"Yes, OK," he said finally. "Thanks."

The task that day was to cut scrub back on the same hillside where I had installed that ill-fated kissing gate years before. The habitat had changed since then; a reduction in grazing had allowed the blackthorn to reclaim the land and the flower-rich grassland we had enjoyed that summer had been lost. In a bid to remove the blackthorn quickly, the Wildlife Trusts had brought in a machine which chewed up and spat out the blackthorn bushes as a rich mulch, which had covered all the delicate grassland flowers and through which only hardy thistles and docks could grow. After realising their error we had been called back in to hand cut the scrub once more.

As I drove down the country lane, the maple leaves were brimstone bright on the wet Tarmac. This time I had all the necessary keys for the car park and we swung through the barriers into one of the abandoned parking bays. The site hadn't got any prettier in our absence: old fridges, long dumped and rusting, were bunched up around the edge of the car park, and the buzz of pylons crackled overhead, but still the site felt like a secret place, one where few people ventured.

We climbed the muddy and pony-printed track up through the brambles, pushing the wheelbarrow, laden with tools, ahead of us. Robins sang tenuously, unsure, as yet, of their territory. The path opened out and we emerged at the top of the hill with the sea cast down below us. There was Laurie's tree, the one he had sculpted into topiary. The haircut he had given it had grown a little wilder, but still it retained its basic shape, symmetrical, pleasingly round. All around it the scrub had been removed but, somehow, this one tree remained, as if Laurie had cast a spell of protection around it. It was his topiary clipping, I'm sure, which had saved it.

We began the slow work of cutting our way through the blackthorn while Roy and Meg set to work on the bonfire. Meg cut the branches into even lengths and stacked them carefully while Roy flapped away with his trademark trusty biscuit-tin lid at the base.

"Never mind that," Jim said, chucking a huge pile of bramble on top of the fire. "Pile it all on. It will burn."

Meg looked a little miffed as her neat pile vanished beneath a voluminous mountain of vegetation. As the flames engulfed the briars, eyelashes and eyebrows singed in the heat and rose hips glowed bonny bright in the hedgerows.

I wandered over to see how our other recent recruit was doing. Jack was only 22, but his email had struck a chord. "I've been struggling with chronic fatigue syndrome for years," it read, "I'm feeling better and would like to come out on some tasks to try out my strength and see what I can manage." I sympathised – I still struggled with the mystery illness, which some days left me too tired to even get out of bed. There were other days when I managed to get to the task but then found that the most I could do was to lie on the grass, while the volunteers worked around me, preserving my energy for the drive back to the farm and the offloading of tools.

Jack had been lucky to get a spot on the group – back at the office I had a waiting list of people wanting a place. I had long ago decided that 16 people was the most I could effectively manage at once. Any more and people would be struggling to get a space on the minibus and, once on site, would be standing around twiddling their thumbs for lack of work or fighting for tools or space, which was the way accidents could happen.

Every week people contacted me asking if they could join but, as hardly anyone left, spaces were limited. I had taken the decision that, instead of slotting in whoever was at the top of the waiting list, I would give the spot to someone who would maintain the balance between men and women, young people and older members. I hadn't asked Kirk's permission to do this; I presumed that he would have refused to let me limit numbers and, besides, I had long ago decided that, when it came to the group, I would do what I thought right. The balance between ages, I felt, gave the group energy and just a little more diversity than your typical wildlife-conservation volunteer group, although we were still a long way from being a melting pot of ethnicity or class.

If I'm honest then, in some ways the group had become my own little kingdom. Hopefully not in the sense that I had become a dictator, but more that I was proud of helping to shape a community that reflected my values. I was proud of how we, as a family, had helped people. I knew what the group had done for my own confidence and I wanted to give the same opportunity to someone else who really needed it. So, when Jack got in touch and explained why he needed the group, he jumped to the top of the queue.

However, it quickly transpired that Jack was no lover of conservation work.

"How are you enjoying the task?" I had asked him a few weeks after he began.

"I find the work boring," he said, without apology, "but it's useful for helping me monitor my progress."

I laughed out loud. "Well, I'm glad you're getting something out of it," I said.

That was the most conversation I got out of Jack during those first weeks. He was morose, sad in a way no 22-year-old should be. I worked hard to wring a smile from him, hamming it up and prancing around him like a clown; the slightest upward curl of his mouth was reward enough.

Today, though, he looked almost happy. He had managed to cycle to the site from the station and had begun to show a little interest in why we were doing the work. That morning I had demonstrated a felling cut, a little cheese wedge sawn out low down on the trunk, to allow the tree to fall in the direction you wanted. I could see Jack was now working hard to saw through a fair-sized tree trunk, sweating, despite the cold. The tree fell neatly with a satisfying rustle.

"Great work," I said.

Jack actually beamed at me before sitting back, exhausted.

"Time for a cuppa, I think," I said.

Rain was coming in, sheeting grey across the hills. We sheltered in the lee of a blackthorn clump while I went through the ritual of putting together the 16 individual orders for tea and coffee. I didn't need to ask the group what they wanted, by now I knew their special requests by heart; Bevan, blue mug, Josie, black coffee, Jim, don't squish the teabag, dolloping Reuben's sugar in with the company spoon as Trevor called it because it was the only one that remained after Alex had pilfered the rest. Jack hung around.

"I wasn't like this before," he said suddenly.

"Before?" I questioned, looking up.

"Before the chronic fatigue. I played football, I was good and then, at fifteen, I started to get ill. Some days I can do nothing but sleep and my brain feels fogged."

This sounded worryingly familiar to me. "What did it feel like?" I asked. "At the outset?"

"Like you're coming down with flu," he said, "repeatedly coming down with flu that never turns into anything."

That was exactly how I felt but, if my mystery illness was chronic fatigue, I was one of the lucky ones. My illness could stop me in my tracks, forcing me to cancel an outing or let down a friend, but a few weeks of taking it easy and I bounced back. Jack it seemed, hadn't bounced back.

I handed him a cup of tea.

"I got worse and worse," he said, "until I couldn't get out of bed. I lay in bed for five years."

We both sipped our tea as the lost years settled on us.

"I can't seem to go back," he said. "I'm feeling better physically but this illness, it robbed me of my personality. I've become much more serious."

"That's a tough break," I said slowly. "How do you manage the illness now?"

Jack straightened. "You've got to pace yourself, look forward, have good times up ahead." He rolled through the words, like he said them often, like a mantra, a recipe to live by. I understood that too. He was old beyond his 22 years.

"The illness took something from you," I said, "but maybe it gave you something else."

"Like what?" he said.

"I don't know," I said, "maturity? A depth of understanding? It might not seem like a fair trade but maybe you've got qualities now that you wouldn't have developed without the illness."

Jack took a slurp of his drink and gazed down at the dregs thoughtfully. "Maybe," he said. "I'm thinking of signing up to college to do physio, sports physio."

"Sounds like a good plan." I clapped him on the shoulder. "Come on," I said. "Let's call a break before the others' tea gets cold."

Jack smiled again and, despite the greyness of the day, the sun came out.

Kit was trickier to please. I found him, later that afternoon, standing over Jack, who was kneeling at the base of another tree.

"This is all wrong," he was saying. "We shouldn't be coppicing the trees in this landscape. We should be pollarding them."

Jack was looking confused. Kit, I noticed, had cut the trees at shoulder height, leaving a little grove of tall stumps. I went across.

"Why do you think we should be pollarding them?" I asked benignly.

Kit flushed and glared at me. "It's like parkland here, not a woodland," he said defensively. He pointed at Laurie's tree. "We should be aiming for trees that look like that. A tree on its own with character. That's why I am doing mine differently."

He was well spoken, I noticed, and his accent became just that little bit more clipped when under pressure.

"And," he added as if he was teaching me the basics, "pollarding prolongs the life of the tree."

I felt a sudden wave of tiredness. I had been working in conservation for 15 years. I wasn't the world's greatest naturalist but I had learned a thing or two. *Was this the way of the future?* I thought. *Young people keen to prove themselves, snapping at your heels and thinking they could do it better?* It had begun to seep in a little lately, this tiredness. When the volunteers moaned because their tea break was late or they had missed the pick-up and wanted me to come back for them or felt they could manage the task better than me.

I looked at Kit. He seemed angry, as if he really wanted me to argue this point with him. It was the same way Laurie had wanted to confront people when he had first joined the group. I knew that if Kit gave the group a chance, it could make life a little less jagged for him too. I had seen it work with Laurie and Bella and Josie and me. The group was big enough and the space we worked in was large enough that it could accept all manner of human quirks. *Give it a chance,* I wanted to say to Kit. *Just chop trees, drink tea, be polite, no one's going to ask any more from you here.* But you can't tell young men, or women for that matter, these things. They just had to keep coming and it would creep into them by osmosis. However, I also knew by now that I didn't need to argue over scrub cutting. I'd earned my stripes and had nothing to prove. I looked back across at Laurie's hawthorn tree. Maybe we didn't all have to do it uniformly. Maybe on a whole hillside of trees we could tolerate a little difference.

"Pollarding is a great idea in the right setting," I said calmly. "You're right, it works really well for parkland and that one tree is distinctive, so maybe it's fine to have some that are a bit different. Why don't you leave the ones that you've already done at that height. Ultimately, though," I said, "we are not aiming at a parkland landscape here. Maybe I didn't explain things correctly. We want to get the trees down to the ground so the livestock can graze them. We want to suppress the trees to benefit the grassland, not preserve them for the future."

Kit shrugged. "Whatever you think best," he said and walked off.

I left him alone to work off his frustrations. Scrub cutting was good for that. Secretly want to batter the leader? Well, that's OK, just take it out on the blackthorn. *He's a funny fish,* I thought, as I watched him bashing a stump with the axe he carried at his belt, another well-brought-up, probably well-educated young man, angry at the world with a story on his tailcoat so heavy it was dragging him backwards.

How did he become this way? I had noticed over the years that the young adults from rather good backgrounds often struggled to live up to their expectations of what life should be like. Josie had recently started a conservation course at agricultural college. She was excelling in every test but her moods still pinballed up and down. A setback was a crisis, an A– on a report was a disaster which made her want to quit. We could all see the progress she was making; she was back in education, she was making friends with people at college, she had come so very far from the silent, socially isolated woman who rarely left her bedroom. *Look back, Josie,* I wanted to say, *Look down from this new height and see how far you've climbed.* But still she would berate herself.

"I'm terrible," she'd cry if she didn't get top grades on every exam.

"But you're not," I'd say. "You're doing fine. No one knows it all immediately."

"I'm just no good," she said stubbornly. "I don't know if I want to continue."

I felt frustrated at how down on herself she was determined to be.

"Josie, everything that is worth having in life takes time to do well. It doesn't just happen. You have to work at it," I'd say.

Kit also seemed to feel a failure because he hadn't been offered a much sought-after apprenticeship at the first time of trying. If you set unrealistically high standards for yourself, maybe you'll take it hard when life falls short of those expectations.

A 2019 article by Anne Helen Petersen in BuzzFeed News called "How Millennials Became the Burnout Generation" suggests that young people are put under far more pressure to perform than previous generations. Instead of just playing, children are now escorted to "play dates, organised activities and classes". Children can no longer just mooch around and be bored, they need to be entertained and doing activities where they succeed or fail.

Things are also likely to get worse with the emphasis on continuous testing in schools. Many have linked the rise in anxiety and depression in young adults to continuous grading as children.

It's small wonder that with all this emphasis on success, many young people are scared to try in case they fail.

Petersen's article continues that "when they are older these same children are constantly told how hard the job market is and that they must be able to compete". With the demise of free university education in England, it is no longer possible for many people to take a degree just because the subject interests them, as I did; now, it seems, you need to be very clear on how that degree will lead to a future career.

Like almost everyone involved in conservation, my first job came about through a residential volunteering stint – six months on an RSPB reserve in Dorset. Nowadays, the requirement to volunteer in order to get a wildlife-conservation job is criticised as prohibiting entry to the profession for those who cannot afford to give their time for free but, in the past, this was really the only route in. My first proper job came about after another bout of volunteering part-time at a local community woodland scheme, while working the rest of the week at a mind-numbing temp job. When a role came up, which involved talking with the communities surrounding the proposed forest sites, I had an added advantage as I was the only person on a team of ten who came from that area. It was felt that someone from the local area would be better placed to get the message across than an outsider. I had earned that job by putting myself in the right place at the right time, but I didn't have a qualification in countryside management when I got it. Now the job market for a poorly paid but rewarding career like wildlife conservation is a lot tougher. If a twenty-something went for a similar role nowadays they would be up against highly educated graduates with appropriate degrees and internships under their belts, a route which is even less viable for people from low-income backgrounds.

Life just seems very competitive for young adults nowadays. You can no longer spend your early twenties bumming around and finding yourself, you seem to have to have it all sorted by 22. The bright young things like Kit and Josie just seemed to collapse under the pressure of their own expectations of where they should be in life by their age. I wanted to say, *As long as you sort it out by 30 then that's OK*. But I also wanted to say, *You do know that no one else is responsible. You are an adult. You have to sort it out for yourself.*

By the end of that day's task, Kit had worked his pollarding annoyance out of his system and helpfully collected and handed the bow saws back to me as I stood on the footplate of the van, counting the tools back in.

"Thanks, Frank."

"Frank?" he said, quizzically.

"Frank Zappa," I said. "You look just like him with that moustache."

He smiled despite himself. "Cool," he said.

We seemed to have called a truce.

Kit began coming into the office on a weekly work experience placement. He helped me with ordering materials for tasks and visiting sites to plan new projects. As the weather warmed a little and spring arrived, the Victorian pheasant-shooting outfit was exchanged for a look resembling a roadie for a prog rock band. Kit spoke little in the office, seemed distant with the other volunteers and gave away no information on his personal life. I couldn't work out whether he was full of himself or the reverse and sometimes I wondered if I had done the right thing in taking him on at all.

"Can you source some hedge plants from a local nursery for next week's task?" I emailed him one week.

His reply came back. "I don't think this is the right approach. You should be using trees of local provenance, not just getting them from the nearest nursery."

I felt a stab of irritation again. It wasn't his job to teach me but the other way around. Did he think I had learned nothing in all my years working in conservation? I sighed deeply and tried again. "Trees of local provenance are obviously the ideal," I typed back, "but as we need to get the hedge planted next week then we don't have time to grow the saplings from seed." I know I sounded cynical when I typed; the reality of working in conservation means that sometimes you have to compromise on the ideal in order to get something done.

The response that came back was a shock. "I've clearly rattled your cage," it said. "I'm sorry if giving you advice has upset you. I just thought I would tell you my opinion but it clearly isn't worth much to you."

I was startled and actually laughed out loud at the cheek of him. By now I'd had a few volunteer assistants, but never one who had answered me like this.

Gemima looked up. There were only the two of us in that day.

"What's so funny?" she said.

Gemima and I had never become friends, but I did respect her knowledge. After all, she was the only other person who understood the reality of running a volunteer group.

"It's Kit," I said. "I want to give him a chance but sometimes he is really cocky." I showed her the message.

Gemima read it and looked thoughtful. "Do you think he could be overcompensating?"

"What do you mean?"

"Well, he seems quite shy to me. Maybe he's acting like he's full of himself to hide that. Maybe he's intimidated by you?"

"Me?" I said. "Who would feel intimidated by me?"

Gemima raised her eyes to heaven and sighed. "Lots of people," she said. "You have all these years of experience. You are really good at managing the volunteer group, you have this great social life and always seem so confident."

"But," I said, thinking of how often I felt out of my depth and lonely, "it's not like that at all. It doesn't feel like that to me."

"Well, it appears like that to the world," she said. "Maybe Kit is just trying to show you how much he knows because he doesn't think he knows enough."

She walked away, leaving me with plenty to think about. Maybe, like me, Kit was showing one face to the world but felt quite different on the inside. Maybe we all were. I was seeing this well-spoken, intelligent guy who seemed to fancy himself, when maybe he didn't feel that way at all.

"Thanks, Gemima," I called after her. "Really, thanks."

I looked at Kit's message again, then came to a decision.

"Apology accepted," I typed. "Here's the tree order. Look forward to seeing you on Thursday."

CHAPTER
THIRTEEN

By February, as the early spring sunshine warmed the earth once more, the wheel of life clicked forward one notch and everything moved on. Despite her early wobble, Josie had stuck at her countryside-management course and was doing well. She had begun talking about a career in wildlife conservation. "I want to do more," she said. "I want to feel that I've got a job that might make a positive difference." She continued to come out to the task days when her course allowed and certainly threw herself into the physical work, always willing to lend a hand to haul the heaviest loads across the site. I knew though that, if she was ever to have a career in conservation, then, ironically, she would need to learn to drive. It just wasn't feasible to travel between sites with public transport and a bicycle.

I saw in Josie the socially awkward teenager that I had been. Josie was talented in so many areas, naturally gifted and sporty and pretty and clever, but she seemed to find it hard to push herself out of her comfort zone. The driving lessons I had agreed to give her were a struggle. We'd arrange a time and I would arrive at her house only to find that she had decided she didn't want to go after all.

"I'm too stupid to do it," she'd say.

"I just want you to try," I would wheedle, and feel a sense of triumph when I encouraged her to leave the house. Once in the car it would be a major task to get her to take the driver's seat and turn on the ignition. "You're doing well," I'd say as we slowly made our way down an empty road but, at the first hiccup, Josie would pull over and put her head on the wheel and refuse to go on.

I despaired.

"She's so isolated in that village," I confided in Meg the following Thursday as we bundled branches together for the faggots.

"She needs to have independence from her parents, be able to get into town. Meet other people her own age." But really these were my goals for her, not hers, and my "help" wasn't purely altruism. I was out to rescue her when really she had to do it for herself.

Bella was also thinking of a new career and was trying hard to draw a line under her past and get some experience to put on her CV. She tried for a job in a bookshop, which was perfect for her – she could have discussed books with the customers all day. I wrote references, flagging up her good points, but the answer came back, "We can't employ someone with a criminal record for a violent crime." I could see their point; on paper Bella was one thing, a person who was unpredictable and possibly violent. There was no getting away from the fact that she had, for one moment, been this person. But she was also sweet and loving and open and vulnerable and needed someone to believe in her. She needed a goal that she wanted badly enough to stick at and work hard for. Without this, I felt, she could easily become disillusioned and drift back into negativity and flash points.

Bella had always been a bit of a sporadic member of the gang, and soon she vanished for a while. The news was she had found a job cleaning in a pub. I was doubtful that there was enough in this job to keep her motivated, but it was something on her CV, something to keep her busy, and I chalked it up as good news.

The older volunteers were also taking on new challenges. Roy fell in love with the Baltic coast after a family wedding in Denmark and took off on a new wave of exploration, cycling and swimming his way along the coast and islands, learning German and coming back buoyant with enthusiasm over his discoveries. And Esther and Wayland started talking about fulfilling a long-held dream to own a smallholding and keep chickens. Their daughter had recently moved to the West Country and they followed her there on weekends to scout out possible properties. Meg and I secretly wished they would find somewhere closer to home. They were such an integral part of the group and we would miss them terribly if they went. Over the years the group had remained remarkably stable; Laurie had left, of course, along with Alex and sadly Bastian, but otherwise we had remained a steady crew, which helped with the sense of community. If Esther and Wayland left, then it would be the first major departure of the core gang and we knew it would create a hole in our "family".

After our rocky start, my working relationship with Kit had also begun to improve. I felt drawn to Kit because he reminded me so much of Laurie, but Kit was 14 years my junior and my interest in him was only ever going to be platonic. Maybe, though, because he reminded me of Laurie, I wanted to learn more about who he was.

"It's no good," I told him, after one visit to a prospective worksite, where we had driven in silence through the country lanes. "You are going to have to speak to me. It's going to be dead boring if all our journeys are as quiet as this."

Poor Kit – if he wanted to work with me, he couldn't escape. I bombarded him with chatter and slowly, bit by bit, he emerged. A shared love of music helped. We both ransacked our CD collections and played everything from Radiohead to "Tuvan throat gargling", as he called it, which turned out to be Mongolian throat singing and surprisingly funky to listen to while we bounced down the country roads in the Micra. Before long he was recommending bands he thought I might enjoy and bringing out films for me to watch. He sent chatty emails, no longer telling me what I was doing wrong, but letting me know that "I plan to expand your mind, duuuude." These messages seemed to come from a much more confident, jolly chap than he sometimes seemed in person and I began to suspect that a rather lovely man was lurking beneath the self-conscious exterior.

It made me think about my old pony. Fairisle was a pony that my friend Karen and I had taken on loan when we were in our twenties. Taking a pony on loan is basically renting someone else's horse and was as close to our childhood dream of horse ownership as we were likely to get. Fairisle had been mistreated and, when I first met her, she stood in the back of her stable refusing to show an interest in anyone who entered. Unless, that was, you did something she didn't like, and then she would take a swipe at you with her teeth or heels. She had decided that humanity was bad news and not to be trusted and had closed off in response. It took a long time to earn her trust. I took her for walks, not riding her, just leading her, and letting her eat while I read books aloud to her. I would brush tiny bits of her face with a soft brush until her eyes closed in pleasure. I would make no sudden moves, everything was a routine, same words, same movements and slowly, she became a different horse. One who would rest her head on my shoulder as we would just stand together in mutual reassurance and companionship. It is worth the effort to win the trust of a difficult animal. Kit was the same. An untrusting animal that needed coaxing out, but when he emerged he was worth it.

One day we tied up bundles of faggots in preparation for the summer's river work and then sat soaking up the early spring sun with our backs to the wood of the old hen houses. We were talking music again.

"I used to love that band," Kit said, "but then the guy got married. He got all happy and content and it wrecked his artistic abilities."

"So contentment kills art?" I questioned.

"I don't know," Kit said seriously. "I don't know if contentment and happiness are really the same thing."

I laughed. "I hear you. And you?" I said. "Are you a contented person?"

Kit shrugged. "Yeah, right," he said.

He was becoming happier though. I could see that for myself. I would watch him, from behind my sunglasses, as he talked, expanding on his ideas about the world and theories of life. It was like watching a flower uncurl, a pure joy to see this guy lose his inhibitions and forget, for a moment, that he was down on the world.

Spring was here and with it came another season of water vole surveys. During the winter the volunteers had found a kayak long abandoned in the undergrowth by the river. It had a hole in the bottom but, undeterred, Kit and Josie patched it up during one task using duct tape and a hot spoon. The hot spoon was run over the duct tape patch, supposedly melting it enough to create a watertight seal. I was a little sceptical as Kit and I hauled the kayak off the roof of the minibus and carried it through a meadow humming with bumblebees, down to the river, but hopefully it would be a little safer than wading through a waterway, thigh deep in silt.

We found a suitable spot, a cutaway in the bank, and I climbed in. Kit pushed the kayak down the slope, launching me with a splash amid the celandine and into a water vole's eye view of the world. Miraculously, the duct tape patch seemed to work. He pulled the boat along by a rope attached to the front while I punted through the mud of the river bottom using a long hazel pole. As I parted the vegetation looking for water vole poo, my arms soon became scraped with long angry bramble marks.

It had taken weeks before Kit trusted me enough to reveal that he wrote. Now, as he pulled the kayak through the water, he struggled to explain the plot of the short story he was writing.

"It sounds good," I encouraged him. "Can I see it?"

It was a step too far. He shot back into his shell.

"Maybe, one day," he said.

It was obvious that day was not going to come any time soon. It was a dance getting Kit to trust me, one step forward, one back.

After a few moments' silence, while I searched the undergrowth, he spoke again.

"I don't normally tell people about my writing," he said. "I don't normally like talking about myself at all actually. I am normally quite apathetic about people. I mean, there are good people out there but mainly I don't think I like people very much."

I carried on peering into burrows. This, I had learned, was the kind of conversation better conducted without eye contact.

"I think most people are very kind if you give them half a chance," I said. "I know people have been to me."

He sat down, trailing the rope across his legs.

"But people gravitate towards you," he said, "because you're gregarious. I'm not. I'm insular."

I looked up. "That is a label you've put on yourself," I said. "You're not that way with me."

Kit laughed. "You don't give me an option and, besides, you draw it out in me. With most people I've just locked myself off. I've had to get by on my own. I'm no good at asking for help. Needing help is a weakness."

It sounded like the kind of thing I said to myself.

"I get it," I said looking up at him, "one hundred per cent, I get it. I was exactly like that. I thought 'I can cope, I can cope' and then something happened where I thought, actually I really can't cope and I have to let people know that I am going to go under without help."

He stood there for a long time, fiddling with the end of the rope. I waited. *If you just wait he'll tell you,* I thought, but I knew, at that moment, to tell me would cost him.

"So is there a story you want to tell?" I asked bluntly, to deliberately break the spell. He retreated back into himself.

"No," he said. "Not one I want to tell."

There was a story of course. It was written all over him in the faint parallel scars on his arms and the great scar on his leg. I had seen enough troubled young people by now to know what those scars might mean. I got the story out of him in the end and by then our friendship had grown beyond the volunteer group.

In some ways Kit filled the hole that Laurie had left – not romantically; our friendship never became anything more than friends – but because, like Laurie, Kit was at a point in his life where he lacked friends and was as up for sporadic adventures as I was.

"Come and practise cartwheels with me," I would suggest, and he'd agree. We went to a meadow full of flowers and tumbled down a hill with a view of the city. It didn't feel like the kind of thing I could say to a man of my own age. What does this say about me? I didn't want to know; by then I'd had enough of people telling me I had to grow up, settle down, settle for anything. Cartwheeling downhill brought me joy, that was all I knew.

Unlike my pony, it didn't take years of metaphorical face brushing and reading for Kit to open up – it took a night down the pub with too much booze and a well-timed but impertinent question that, if I hadn't been drunk, I would never have asked.

"Tell me your scar stories."

I wasn't thinking.

The scars on his arms, he told me, had been done by a homeless man who mugged Kit for his rucksack at a time when he, too, was living on the streets.

Kit's was another tale of a bright boy from a good, successful family, struggling with insecurity and shyness. He'd got good grades at school, he told me, and had been given a place at a top London university, but from there things began to unravel.

"I was always a loner," he said. "And I didn't like living in London with all the noise and people. I had cabin fever, so I started taking walks at night. I was also, it has to be said, taking a lot of drugs," he admitted, and laughed dryly. "I had some good times while taking drugs and they helped me fit in, but there is a difference between taking drugs with friends as a social thing and taking drugs on your own to escape."

It was around the time he started taking drugs regularly, alone, that his behaviour became a bit more erratic.

"After a bit I started avoiding people," he told me. "I would just walk further and further until there seemed little point in returning, so I would just sleep in a doorway."

Eventually, no doubt appalled by their son's behaviour, his parents had stepped in and taken Kit back home. Somehow he had managed to graduate but things had continued to spiral. He was put on antidepressants, which he hated, saying they just made him feel like he was living at the bottom of a well. He was also sent to a psychiatrist.

"I didn't trust the guy they sent me to, so I asked to see my medical records."

Here Kit had read, "The first experience this young man has with mental health care should not see him end up on a secure ward."

Seeing the words "secure ward" applied to himself had scared him, and in fear that he was about to be sectioned, Kit made a plan, took the family dog and his axe and headed to the woods to live a more natural life.

"I'd always loved Ray Mears and, that first night in the woods, I got a fire going and felt better. Life suddenly had become reduced to the basic elements of survival. Things felt more real."

I could see how this life would appeal to Kit. I could picture him wandering the woods with his pheasant-shooting coat, an axe and his dog. After that first night in the woods Kit had begun to move around the country, sleeping rough, sometimes in the woods, sometimes in hostels. It was in one of the hostels that the police caught up with him.

"My parents wanted the dog back," he said.

I was fairly sure they wanted him back too.

After the police visited the hostel, where he and the dog were sheltering, Kit had been persuaded to return to the family home.

"I went back because of my dog," he'd told me. "I didn't want to be without her."

Once back home, he returned to therapy and started a countryside-management course, and a new path had begun. Kit's relationship with his parents, when I first met him, was still rocky; things had undoubtedly been said on both sides and it would take more time before they could be set to one side.

I was profoundly moved when Kit placed his trust in me and told me this story. Until that moment all I had seen was this blazing boy with his music and opinions. His story made me feel, once again, how little we can judge a book by its cover. I admit there was a part of me that wanted to help Kit because of Laurie. Laurie had vanished from my life and as far as I knew his problems remained unresolved but Kit was young, the damage didn't run so deep and I felt that maybe, with him, I could make a difference. Beyond that though, I just loved those summer days with Kit. I wanted to be forever driving through the country lanes with the music playing, forever cartwheeling in a field with the future far away.

As autumn and bonfire season began once again I knew that life with the volunteers made me happy, and some days I would sit on a hillside, resting on my elbows, listening to the chatter of the others, and realise how much I loved this little world we had created. Some days I felt so lucky to be paid to do this, to spend the day on a hillside with my friends, laughing and swapping stories. It was a privilege, as well, to do a job I believed in, which I felt contributed something to the world. *What more is there to life?* I thought. *What more really than that?* But at the same time, I knew that there was something else I wanted, something which I hadn't told the volunteers.

A few weeks earlier I had sent a proposal for a book I was hoping to write to a number of literary agents, along with one chapter. I had tried this before with previous manuscripts and fully expected to work my way down a long list of agents and receive endless polite rejection letters. However, this time, I got a response within hours. "I love it," one agent wrote, "send me the rest." This had been followed by a positive response from a second agent the next day and another a week later. The problem was I had nothing else to show them. I had worked evenings and weekends to write one chapter and a proposal. I was never going to be able to take the journey I needed to or write the book while working full-time. Something had to give.

I felt a change in the air. *The time is now,* I told myself. *You have to grab this opportunity.* The trouble was, I didn't know how I could do that and support myself as well. I knew it would take me time to figure that one out. *It's OK,* I told myself, *there's no rush, nothing has to change just yet.* Even so, as autumn turned to winter, I held each precious moment with the gang a little tighter to my chest.

The last task of the year took place on a bright December day. The path to the woods was pitted with potholes the size of bomb craters as I wove the heavily laden minibus to and fro, tools, food and gifts rattling about in the back. The volunteers were waiting, this time in the woodland car park, chatting as they bounced on one leg while they pulled on waterproofs and wellies. I pulled over in front of the gate that led to the woods and the others ambled across. Today the whole gang was reunited, Bella and Josie returning for this one task to join our newer recruits, Kit and Jack. Bevan and Jim were deep in conversation, Roy had taken the gate key from me and was fiddling with the lock, supervised by Val. Esther and Wayland had brought a big black cooking pot for the fire. Bella was waving marshmallows at me and yelling with laughter close to Reuben's ear. They all scrabbled into the minibus among potatoes and satsumas for the ride down to the worksite.

The woods were pared down into a winter palette. Dead leaves were mulched into a thick stew, and ice crisped the puddles. I'd judged it an "eight items of clothing" day, sharp enough that the breeze sent a shiver along your arms but not ice-in-the-blood cold – that was a 12-layer day. Grey squirrels eyed us, chattering and wheezing in protest as we drove along the main path. Black pools lay like oiled mirrors alongside the track, inverting the canopy in their depths.

We didn't need to drive far today. Christmas tasks required only a spot where we could coppice enough wood to create a fire and keep everyone warm until lunch. As the others set about sawing and lopping, I got to work unloading the food from the minibus. Bella sidled up to me.

"I had a row in the street the other night," she said quietly, no longer seeming the buoyant girl who had appeared in the car park that morning. "The police were called."

I worried for her. When was I going to stop worrying for her? I felt she needed the group to keep her on the straight and narrow, but everything in life changed. What if Kirk failed to find the next bit of funding and the Partnership folded? What if I left my job to write the book?

Either way, the volunteer group wasn't really the solution Bella needed. What we offered did help because it provided healthy exercise, access to nature, space to talk, a useful purpose and a chance to be part of a community – those ways to well-being that help us all – but that wasn't the whole answer for someone like Bella. Ultimately, I felt, she needed good ongoing support and counselling.

Mental health trusts in England had seen their budgets cut by 8 per cent year-on-year since 2011, according to Dr Mona Kamal in an article entitled "Austerity and NHS Cuts: Wrecking our Mental Health". Almost a third of NHS mental health beds had been lost and 6,800 mental health nurse posts had vanished. It was hard to see how Bella was ever going to get back on with the life that she should be having, the one where she played a full role in the world and contributed her many gifts to it, unless mental health provision was better funded. There wasn't much I could do for Bel in the long term, but in the short term I could at least offer her a way of releasing her stress.

I handed her a bag of potatoes and a fork. "Stab these," I said, "but not too hard, and then wrap them in foil and put them on the fire."

When I looked back Bella was looking cheerier and had roped in Jack to assist, who was laughing, actually laughing out loud, at one of Bella's stories. The others were busy as well. Wayland was stirring beans and chilli into the cooking pot. Esther and Meg were setting up trestle tables and lining them with the food the others had brought along. Jim and Roy teased the fire into life, flapping with the biscuit-tin lid and blowing at the coals with reckless disregard to eyebrows and lungs. Bevan raked out the embers and put split chestnuts on an iron shovel. Bella worked on creating marshmallow sticks. Kit was constructing a tripod over the fire with Josie.

Josie was in her second year of her countryside-management course by now. "I'm doing really well," she told me. "Particularly with the plant ID. I got a hundred per cent in my test."

"I'm glad to hear it," I said. I was but, beyond her good results, it was great to hear her acknowledge her own success. She'd worked hard, stuck the course out even when it was difficult and had every right to feel proud of herself.

"How about the driving lessons?" I asked hopefully. After our few lessons, Josie had decided to continue with a qualified instructor.

She shrugged. "I'm rubbish. I can't do it. I've given them up."

Oh well, I thought. *You can't win them all.* Part of me wanted to stamp the lesson of perseverance into Josie but I had learned too, sometimes the best way to help someone is to stand back and trust them to work it out for themselves.

The other volunteers spent the morning coppicing the birch to keep warm until lunchtime, working at the never-ending task of opening up clearings and widening the rides to allow the cow wheat to grow, creating the sunny pools where Duke of Burgundy butterflies would court in chequerboard beauty in the summer.

Stripped of its vegetation, the woodland revealed an ethereal beauty and, for one moment, looking out over the scene, I felt again that link with the ancestors. With the people who had lived in the woods and stood at the door of a hut on a dark night, as winter crept its fingers towards them. For one moment I felt the long dark of winter before electric lights, when we still had the wonder of a star-filled sky. It is this connection with who we had been in the past and naturally still were that helped put our feet back on the earth. Not an outsider to nature, as the people jogging and dog walking on the main path through the woods were, but a working part of the woods and the seasons. Here was work to be proud of which made your soul ring.

The memory of this past is written into us, all of us, you as well. American biologist E. O. Wilson called it "biophilia" (love of nature). We are part of the mycelium that dwells beneath the forest floor and bursts into fungi in the autumn. We are the trees, created from carbon, just like us. We are air and bird and sky and fire and dirt and death beneath the canopy. We are the running deer and the yellow eyes of the wolves that once roamed. Dust to dust, come from the earth, back to the earth. Divorce yourself from nature, don't embrace it, and you are turning your back on yourself. Dig your hands in the soil, swim in a river, work up a sweat while felling a tree for a fire to create a feast with your friends and you are alive again. If you haven't already experienced this, I urge you to just get out there and find the truth of it for yourself.

So we feasted, as our ancestors had done, to celebrate the turning of the year, the return of the light, the halfway point of bonfire season. Baked potato with butter speckled with wood ash, dollops of chilli, mince pies, hot apple punch, marshmallows crisped on the outside with hot gooey centres.

Afterwards, the tables were cleared and there were photo competitions: guess the baby, guess the teenager. Fantastic photos from the 50s and 60s of volunteers with quiffs, pixie cuts and unimaginable beards. Then there was Bevan's quiz, fiendishly tricky questions full of news items, literature and classical music. Cards were swapped, mine written surreptitiously during work while Kirk wasn't watching. Each one needed a personal message. "Jim, thanks for having my back", "Reuben, I enjoy our chats". "Val, your cakes are a lifesaver", "Bella, continue to sparkle". Finally, I gave a speech, remembering the past year and our achievements, thanking everyone for their support. It was nothing really, a Christmas bash in the woods, but it was fun and free for everyone, the one time in the year I persuaded Kirk to release some petty cash to pay for the chilli, spuds and quiz prizes.

The light mellowed as the afternoon wore on, becoming honeyed like the golden ends of the logs, freshly cut and stacked high along the path. Then, as the light faded, we watched the embers and talked of nothing with an ease brought on by fresh air, exercise and the long knowing of each other.

Over Christmas, the question of how I was going to write the book occupied me and, by the new year, I had a rough plan. I would apply for an Arts Council Development Grant to support me while I wrote and I would supplement this with freelance work. Years before, my dreams of running a business had come to nothing. The time hadn't been right but, more than that, the business hadn't been right. I knew that now. I hadn't looked hard enough at the figures or questioned whether there was really enough demand for what I wanted to do. This time it would be different. I contacted a chamber of commerce, signed up for business start-up courses and began to tentatively ask around about freelance ecology work.

When I had begun working for the Kingsdown Partnership I didn't think I knew nearly enough to call myself an ecologist. I was just the publicity officer who knew a bit about wildlife. Actually, I still feel that "proper" ecologists are experts and these are increasingly thin on the ground, but my work with the Partnership had given me confidence. If I hadn't been thrown in at the deep end, I would never have had the opportunity to learn on the job. Now I was giving advice on management to the local drainage board, commanding men with machines to do my bidding and create river improvements and wetland meadows. I was discussing farmland conservation in front of rooms of tweed-coated men. Some of them would undoubtedly be nodding off in a corner, but there were others who listened and supported what I did. Many days I still drove to work frustrated beyond belief at the boss's petty rules and endless admin, but I knew that, without the chance he had given me, I would never have come so far.

I owed my newfound confidence to the volunteers, too. I would still struggle to install a kissing gate, but I had tried hard to learn the skills I needed, and I had other talents which had earned me their respect and, more importantly, their friendship. They had become both my support crew and my mentors.

Yet, all the same I felt that I would regret it if I never took the time to write my book. Something had been put in motion and I felt the clock ticking down to a time when I would leave these happy days behind.

CHAPTER FOURTEEN

Six Years Later

All along the valley, the beech woods are running to gold as I plunge up and down the road towards Greengate Farm. I chuck the Micra into a gap in the hedge at the back and clamber over the rusting gate, hoping to avoid the eyes of the security firm that now occupies the site.

The tool shed is open at both ends. The tools have been removed and the electricity has finally packed up. A giant wasp nest hangs like a lantern from the ceiling. An old tool list is still tacked to one wall. I debate whether to pocket it as a souvenir. Painted words run along the top of the old tool rack: "rakes", "shovels", "shuv holers".

It's strange coming back here. The Kingsdown Partnership has long abandoned the site. About a year before my departure we had moved to the new accommodation in a hermetically sealed office on the edge of a commuter town, among other council staff who wore suits to work. It was safe, warm and dry but felt disconnected from the natural world we were dedicated to. However, we still carried on using Greengate Farm to store our tools and vehicles. Without a regular presence on site though the tool shed became a target of thieves who stole what little equipment we had and smashed the windows of the ancient Land Rover. Soon after I left, Kirk was finally offered alternative storage for the equipment and the team left the farm behind for good.

I would be lying if I said I had fond memories of my days in the porta cabin. My recollections are of long hours sitting in silence, typing in fingerless gloves as water dripped slowly from the ceiling into a bucket. However, as I walk through the abandoned tool shed, I think of happier times, loading up barn owl ladders with Roy, tying bundles of faggots in the sun with Kit. Stacking sandbags at the back of the site with Esther and Wayland. Moments of fun, friendship, support and companionship with people I came to love.

I sit on the moss-covered step of the outside loo in the growing autumn dusk. The buildings are collapsing, the cherry trees dying. The path to the minibus shed has grown spiky with docks and teasels. Nature is consuming my memories, both good and bad.

Six Years Earlier

I got the letter from the Arts Council as I headed out of the door for a spring day's survey work in the fields. I hadn't got the grant. The door swung shut behind me.

Kit was waiting in the car park with the family dog, the one he had run away with.

"I can't have her full-time," he said, "but my parents are on holiday this week so I've got custody."

Kit's relationship with his parents, it seemed, was improving, just a little.

The dog, at the centre of all this, sat looking innocently up at me. She was a schnauzer. She sat on Kit's lap as we drove through the country lanes, with her head on my hand as it rested on the gear stick.

"She does that with me," he said.

It was only May but a hot day for survey work. We trudged miles across exposed wheat fields, looking at reed-lined ditches. Grass wrapped around our legs as we scrambled down banks to take water samples or dip for insects. Our survey would help decide the best form of management for this watery world. The sun beat down, and by lunchtime I was sticky with factor 50 and tired of being harassed by horseflies, who refused to give up as we swatted at them with nets and maps.

"Let's go and find some shade," I suggested.

We stumbled by accident upon the spot where, many years before, Laurie had almost drowned. Somehow it seemed suitable. With the Arts Council rejection, my plans to leave work and write my book also felt as though they had sunk without trace. I told Kit about the letter as I lay on my stomach on the riverbank with his dog licking my face. I knew it was OK to discuss it with him. He was no gossip and, unlike the other volunteers, he wasn't going to be upset by the news I was considering giving up the job. He would be gone soon, too. He was applying for work and sooner or later he would strike lucky. He wasn't as invested in the group as, I felt, the others were.

"What would you do, Kit?" I asked. "I was relying on the money from the Arts Council to support me while I wrote. Now, if I leave, I have to survive entirely on any freelance work I can pick up."

Kit didn't give opinions unless pressed. Now though, he looked thoughtful.

"I think," he said finally, "that in any decision in life there is always a do and a don't do, and taking action instead of not may lead to fewer regrets."

I sat and thought. I could think of numerous incidents where this was not the case. Deciding whether to have an affair or commit a crime or do away with your annoying boss. All of these actions were likely to lead to regrets. Still, it was the kind of advice I liked: simple, clean cut and, like all the best advice, it chimed with my own thoughts. *Nothing worth having in life comes without sacrifice,* I told myself. Giving up the volunteers was, without doubt, going to be my sacrifice.

Six Years Later

The porta cabin has long since collapsed and been removed. I stand on the concrete foundations at the spot where Kirk's desk used to be. I think of all the times I stood there, like a naughty schoolgirl, being told off for buying the volunteers expensive biscuits or using the work vehicle to drop one of them home after they had spent a long day volunteering. I think of Marley in his basket, his great hairy eyebrows raised in question when I sighed deeply at Kirk's lecture. Sycamore seeds are feeding into the concrete slab. I dare not go into the building that housed the kitchen. Russian vine is climbing up the flaking white paint of the door, and the roof looks close to collapse.

I edge forward slowly, not wanting to be spotted by the people in the shiny new porta cabin which sits to one side of the site. There are plans for housing. This is a lovely spot in a charming countryside setting, of course some developer wants to cover it with concrete and ugly, urban, four-bedroom, luxury houses.

I hear the door of the new porta cabin open and I scurry across to hide in the entrance to what used to be the men's loo. A girl emerges and runs across the yard to fling a bag of rubbish into a skip. She is bent against the rain. She looks cold. She skids on wet mud. Some things don't change but sometimes everything changes at once.

Six Years Earlier

I knew I had to leave the job but still I hesitated to make a definite move. As spring turned to summer, the days were full of sunshine. I scythed hay in the field with the volunteers. Roy somehow managed to bring us all ice creams on the back of his bike. Wayland spun me around in the air as hay dust swirled in shafts of sunlight. How could I leave?

On other days when I felt I had produced a really good piece of work and still received a long list of petty criticism from Kirk, I felt myself ready to step over the edge and be gone.

"What do you want, Kirk?" I said in exasperation after one altercation with him. "I am never going to be a 'yes sir, no sir' sort of person."

To my surprise he laughed. "I know," he said. "That's what I like about you."

Why, why then did he seem to take delight in forcing me to do his bidding and watching the sparks fly when I invariably rebelled? I was tired of it. I wanted to run with my ideas, succeed or fail on my own merits, not be led by the nose along a path I disagreed with. Autonomy was a word that felt like a beacon to head towards. I stood on that diving board looking down at self-employment, wanting to jump but afraid to do so.

I went to visit Graham, meaning to ask his advice. I'd been told by some of the volunteers at College Lake that his illness had progressed but, when he opened the door, he looked the same to me, still tall, upright and dressed like David Attenborough.

"You look good," I said, surprised.

"Finally," he said. "Someone who doesn't treat me like I'm dying."

He drove us to a garden centre for lunch, and on the way Graham revealed that his doctor had advised him not to get behind the wheel. I knew better than to argue; it wouldn't have helped or stopped him driving the next time. As the day wore on though, his defiance at his illness began to fail him. He became pale and drawn. He struggled out of the car and we almost toppled into the rose beds together as I tried to support him, while he leaned heavily on a walking stick – a beautiful thing with the handle shaped into the head of a dog with inset green, jewelled eyes.

He told me he had recently walked up Pitstone Hill. "I wanted to see the views again," he said. At the top he had collapsed and been carted off to hospital by air ambulance. "I'm not going to die in a hospital bed," he said. "I'm going up there again."

So many people who cared about Graham were worried and exasperated by him, but I loved him, pure and simple, for all that he was, even his single-minded stubbornness. I didn't want to diminish him by telling him not to go.

"Call me," I told him. "If you are determined to walk up there again then call me and I will walk behind with a wheelbarrow. Then, if you collapse, I can freewheel you down. Save the air ambulance coming out again."

Graham laughed. It was the sort of tough love he could cope with.

For so long Graham had been my touchstone, my centre point, the person who made me feel it was OK to be me. The least I could do was offer him the same support in return. By the time I dropped him off he was clearly in pain. I left without asking him for advice. Maybe, if I had, then I wouldn't have made my next move. A move that surprised even me. Instead of taking the plunge and leaving my job, I asked for a promotion. Looking back, I wonder if maybe this was a way of knocking me out of my comfort zone. Kirk said he would think about it and let me know in a fortnight.

A lot can happen in two weeks.

First of all, Kit left. He appeared on his bike in the car park that Thursday just as the volunteers were boarding the minibus. We were heading to the river for a day of pulling Himalayan balsam and I had climbed onto the roof and was trying to strap the unwieldy kayak tighter to stop it sliding off and impaling a passing tourist. I hung over the side with a ratchet strap in my teeth as Kit called up to me.

"I'm off for a bit," he said. "I've got a gardening gig by the coast. I am going down there and after that I don't know. I'll be back, I think, in a couple of months. Maybe."

It was typical Kit casualness.

I had expected him to leave but his sudden departure was a surprise. Over the last few months I had begun to rely on him, not only for practical help, but also for the kind of support that Laurie had once provided, a confidant and pal. Now he spun a circle on his bike.

"Cheery bye," he shouted and was gone.

That evening, having offloaded the tools at the farm, I was driving back home when my mobile rang. I pulled over by the village green next to the fish-and-chip wagon that came to the village every Thursday. Kids on scooters zigzagged down the long path that led across the green, teenagers sat in circles on the ground, gossiping in pools of shade beneath the horse chestnut trees, grandmothers walked excitable toddlers. It was a happy scene in which to receive sad news. The caller was one of the volunteers from College Lake. As soon as I heard his voice I knew why he was calling. Graham had died, not on top of Pitstone Hill, as he had wished, but in a hospital bed from a heart attack.

It was Graham who taught me how to treat volunteers. His philosophy had been "work a little, rest a little, laugh a lot". Each working day at College Lake had begun with a cup of tea and a chat. He encouraged me to finish work early on a beautiful day and enjoy the wildlife of the reserve. He always thanked me for what I had done and, in return, I had given him my loyalty and willingly threw myself into the job. Graham taught me the fundamentals of running a volunteer group. Treat people with respect. Listen to their ideas. Be prepared to do the mucky jobs yourself. Let people use their talents and do the job that makes them happiest. Let everyone have a go. Feed them plenty of tea and biscuits.

Working with Graham at College Lake had made me feel part of a supportive community. Back in the days when most people worked close to home, we all knew this sense of community. We worked alongside our neighbours, we helped each other out in times of trouble, we celebrated and offered thanks together. But even in the twenty-first century it is possible to still experience this sense of community. I had found mine among the volunteers.

The news of Graham's death brought my indecision over leaving my job into sharp focus. For the last few years the Kingsdown Partnership had been a safety net, a place to recover from my break-up, redundancy and financial insecurity. Kirk had given me an opportunity, and with the volunteers I had found generosity, support and love that wasn't self-regarding or self-seeking. The safety net had helped build my confidence but I knew if I wallowed in it forever then it would become a trap. All those years ago I had been hiding out at College Lake too. Part of me had wanted to stay in the world of feeding the chickens and mending the hides with no hard decisions. Graham had known that and urged me to leave and get out into the world.

"It's not life," he'd said. "At least it's not the life for you. You have to move forward, get a career. Step out into the world again." I knew now what he would have said if I had asked him during my visit. Move forward, don't stagnate, trust in yourself and your own instincts and go for it. The following Monday I sat in front of Kirk, waiting to hear his decision about my promotion. *Say no,* I thought, *please say no.* Kirk didn't disappoint.

A few days later I posted my resignation letter to him. There was a sun dog above the postbox, a refraction of ice crystals in the atmosphere causing a little rainbow to appear in the sky. I took it to be a good sign. When Kirk called me into his office and shut the door the following Monday, I was expecting sarcasm and anger, but instead, the man wrong-footed me once again.

"You're doing a really brave thing," he said. He had tears in his eyes as he said it. To see such a basically unemotional man show emotion moved me. Suddenly I realised that Kirk did value me, did think highly of my work, but it would never have crossed his mind to say it or understand that the occasional word of praise instead of criticism may have made me more motivated. I told him about the book I planned to write.

"I can quite see why you want to leave," he said. "It sounds a great idea and I'm sure you can continue to do some work for us as a freelance."

"Thanks," I said, amazed. I took a deep breath. "I also want to thank you for taking me on, giving me the opportunity to learn so much."

We shook hands. It seemed I had finally grown up from that woman who walked away from jobs with bad feeling and fiery speeches.

Six Years Later

My walk across Greengate Farm has made me sad. Why have I come here? What am I looking for on this derelict site? I am looking for us, for signs of us.

I told the volunteers I was leaving at the end of August. By then I had begun picking up freelance work, not just from Kirk but from my former employees at the RSPB and other people who I had worked for over the last few years who valued my experience. I felt confident and positive about the way ahead. I had also begun my journey across the marshes, which would become the backbone of my first book.

I chose to tell the volunteers on that year's jolly. I didn't want to ruin the day, but I knew the whole gang would be out and I wanted to tell everyone at once. I also hoped we could celebrate what we had achieved. We had gone to the seaside, the volunteers and I, for that year's outing. We hunted crabs, had lunch in the pub and took a stroll across a nature reserve. I felt sick all day, knowing what was to come. The axe had to fall. Bella cried, Meg and Esther sat in glum silence. Val became matter of fact with plans for the future. Bevan came up and told me I was doing the right thing. Jim said he was proud.

"Don't worry about us," Roy said. "You've created a legacy here that will last."

A legacy, I think about that now as I shelter in the old tool shed from the rain. On the day I had visited Graham he had told me the story of the dog-headed walking stick he carried. The stick had been given to him by one of the founders of the Wildlife Trusts. Graham had made an impression on this woman and, after she died, the stick had been delivered to him in the post. The stick was meant to be passed on, he told me, to whoever carried on the legacy but, when Graham died, the walking stick vanished. Some said he had lost it on a hillside, others said it had been buried with him. Either way, it made me sad that the line had been broken. In the end though, it wasn't the stick that was the legacy.

Graham's legacy, passed down to me, was the lesson on how to treat the people that turn up to volunteer, week in, week out, in all weathers. When I left my job I wasn't sure who I had passed this legacy on to, but to my surprise it was Kit. I say surprise because, at the time he left the group, he was still a bit flaky. He bounced to the gardening gig and later I put his name forward for some lizard-trapping work for an ecology firm. We lost touch, we got back in touch. We remain friends.

Kit finally got his apprenticeship with the Wildlife Trusts and afterwards went on to take a job running a volunteer group. He has changed in the intervening years. He has become comfortable in his skin. He has learned to show all his colours, and how fantastic those colours are. Somehow I have ended up on the mailing list for Kit's volunteers and, each week, I see the email he sends to the group telling them how the work they are doing is making such a difference. He thanks them for their efforts cutting scrub in the rain. He promises to bring them carrot cake, he organises jacket potatoes around winter bonfires. It makes me giddy with pride. What fun it must be to be part of his gang.

It won't be long before the site at Greengate Farm is cleared. The old ash trees felled, the chicken sheds pulled down, the toilet block and kitchen crushed by diggers. Fancy houses built, the village urbanised. It's no good reminiscing, they are not here, the volunteers. I shut the door of the tool shed before I leave. I don't take a souvenir, I don't need to.

Outside I climb into the Micra and head away. My time as volunteer group leader had ended but, at the last minute, an idea came to me. I asked the new group leader if I could become a volunteer and, to my delight, he agreed. I am heading to town to meet the others for a day out in the woods. There I will lean on a rake and gossip with Bevan, I will be bossed around by Val. I will flap hot coals into a holy blaze with a biscuit tin alongside Roy. Jim will give me advice and I will listen. The smoke will reach up into the trees above us, the birds will call, my feet will rest upon the earth and I will know that this is where I belong.

ACKNOWLEDGEMENTS

ACKNOWLEDGEMENTS

Running the volunteer group will forever be one of the happiest times of my life, a testament that sunshine can come after grief. I would like to thank my beloved friends of the volunteer group for all their support and kindness to me over the years, which continued long after I left the job.

Young and old, you are a truly inspirational bunch of people and it is my good fortune that I stumbled into your midst. Sadly I can't acknowledge you by name but you know who you are and I am hugely grateful for the trust you have placed in me in allowing me to write our story.

I would also like to thank "Kirk" for seeing something in me at that interview that made him feel I was up to the job, and for giving me the opportunity to spend part of each week in such happy company.

Thanks to my early readers, Angie Murray and Lynn Yardley and my mum, for all their advice and early editing.

Many thanks to Joanna Swainson, my glorious agent at Hardman and Swainson, who backed the manuscript and worked so hard to find me a fabulous publisher. Thanks also for the loan of your beautiful house to complete the edit.

Thanks also to Debbie Chapman for championing the book at Summersdale and working hard, along with Claire Berrisford, on the edit, and to Jasmin Burkitt for all her help with publicity.

Lastly, to "Laurie", you may or may not ever read this book and even if you do, you may not recognise yourself, but just to let you know I will always wish the best for you wherever you are.

ABOUT THE AUTHOR

Photo © Mimi Donaldson

Carol Donaldson is a writer and naturalist. Originally from Essex, she has worked for many of Britain's best wildlife charities and currently works as a freelance ecologist advising farmers across Kent and Essex to restore wetlands and rivers and manage land for waders.

Her first book, *On the Marshes*, was published by Little Toller in 2017. She is a regular contributor to the *Guardian* travel pages and was *BBC Wildlife Magazine*'s Travel Writer of the Year in 2011.

Carol lives in a very old and slightly crumbling house in Kent and enjoys wild swimming and dancing the Argentine Tango.

Have you enjoyed this book?

If so, why not write a review on your favourite website?

If you're interested in finding out more about our books, find us
on Facebook at **Summersdale Publishers**, on Twitter/X at
@Summersdale and on Instagram and TikTok at
@summersdalebooks and get in touch.
We'd love to hear from you!

Thanks very much for buying this Summersdale book.

www.summersdale.com

IMAGE CREDITS